Amorphous Dissent

JAPANESE SOCIETY SERIES
General Editor: Yoshio Sugimoto

Lives of Young Koreans in Japan
Yasunori Fukuoka

Globalization and Social Change in Contemporary Japan
J.S. Eades, Tom Gill and Harumi Befu

Coming Out in Japan: The Story of Satoru and Ryuta
Satoru Ito and Ryuta Yanase

Japan and Its Others:
Globalization, Difference and the Critique of Modernity
John Clammer

Hegemony of Homogeneity: An Anthropological Analysis of Nihonjinron
Harumi Befu

Foreign Migrants in Contemporary Japan
Hiroshi Komai

A Social History of Science and Technology in Contemporary Japan, Volume 1
Shigeru Nakayama

Farewell to Nippon: Japanese Lifestyle Migrants in Australia
Machiko Sato

The Peripheral Centre:
Essays on Japanese History and Civilization
Johann P. Arnason

A Genealogy of 'Japanese' Self-images
Eiji Oguma

Class Structure in Contemporary Japan
Kenji Hashimoto

An Ecological View of History
Tadao Umesao

Nationalism and Gender
Chizuko Ueno

Native Anthropology: The Japanese Challenge to Western Academic Hegemony
Takami Kuwayama

Youth Deviance in Japan: Class Reproduction of Non-Conformity
Robert Stuart Yoder

Japanese Companies: Theories and Realities
Masami Nomura and Yoshihiko Kamii

From Salvation to Spirituality: Popular Religious Movements in Modern Japan
Susumu Shimazono

The 'Big Bang' in Japanese Higher Education:
The 2004 Reforms and the Dynamics of Change
J.S. Eades, Roger Goodman and Yumiko Hada

Japanese Politics: An Introduction
Takashi Inoguchi

A Social History of Science and Technology in Contemporary Japan, Volume 2
Shigeru Nakayama

Gender and Japanese Management
Kimiko Kimoto

Philosophy of Agricultural Science: A Japanese Perspective
Osamu Soda

A Social History of Science and Technology in Contemporary Japan, Volume 3
Shigeru Nakayama and Kunio Goto

Japan's Underclass: Day Laborers and the Homeless
Hideo Aoki

A Social History of Science and Technology in Contemporary Japan, Volume 4
Shigeru Nakayama and Hitoshi Yoshioka

Scams and Sweeteners: A Sociology of Fraud
Masahiro Ogino

Toyota's Assembly Line: A View from the Factory Floor
Ryoji Ihara

Village Life in Modern Japan: An Environmental Perspective
Akira Furukawa

Social Welfare in Japan: Principles and Applications
Kojun Furukawa

Escape from Work: Freelancing Youth and the Challenge to Corporate Japan
Reiko Kosugi

Japan's Whaling: The Politics of Culture in Historical Perspective
Hiroyuki Watanabe

Gender Gymnastics: Performing and Consuming Japan's Takarazuka Revue
Leonie R. Stickland

Poverty and Social Welfare in Japan
Masami Iwata and Akihiko Nishizawa

The Modern Japanese Family: Its Rise and Fall
Chizuko Ueno

Widows of Japan: An Anthropological Perspective
Deborah McDowell Aoki

In Pursuit of the Seikatsusha:
A Genealogy of the Autonomous Citizen in Japan
Masako Amano

Demographic Change and Inequality in Japan
Sawako Shirahase

The Origins of Japanese Credentialism
Ikuo Amano

Pop Culture and the Everyday in Japan: Sociological Perspectives
Katsuya Minamida and Izumi Tsuji

Japanese Perceptions of Foreigners
Shunsuke Tanabe

Migrant Workers in Contemporary Japan:
An Institutional Perspective on Transnational Employment
Kiyoto Tanno

The Boundaries of 'the Japanese', Volume 1:
Okinawa 1868–1972 – Inclusion and Exclusion
Eiji Oguma

International Migrants in Japan: Contributions in an Era of Population Decline
Yoshitaka Ishikawa

Globalizing Japan: Striving to Engage the World
Ross Mouer

Beyond Fukushima: Toward a Post-Nuclear Society
Koichi Hasegawa

Japan's Ultra Right
Naoto Higuchi

The Boundaries of 'the Japanese', Volume 2:
Korea, Taiwan and the Ainu 1868–1945
Eiji Oguma

Creating Subaltern Counterpublics: Korean Women
In Japan and Their Struggles for Night School
Akwi Seo

Aftermath: Fukushima and the 3.11 Earthquake
Yutaka Tsujinaka and Hiroaki Inatsugu

Learning English in Japan
Takunori Terasawa

Others in Japanese Agriculture
Kenichi Yasuoka

Fighting Prejudice in Japan: The Families of Hansen's Disease Patients Speak Out
Ai Kurosaka

Living on the Streets in Japan: Homeless Women Break their Silence
Satomi Maruyama

U. S. Occupation of Okinawa: A Soft Power Theory Perspective
Hideko Yoshimoto

The State Construction Of 'Japaneseness'
Masataka Endo

Amorphous Dissent: Post-Fukushima Social Movements in Japan
Takashi Horie, Hikaru Tanaka and Kiyoto Tanno

Baseball in Occupied Japan: US Postwar Cultural Policy
Takeshi Tanikawa

Amorphous Dissent
Post-Fukushima Social Movements in Japan

Edited by

HORIE Takashi
TANAKA Hikaru
TANNO Kiyoto

TRANS
PACIFIC
PRESS

This English edition published in 2020 by:

Trans Pacific Press Co., Ltd
2nd Floor, Hamamatsu-cho Daiya Building
2-2-15 Hamamatsu-cho, Minato-ku,
Tokyo 105-0013
Japan

Telephone: +81-(0)50-5371-9475
e-mail: info@transpacificpress.com
Web: http://www.transpacificpress.com

© Trans Pacific Press 2020.

Edited by Miriam Riley, Armidale, Australia.

Designed and set by Sarah Tuke, Melbourne, Australia.

Distributors

USA and Canada
Independent Publishers Group (IPG)
814 N. Franklin Street
Chicago, IL 60610
USA
Telephone inquiries: +1-312-337-0747
Order placement: 800-888-4741
 (domestic only)
Fax: +1-312-337-5985
Email: frontdesk@ipgbook.com
Web: http://www.ipgbook.com

Japan
Kinokuniya Company Ltd.
3-7-10 Shimomeguro
Meguro-ku
Tokyo 153-8504
Japan
Telephone: +81-(0)3-6910-0531
Fax: +81-(0)3-6420-1362
Email: bkimp@kinokuniya.co.jp
Web: www.kinokuniya.co.jp

Europe, Oceania, Middle East and Africa
EUROSPAN
Gray's Inn House,
127 Clerkenwell Road
London, EC1R 5DB
United Kingdom
Telephone: +44-(0)20-7240-0856
Email: info@eurospan.co.uk
Web: https://www.eurospangroup.com/

All rights reserved. No reproduction of any part of this book may take place without the written permission of Trans Pacific Press.

ISSN   1443–9670 (Japanese Society Series)
ISBN   978–1–920901–85–1 (paperback)
ISBN   978–1–920901–87–5 (eBook)

Cover photo: Demonstration against the National Security Legislation in front of the National Diet building on 30 August 2015: many people gathering. Source: mkimpo.

Contents

Tables	viii
Photographs	ix
Preface *Katō Tetsurō*	x
Contributors	xiii

	Introduction – Post-Fukushima Social Movements in Japan: An Overview *Horie Takashi, Tanaka Hikaru and Tanno Kiyoto*	1
1	Amorphous Dissent – a Conceptualization *Horie Takashi, Tanaka Hiraku and Tanno Kiyoto*	26
2	What Have Post-3.11 Social Movements Changed? *Kinoshita Chigaya*	59
3	Post-3.11 Social Movements and Politics *Horie Takashi*	81
4	Amateur Revolt: The Amorphous Social Movement Resisting the System *Tanaka Hikaru*	114
5	Twenty Years of Confrontation: Against the Ossification of US Military Bases in Okinawa *Toriyama Atsushi*	143
6	Opposing Hate Speech in Japan: Valuing Differences and Breaking New Ground for Human Rights *Tanno Kiyoto*	167

Notes	190
Bibliography	197
Index	215

Tables

3.1 The number of articles in the *Asahi Shimbun* featuring the term 'constitutionalism'   101

3.2 The numbers of articles in the *Asahi Shimbun* that contain the term 'outside the PM's official residence' (*kantei mae*) or 'outside the Diet building' (*kokkai mae*)   107

Photos

0.1 'Do not change Article Nine! No to the Abe regime!' demonstration on 2 March 2019 — 2
1.1 Fukushima nuclear power plant after the accident of 2011 — 42
1.2 Demonstration against the National Security Legislation in front of the National Diet building on 30 August 2015: people with drums and a megaphone — 49
2.1 Anti-nuclear demonstration in Osaka on 15 June 2011 — 73
3.1 Demonstration against the National Security Legislation in front the National Diet building on 30 August 2015: many people gathering — 86
4.1 'Give back my bike' demonstration in 2005 — 125
4.2 Cut-out headshot of punk rocker Machida Machizō — 128
5.1 Henoko seashore and fence before the beginning of construction in 2011 — 152
5.2 The office of the Association for Protecting the Life of Henoko (Council to Stop Helicopter Base Construction) in 2011 — 156
6.1 Sakuramoto anti-war demonstration — 175

Preface

Japan witnessed waves of street demonstrations immediately after the meltdown of a nuclear power plant in Fukushima in 2011. These were followed by a series of protests in 2015 over the National Security Legislation and a chain of anti-government actions thereafter. Suddenly, after a long dormancy up to the first decade of the twenty-first century, a variety of social movements broke out in urban Japan, shaping a new landscape in civil society. This book sheds light on these contemporary social movements from political, social and historical perspectives, analysing their demands, demographic backgrounds, organizational structures and styles. It also investigates the meanings of these movements for Japanese society and for social movement theory.

This book is based on a unique study collectively conducted by social scientists who are participants in the movements themselves. All based in Japan, the contributors took part in the demonstrations, some as their leaders and others as fellow travellers, walking on the streets with other protesters and sharing the views on the ground. At the same time, the authors also attempted to develop panoramic perspectives, conceptualizing and theorizing the protest actions as social scientists. They shuttled between the two levels – between worm's-eye views and bird's-eye views – as activists and analysts.

As participant observers, they formulated a framework to explain these movements by characterizing them as 'amorphous dissent', arising from increasingly amorphous Japanese society at large, as the title of the book suggests. The post-Fukushima movements represent fresh styles of disobedience which depart from the more structured and organized forms of protest at play in the pre-Fukushima years. The more recent amorphous configurations differ from older types

Preface   *xi*

which have crystalline structures. This project attempts to detail the rise of these amorphous movements in a variety of areas – revolts not only against nuclear power policies and the National Security Legislation but also against hate speech and the governmental programs concerning US military bases in Okinawa. Anarchist rebellion in Tokyo vividly displays the amorphous attributes that have now spread across many other street protests around the country.

This book scrutinizes the post-Fukushima social movements as the products of independent networks of civic activism, combining empirical data, interviews, participant observation and media records. We found that the conventional theories of social movements – such as social structure theory, resource mobilization theory and new social movement theory – were not fit for purpose in the analysis of contemporary social movements in Japan. Therefore, we endeavored to pursue a different model which emphasizes their non-partisan, non-institutional qualities. With no clear center, these new social movements showed non-hierarchical, non-organizational and non-ideological tendencies. As privatized individuals, participants emerged through horizontal communications, social networking services (SNS) in particular. Fragmented and liquated, they shaped a new public platform, which we call 'amorphous dissent'.

I have known the authors of this book for many years through my seminars in the Graduate School of Social Sciences at Hitotsubashi University. In recent years, we came to share an interest in social movements in Japan and pursued our research on post-3.11 activism in Japan in particular. Emeritus Professor Yoshio Sugimoto of La Trobe University in Melbourne, Australia, often encouraged us to develop our studies in full.

This book derives from conference papers presented at the 2017 Biennial Conference of the Japanese Studies Association of Australia (JSAA), held at the University of Wollongong, Sydney, Australia, from 27 to 30 June 2017. I was honored to chair the session entitled 'The ideas and practices of social movements in contemporary Japan' to which Horie Takashi, Kinoshita Chigaya and Tanaka Hikaru presented the original versions of their papers. We would like to thank

Dr. Rowena Ward, Senior Lecturer in the School of Humanities and Social Inquiry at the University of Wollongong, for her great help and cooperation at the JSAA conference. After the conference, we held several workshops in Tokyo, seizing the occasions of Emeritus Professor Sugimoto's visits to Japan, and were able to put together additional chapters by Tanno Kiyoto and Toriyama Atsushi for inclusion in this book.

This study seeks to provide building blocks for universal concepts and theories derived from the Japanese experience in the hope of generating debate for the enhancement of research on social movements in general. To this process, the translators of Trans Pacific Press, including Teresa Castelvetere, Barbara Hartley, Minako Sato and Leonie Stickland, made invaluable contributions, for which we are sincerely grateful. Thanks are also due to Miriam Riley who not only edited all the chapters judiciously but gave us thoughtful comments and suggestions.

KATŌ Tetsurō
September 2020
Tokyo

Contributors

Horie Takashi
Professor of Political Science in the Graduate School of Humanities, Tokyo Metropolitan University. He specializes in Japanese politics and the welfare state. His publications include *Gendai seiji to josei seisaku* (Contemporary Japanese politics and gender policies), Keisō Shobō, 2005; and *Japanese Politics Today: From Karaoke to Kabuki Democracy*, Palgrave Macmillan, 2011 (co-author).

Katō Tetsurō
Professor Emeritus at Hitotsubashi University. Specializing in Japanese political history, he published dozens of books, the latest of which is *Pandemikku no seijigaku* (Politics of pandemics), Kadensha, 2020.

Kinoshita Chigaya
Researcher in the International Peace Research Institute at Meiji Gakuin University. He specializes in the studies of Japanese political history. His publications include *Popyurizumu to 'min-i' no seijigaku: 3.11 igo no minshu-shugi* (The politics of populism and the 'will of the people': Post-3.11 democracy), Ōtsuki Shoten, 2017.

Tanaka Hikaru
Professor of History in the School of Law at Meiji University. His current research focuses on the history of German, Jewish and Japanese anarchism. His publications include *Doitsu anākizumu no seiritsu* (Making of German anarchism), Ochanomizu Shobō, 2002; and *Japan and the High Treason Incident*, Routledge, 2013 (co-author).

TANNO *Kiyoto*
Professor of Sociology in the Graduate School of Humanities, Tokyo Metropolitan University. He specialises in studies of international migration. He authored *Migrant Workers in Contemporary Japan: An Institutional Perspective on Transnational Employment*, Trans Pacific Press, 2013; and *Gaikokujin no jinken no shakaigaku* (Sociology of foreigners' human rights in Japan), Yoshida Shoten, 2018.

TORIYAMA *Atsushi*
Professor, Research Institute for Islands Sustainability, Ryukyu University. He has published in the area of the history of modern Okinawa, including *Okinawa: Kichi shakai no kigen to sōkoku* (Okinawa: The origins of military base society and its conflict with the US, 1945–56), Keisō Shobō, 2013.

Introduction
Post-Fukushima Social Movements in Japan: An Overview

Horie Takashi, Tanaka Hikaru and Tanno Kiyoto

When disparate movements conjoin

At 2.00 p.m. on 2 March 2019, a crowd of demonstrators numbering about 1,200 departed Kōenji Central Park at the southern entrance to JR Kōenji Station in Tokyo's Suginami Ward chanting the slogan 'Do not change Article Nine! No to the Abe regime!' and marched along the Ōme Highway as far as Asagaya Station. Slogans opposed to the revision of Article Nine of the Constitution and the construction of a new military base at Henoko in Okinawa were printed on flyers distributed in advance, and many of the participating groups named on the flyers were from the Article Nine Association (Kyūjō no Kai) composed of people active in Suginami Ward and elsewhere who supported the former Japanese Socialist Party and Communist Party, and who advocated for the protection of Article Nine. Others listed as participants in this demonstration included anti-war peace movement groups, women's groups, labor unions, pensioners' associations and chambers of commerce and industry and suchlike, in addition to branch organizations belonging to such political parties as the Communist Party, New Socialist Party, the Greens, the Constitutional Democratic Party and the Social Democratic Party ('*Kyūjō kaeru na! Abe seiken NO! 2019/3/2 Suginami demo*' 2019).

The demonstration was divided into two groups: the first adopted an orthodox style of protest, brandishing a horizontal banner inscribed with the words 'Peace and democracy are in peril. Stop the Abe regime now!' at the head of the march, with a chorus of women's voices chanting the rallying call from a loudspeaker van, and participants in the demonstration then repeating it as they marched along holding up horizontal banners, labor union flags and so on. The lead vehicle

Photo 0.1: 'Do not change Article Nine! No to the Abe regime!' demonstration on 2 March 2019. Source: mkimpo.

of the second group, which followed the first, was called a *saund kā* (sound truck). On its tray, three bands took turns playing live music at high volume all the way to the end point of the march. The vehicle was hung with horizontal banners, saying 'Abe cannot sing rock' and 'Abe guillotine rock'; unlike the first group, there was no uniformity, it being a collection of diverse individuals. Behind the sound truck came a procession of young people dressed as Prime Minister Abe or as the 'super-rich', or carrying the LGBT rainbow flag or the anti-fascist (Antifa) flag, or holding signs calling for opposition to the construction of a military base at Henoko and so on, and here and there the chant of 'Abe, quit!' erupted sporadically. Out of the six people listed as eliciting participation in this demonstration were three university professors, one translator of German literature and one video journalist, with ages ranging from their fifties to their seventies. The sixth, in his forties, was titled 'Owner of Amateur Revolt [Shirōto no ran] Shop Number Five'.

This last individual, the youngest among the recruiters, was Matsumoto Hajime, neither an intellectual nor a journalist, but the 'owner' of a recycling shop called Amateur Revolt Shop Number Five. The group that he and his companions organized was the second one, led by the sound truck. As noted above, the first group, formed by people of the older generations who had appealed to the second group for participation, was made up of various organizations that supported political parties. Their style of demonstration consisted of repeating the same chant, and their unified ideal of 'peace and democracy' was hoisted aloft on their horizontal banner. By contrast, in the second group, a diverse assortment of individuals displayed different messages; feelings towards the Abe regime were expressed in an extremely abstract way on the horizontal banner attached to the sound truck, and more direct messages were conveyed by the music played by the three bands as well as via the vocalists' speeches.[1]

In Kōenji, since 2005, Matsumoto and his companions had created the special features displayed by this second group, which could be described as the Japanese version of European autonomous movements. Unlike its European counterparts, the Japanese movement does not occupy empty houses, but instead operates a variety of shops with cheap rent. In these spaces, small 'gatherings' consisting of diverse people and a form of 'autonomy' came into being, and a subculture based on people freely interrelating and alternative values and attitudes was born. Furthermore, a network that loosely connected such multiple spaces took shape (see Chapter Four by Tanaka). Through people's engagement in this network, demonstrations and gatherings were sometimes formed, and it became possible to mobilize from several hundred to several thousand participants for these purposes. This was because Amateur Revolt had no unified ideology or constant structure and pursued 'fun' at demonstrations as a 'stir'. As a result, the street became a free and open space, and a diverse and motley group of people took part as individuals or with invited friends, either in pursuit of such spaces, or motivated by agreement with the demonstration's intent.

Assuming that each of the organizations that joined the first group mentioned above fit the definition of classical social movements in the sense that they have a constant structure, theme or goal, then Amateur Revolt would be classified as a 'submerged network' as specified by Melucci in his research on new social movements (1989: 70). In Amateur Revolt's network, values, attitudes and subcultures that resist being integrated into the system are formed amid the everyday; and on this basis, demonstrations and gatherings with the abovementioned unique characteristics have at times taken shape. The fusion of movements and subcultures was evident, for example, when the 'Punk Rocker Labor Union' that performed on the sound truck was organized at a police station while Amateur Revolt's application to hold a demonstration was in process.[2] Movements with this kind of unique style are brought into being with a consciousness of holding 'interesting' demonstrations with a sense of 'revelry', counter to the student and anti-war movements shaped by previous generations that were 'serious' rather than fun, making them unappealing to young people. In spite of this, why did Amateur Revolt take part in the demonstration in Suginami Ward in response to an invitation from the older generations whose movements they viewed so negatively?

According to Matsumoto, the older generations include those who experienced the student movement of 1968. Until the Suginami demonstration, they had been disconnected, and were divided into an assortment of cliques. However, impelled by the thought that it was now the time to oppose the Abe government's misrule, they joined hands for a 'final battle'. The person who urged Matsumoto to participate was an activist from this older generation who ran an electrical shop in the same street as Amateur Revolt Shop Number Five. This person had also previously stood unsuccessfully as a Socialist Party candidate on numerous occasions in the Suginami Ward Assembly elections. When passing Matsumoto on the street, he had told Matsumoto that they were going to hold a demonstration to oppose the Abe regime, saying, 'Everyone is angry', and 'You come, too!'. Such a scene, in which a member of the older generation took the lead and called on younger ones to rise up, is a 'new' phenomenon (Matsumoto 2019). The reason why Matsumoto responded to the invitation is as follows.

While Matsumoto had viewed older generations' demonstrations in a critical light, he had also discovered some commonality between the generation of young people that lived in Kōenji, including himself, and the 'bunch of elders'. After retiring from the student movement in the late 1960s, the 'generation of elders' had not only continued to demonstrate, but had also 'opened rice-cracker bakeries or greengrocers or electrical shops, and continued to speak out while building people's livelihoods and communities' (Matsumoto 2019). 'Thanks to those who created spaces for people to congregate' in that manner, 'a phenomenon has arisen in which the oldies still shuffle along to get together'. According to Matsumoto, it is precisely such 'turning one's back on authority, and making one's own community and neighborhood' that constitutes 'rebellion'. Moreover, such demonstrations that are based in community are the very things that pose a threat to the powerful (Matsumoto 2019).

What Matsumoto terms 'community' does not signify a traditional collective, but rather a livelihood sphere created by the alignment of the common values and interests of disparate individuals who have congregated in an area of a city: Matsumoto sometimes simply calls this a 'gathering' (*atsumari*). Matsumoto's emphasis on 'community' in this way is probably due to the fact that in Kōenji they created a 'community' through engagement in all kinds of activities, and this formed the basis of the success of the huge anti-nuclear power demonstrations held from April 2011. The 'community' they built, starting in 2005 and continuing to the present day, has been shaped by an extremely random assortment of people – seemingly incompatible – assembling in Kōenji and elsewhere, and through social movements such as demonstrations and the operation of recycling shops and the like (see Chapter Four). Matsumoto also stresses 'autonomy' (*jichi*), and on this point, too, Amateur Revolt is very similar to European autonomous movements. In Europe, importance has also been placed upon creating places for 'gathering' – mainly the empty houses occupied by movements – and the 'autonomy' (*jiritsu*) of this kind of gathering. Those who assemble at Amateur Revolt, too, are uneasy about the systems in Japanese society that control their thoughts and attitudes in their everyday lives or force them into a mold, and seek to escape from such control and 'live as they please'. For that reason, they share an awareness that the Abe government, which promotes policies such as constitutional amendment, increase in military spending, expansion of US military bases, preferential treatment of large corporations and the wealthy and the promotion of nuclear power, threatens their livelihoods. Accordingly, if they are invited by the older generations to demonstrations calling for the overthrow of the Abe regime, they will respond.

However, unlike the older generations' movements, Amateur Revolt has emphasized 'fun' and 'revelry' at its demonstrations and gatherings since its beginning in 2005: expression via music and performances, etc., has been much employed, fusion with youth subculture has occurred and slogans are rarely political in nature, instead highlighting issues more relevant to people's everyday lives. For that reason, it created an open, free space in which even people who did not understand the political intent could participate. On the other hand, diverse individuals and places connected to Amateur Revolt's network through everyday interactions functioned as the basis for information transfer and transmission. Herein lies one of the reasons Amateur Revolt has been able to mobilize more than ten thousand people to participate in the anti-nuclear power demonstrations it has organized since April 2011.

Amateur Revolt has always had fluctuations among key members, and in recent years, has started to attract attention from activists from such places as Hong Kong, Taiwan and South Korea. As Kōenji became a place frequented by Asian activists, participants in Amateur Revolt became increasingly diverse. In 2018, Amateur Revolt began a movement to oppose the redevelopment of the Kōenji Station precinct and has held multiple demonstrations and speaking events on this issue. Those who spoke at the events were of diverse backgrounds, of different generations and occupations: Indonesians residing in Kōenji, members of the generation that Matsumoto calls 'the elders' (*chōrōshū*) – including electrical appliance shop owners, recycling shop owners and lawyers – as well as 'punk chicks with heavily-pierced faces', musicians, childcare workers and so on.[3] The reason that an amorphous movement linking diverse and motley individuals and transcending generation, occupation and national boundaries was able to be formed is because Amateur Revolt has from the outset had as its ideal an 'autonomy' that allows people to enjoy such 'gatherings' fostered by their 'selfish' pursuits.

From 2005, Matsumoto connected with the older generations, in addition to his local shopping strip. In the post-2011 anti-nuclear power movement he organized demonstrations with participants from all generations; and after 2018, along with local residents, he started an anti-redevelopment movement that transcended both generation and occupation. The basis for Matsumoto's response to the call from 'the elders' at the March 2019 demonstration noted at the beginning of this chapter was shaped during those fifteen years. In this way, Amateur Revolt came to form loose ties with the movements of older generations, despite the latter's strict structure and ideology.

In this manner, old movements grouped according to political parties, championing causes from decades past such as peace or protection of the Constitution, have begun to hold demonstration rallies alongside the new-style movements involving younger generations that have come to the limelight since the 2000s. Underpinning such circumstances lies the reactivation of social movements which took momentum from the movement opposing nuclear power generation, triggered especially by the 2011 Fukushima Dai-ichi nuclear power plant accident. Amid the vibrancy exhibited by Japanese social movements for the first time in several decades, a motley collection of people has come to participate in demonstrations, transcending not only generations but also the boundaries of diverse attributes.

This phenomenon in which a movement is formed by diverse and disparate people is evident in other cases beyond Amateur Revolt – there have been diverse, disparate, disorganized and undefined elements among recent resurgent social movements in Japan. This forms the basis for our argument that social movements in Japan today can be considered 'amorphous' (see Chapter One).

This book conducts a multifaceted investigation into the reactivation of such 'amorphous' social movements, and this introductory chapter offers an outline of the overall perspective presented within. We next provide an overview of the general sequence of events relating to the social movements that followed the accident at the Fukushima nuclear power plant, and then move on to classify the characteristics of earlier social movements in order to consider the ways in which these differ from the later ones. In the penultimate section, we seek hints from among existing studies as to how to characterize participants in the social movements of recent years, before providing a summary of the chapters of this book.

A general chronology of post-3.11 movements[4]

In this section, we review the general sequence of events relating to recent movements that have attracted societal attention – specifically, the anti-nuclear power movement and the movement against the National Security Legislation. In addition, we provide a simple introduction to a counter movement against the racist movement that targets Japan-resident Koreans by means of hate speech and so on as a critical movement in the same era (although its participants are not as numerous in comparison to those involved in the movements noted above). In terms of post-3.11 social movements, the former two are often seen as representative (Satō 2018), but all three, including the counter-racist movement, are considered to have similarities (Tamura and Tamura 2016). As for the movements against nuclear power plants and the National Security Legislation, see Chapter Two by Kinoshita and Chapter Three by Horie, and on movements against racism, see Kinoshita's chapter as well as Chapter Six by Tanno.

The anti-nuclear power movement after the Fukushima accident

Up until the Fukushima accident, there were fifty-four nuclear power stations in Japan, but no major opposition movements arose in the process of their construction outside the areas where the facilities were located, and nuclear power generation did not become a national political issue. However, when the accident at the Chernobyl nuclear power plant in the former Soviet Union occurred in 1986, anxiety regarding nuclear power generation spread. At that time, especially, spontaneous civic movements emerged that centered on highly-educated urban housewives that differed from systematic mobilizations, and these were called 'new wave' to differentiate them from pre-existing movements (Hasegawa 2018; Andō 2019). However, in comparison with European countries, there was both geographical and psychological distance from Chernobyl, and concern about the danger of radiation did not turn into a strong call for the abandonment of nuclear power generation in Japan. It wasn't until the 2012 lower house elections, after the Fukushima accident, that major political parties made nuclear power generation a point of contention in their electoral campaigns (Honda 2014).

For most Japanese, the Fukushima accident became the impetus for serious thought about the dangers of nuclear power generation. A number of demonstrations seeking the cessation of nuclear power generation were held just a few days after the accident. Among the movements in that early stage, the most significant was the 'Stop nuclear power!!!!!' (*Genpatsu yamero!!!!!*) rally, planned by members of Amateur Revolt on 10 April in Tokyo's Kōenji, which drew 15,000 participants, far exceeding the organizers' expectations.[5] On 11 June and 11 September that same year, large-scale demonstrations were held in multiple locations, even in Tokyo alone.

Moreover, in September, thirteen groups that had hitherto been acting in isolation formed the Metropolitan Coalition Against Nukes (Hangenren). Hangenren started to hold protest rallies every Friday from March 2012, and these continue to this day. They are called 'Friday protest in front of the prime minister's official residence', but in actuality, rallies are also held in front of the main gate of the National Diet of Japan, and other small-scale gatherings are held at several places in the vicinity of the Diet as well. The largest venue for protest is the *supīchi eria* (speech area) facing the main gate of the Diet, and there, anyone who wishes to do so can make a speech. The speeches and speakers are diverse, from evacuees from Fukushima expressing their feelings to specialists in nuclear power and energy policy accusing governmental explanations of deception, based on scientific observations. Newspaper and television reportage have also been singled out for criticism, and the speeches play the role of 'alternative media'. Some participants come from areas other than Tokyo, and on occasion there are guests from overseas. Although it is called the 'speech area', the chanting of slogans to music also occurs. The Friday protest rallies are punctual, starting at 6.00 p.m. every week (6.30 p.m. in winter), and ending at 8 p.m.

Participants in the first Friday protest rally held in March 2012 numbered 300. The number of participants from April that year through May was over 1,000, but from June, when the Noda Yoshihiko government announced a positive stance towards restarting the Ōi nuclear power plant, numbers increased dramatically.

Each reactor in a nuclear power plant needs to be switched off every thirteen months for regular inspection, but after the Fukushima accident, the restarting of non-operational reactors was suspended. For that reason, the number of nuclear power plants in operation in Japan gradually dwindled, and in May 2012 all nuclear power generation ceased. However, claiming that a serious shortage of electric power would occur in the summer, the Noda government stated that it would restart the Ōi nuclear power plant in Fukui Prefecture, igniting the protest movement.

On the first Friday following Noda's announcement of the restart, participants swelled to 45,000, and by the end of June, a peak of 200,000 was reached. This number far exceeded the projections of both Hangenren and the police. There were so many participants that they spilled over from the footpath onto the road, and this was widely reported in the mass media. Moreover, 200,000 people also attended the rally held in the vicinity of the Diet on Sundays in July (numbers according to Kinoshita 2013c). Protest action against nuclear power generation after the Fukushima accident was not confined to Tokyo – the Friday protests spread like wildfire across the entire country.

In this manner, the idea of the 'demonstration' that had long remained dormant in Japanese society began to be realized. This formed the backdrop for yet another movement that reached its peak in 2015.

The movement against the National Security Legislation

Prime Minister Abe Shinzō of the Liberal Democratic Party (LDP), who was returned to power in the December 2012 general elections, both showed a positive stance towards the restarting of nuclear power plants and embarked upon his cherished aim of constitutional reform. In 2013, he tried to amend Article Ninety-Six which stipulated the conditions for constitutional reform, lowering the number of Diet members necessary for proposing change to the Constitution from two-thirds of both houses to a simple majority, but this was received with negativity and abandoned. In the following year, 2014, he changed the government's traditional view relating to Article Nine of the Constitution, making a cabinet decision deeming the right of collective self-defense to be constitutional. Until then, the government had repeatedly stated in the National Diet that it could not exercise the right of collective self-defense. With this in mind, in 2015, the ruling party submitted bills relating to peace and security (the National Security Legislation) to the Diet. The passing of this legislation would mean that even if Japan were not exposed to direct attack, its Self-Defense Forces would be able to assist the US military.

During discussion on the bills, three constitutional scholars, including one recommended by the LDP, testified in the Diet that the National Security Legislation was unconstitutional, and interest in the bills increased. Even so, as the government aimed to pass the legislation during the current Diet session, an opposition movement started to draw a large number of supporters.

What especially courted attention was a university students' body called SEALDs (Students Emergency Action for Liberal Democracy), created in May 2015. SEALDs evolved from a student body called SASPL (Students Against the Secret Protection Law), which was formed by a group of college students who had toured anti-nuclear demonstrations and held events at clubs that also hosted study sessions. SEALDs was frequently discussed in the media including newspapers, magazines and television, and there was no dearth of individuals taking part in the movement and emergent activist bodies due to exposure to the extensive reportage. 'SEALDs' was chosen among the top ten buzzwords of 2015.

Even prior to moves around the National Security Legislation reaching their peak, however, the 'Sensō sasenai: kyūjō kowasu na! Sōgakari kōdō jikkō iinkai' (known as 'Sōgakari kōdō') ([We] will not allow [Japan] to wage war: Don't destroy Article Nine! All-Out Action Implementation Committee), formed in December 2014 by the older-generation groups that had long continued their movement, started to attract large numbers of participants. Since its promulgation in 1947, the Japanese Constitution has never been revised, but the conservative LDP government has been enthusiastic regarding constitutional reform and rearmament. In response, in post-war Japan, the constitutional protection movement that defends Article Nine, which stipulates the renunciation of war, was integrated with the peace movement. Amid the gradual expansion of the Self-Defense Forces' sphere of activity, the constitutional protection faction, which felt a sense of impending crisis, founded a new movement in 2004 called the 'Article Nine Association' (Kyūjō no Kai), which spread across sympathetic movements in all areas of the nation.

This pre-existing constitutional protection/peace movement was revitalized by the moves of the Abe administration that successively deviated from the consensus in post-war Japanese society. In addition to the revitalization of pre-existing movements, numerous new movements emerged in response to the National Security Legislation. Apart from SEALDs, opposition toward the National Security Legislation gave rise to all kinds of movements according to their participants' attributes. The Association of Scholars Opposed to National Security Legislation (Anpo hōsei ni hantai suru gakusha no kai; hereafter, Gakusha no Kai) was formed, and in conjunction, more than 150 supporters' groups were established at universities across the country. Other newly founded bodies included the Anti-National Security Legislation Mothers Against War (Anpo kanren hōan ni hantai suru mama no kai; hereafter, Mama no Kai), groups including OLDs (seniors) and MIDDLEs (middle-aged people) whose names were a pun on SEALDs, and T-ns SOWL (formed by upper-secondary students), which began their activities one after another.

Due to the power from the combination of these old and new movements, the movement opposing the National Security Legislation was able to draw more than 100,000 people in Tokyo alone. Among them were many who had no organizational background and were neither students nor academics, but who gathered after having viewed news media or social networking sites. Hangenren's Misao Redwolf testifies that in 'Sōgakari kōdō', classified in the news media as being of the 'organizational mobilization type', there were 'lots of participants who did not belong to any organization' (Okuda, Oguma and Redwolf 2016: 42).

People who participated individually rallied to the call of these various movement bodies, and at the 30 August 'Reject the war bill! Abe government, resign! 8/30 100,000 at the Diet, 1 million nationwide massive action', demonstrations and rallies were held at more than 300 venues around the country, with 120,000 deemed to have participated in front of the Diet building, with an aggregate of 350,000 in its vicinity. Day after day until the establishment of the bill on 19 September, multitudes surged into the area in front of the Diet building.

The racist and anti-racist movements

The above two movements drew attention to social movements in general by drawing many participants in the 2010s. Though smaller in scale than the above, another important social movement came into being in this period.

From the 2000s, a xenophobic movement that engaged in hate speech against Japan's Korean residents became active, causing significant damage in Korean towns and the like. At its center was a movement formed in 2007 called the 'Citizens' Group that Will Not Forgive Special Privileges for Koreans in Japan' (Zainichi tokken o yurusanai shimin no kai; hereafter, Zaitokukai). Counter-movements arose in response, and of these, 'Corps of Racist-Bashers' (Reishisuto o shibaki tai; hereafter, Shibakitai), in particular, played a central role. Noma Yasumichi, a core activist in Hangenren, instigated the creation of Shibakitai.

In this introductory chapter, we do not have the space to explain the circumstances in detail (see Noma 2018), but in the description below, we touch upon this anti-racist movement as an important social movement in contemporary Japan, along with those opposing nuclear power and the National Security Legislation.

Post-war social movements and their transformation

From the impact of aerial photographs of the crowds of demonstration participants, post-3.11 social movements are often talked about in contrast to the 1960 campaign against the US-Japan Security Treaty,[6] and occasionally to the student rebellion of 1968. There are also scholars who argue that Japanese society has entered a new phase in its protest cycle after a period of stagnation that lasted for about thirty-five years from the mid-1970s (Chiavacci and Obinger 2018). However, post-3.11 social movements are completely different from post-war and 1960s movements on a number of fronts. This section surveys the characteristics of post-war Japanese social movements in an effort to understand the characteristics of post-3.11 social movements.

Post-war democracy and 1960s movements

After World War II, an upsurge was seen in the social movements that are today referred to in concert with 'post-war democracy'. Movements at that time were also called 'progressive national movements' (*kakushin kokumin undō*), and attracted many participants, culminating in the 1960 campaign against the US-Japan Security Treaty. They accomplished a certain amount, such as occasionally winning concessions from the government. The mass participation of the young urban dwellers who enjoyed peace and democracy demonstrated their strong rejection of the government's drive to return to the pre-war form of rule it was trying to implement.

Political scientist Takabatake Michitoshi called the consciousness that brought about an upsurge in post-war social movements the 'modernization = peace consciousness complex' (*kindaika=heiwa ishiki fukugō*), incorporating the sense of anticipation for 'modernization' since the Meiji era – modernization leading to urbanization and then to rising living standards – and the sense of hope for 'peace' that comes from experiencing the calamities of war and defeat. This consciousness is deemed to have been formed and expanded through the 1950s, especially centering upon youth, women and people who had flowed into the cities. Under these circumstances, the new Constitution both guaranteed peace in Japan and peace in the home, focused on the nuclear family, and post-war democracy acknowledged the pursuit of happiness in private life, while suppressing the tyranny of the military clique. For the social strata that became the beneficiaries of the post-war democratic reforms, their escape from the shackles of the traditional community of pre-war society and new freedom to pursue their respective personal goals framed both the meaning of 'modernization' in post-war society and the urbanization of their lifestyles. For that reason, a 'reverse course' that went against post-war reforms triggered widespread structural tension that threatened these accomplishments (Takabatake 1979: 327). Here, there is also an aspect of the mobilization of conservative sentiment backed by remnant memories of the war.

Moreover, factors in the social structure enabled broad-ranging mobilization. Ishida Takeshi points out that organizations and groups such as labor unions and various cultural groups, student groups and so on that were originally formed for different purposes produced immediate results through their mobilization in movements in an 'all-embracing' manner (Ishida 1961). The movement petitioning for the banning of atomic and hydrogen bombs initiated in 1954 by Suginami housewives spread to the extent that it amassed the signatures of more than thirty million people, but in one sense the collection of signatures functioned through the existing network of neighborhood associations and the like. The '*Sayonara genpatsu issenman-nin akushon*' (Goodbye nuclear power generation ten-million-person action) campaign which started up in June 2011 in response to the Fukushima accident had collected about 8.8 million signatures as of July 2019 (http://sayonara-nukes.org/), and so could be said to be an extremely successful campaign; yet it came nowhere near the movement of the 1950s. The persistence of a solid network of neighborhood associations is a feature of Japanese society (Pekkanen 2006), but these days it is rare for there to be sufficient connections to enable movements to exercise influence upon political petitioning. In the 1970s, residents' movements were active in every area, but these, too, are assumed to have relied upon local organizations (Krauss and Simcock 1980).

In the post-war era, the mechanism by which the desire to conserve newly-acquired rights connected to participation through the medium of existing community and social groups and organizations changed significantly from the 1960s onwards. Firstly, from the shock of the movement opposing the 1960 US-Japan Security Treaty, the LDP, the ruling party which until the 1950s had aimed for the restoration of a pre-war form of social order, revised its method of governance (restraining its stance on constitutional amendment, switching to economocentrism and so on). Secondly, in concert with Japan becoming a prosperous society through rapid economic growth, the shape of existing groups changed (see Chapter One); and thirdly, the experience of war gradually weathered away.

In the 1960s, however, new movements organized by the younger generation arose and attracted attention. Firstly, the Citizen's League for Peace in Vietnam (Betonamu ni heiwa o! Shimin rengō; hereafter, Beheiren) was formed in 1965, captivating many young people. Furthermore, from the late 1960s to the early 1970s, the student movement reached its peak at universities across the country. In comparison with the 1960 campaign against the US-Japan Security Treaty, which drove the prime minister to resign and prescribed the subsequent direction of LDP politics, Beheiren and university-based movements had only a small impact upon the political process in a narrow sense – their cultural influence, however, was more significant.

These movements inherited much from the conventional citizens' and student movements, but in some respects they repudiated them. For example, Beheiren was based upon the participation of individuals, and the Zenkyōtō undō (the All-Campus Joint Struggle movement; hereafter, 'the Zenkyōtō movement' or simply

'Zenkyōtō') that erupted across many universities in the late 1960s criticized the conventional type of student council with which all students were automatically affiliated, referring to them as 'Potsdam student councils' (*Potsudamu jichikai*). The Zenkyōtō movement, initiated in response to separate problems at each university – such as hikes in tuition fees, student punishments and issues around student dormitories – led to a drive to question post-war democracy and the behavior of progressive intellectuals. In that sense, it differed in character from movements from the previous era which had been understood as part of 'post-war democracy'.

Moreover, an awareness sprouted that was different again from the desire, rooted in the reality of being 'victims' of war, to preserve the peace and freedom gained in the post-war period. Firstly, at the time of the 1965 conclusion of the normalization treaty between Japan and Korea, an opposition movement arose out of the guilt of Japan's aggression in the region that emerged in the peace movement around that time. Many young people took part in the movement opposing the Vietnam War that posed no direct personal threat to them. Amongst those who had experienced the student movement from the late 1960s into the 1970s, there was no small number who had later participated in movements for Third-World and minority rights. In a similar manner to many Western countries, the student movement of the late 1960s also involved developments that linked with the feminist movement that came later.

The stagnation of movements and citizens' depoliticization

In the 1980s and 1990s, countless small-scale movements existed at the local level. One cannot underestimate the significance of the involvement of people who had taken part in the student movement in the 1960s in various later movements (Andō 2013), but in Japan the recognition that social movements had stagnated was widely accepted.

In Japan, movements spearheaded by baby boomers who had been responsible for the student movement around 1970 did not succeed in attracting members of the younger generations (Steinhoff 2018). It became rare for these movements to draw the interest of the media and the general public broadly, and neither were they perceived as part of a national movement. This contrasts with the situation in other advanced countries where the legacy of the 1960s' New Left later became established as a social movement, giving rise to environmental parties and the like (Chiavacci and Obinger 2018).

Various explanations have been given as to why the youth movement of the 1960s was not carried on by succeeding generations in Japan. A widely-held view stresses that the student movement's engagement in a fiercely violent struggle which culminated in internal strife implanted a negative image of demonstrations and social movements in the populace (Andō 2013; Cassegård 2013; Chiavacci and Obinger 2018; Steinhoff 2018). Although not limited to the question of violence, it has been argued that for the current younger generation, the image of past social movements is entirely negative (Tominaga 2017).

Moreover, there is also a tendency to read Japan's transformation into a corporate society as it became an economic superpower and the proliferation of individualism and consumerism as underpinning the development of conservatism since the 1980s. A growing conservatism and disaffection with politics was particularly identified in the younger generation, who were once the key leaders of progressive social movements.

From the 1970s onwards, as protest activities in the West were undertaken by a broad spectrum of the population, including the highly-educated middle class, social movements and public protest became accepted as part of the democratic policy-making process. In contrast, in Japan, social movements lost leverage in the national policy-making process, and protest activities became tinged with social stigma. As a result, even though Japan is not bereft of social conflict, it became a society where public protest was invisible, and the participation rate in legitimate demonstrations and boycotts became the lowest among advanced industrial societies (Dalton 2014: 54).

The failure of large social movements up to the 1960s to leave a systematic legacy is also cited as a Japanese characteristic. Movements like Beheiren, which were averse to the creation of a formal hierarchical structure, did not take a positive attitude towards succession to the next generation in contrast to Western movements which stockpiled their resources and progressively institutionalized (Chiavacci and Obinger 2018: 11). It has also been argued that movements that aimed at self-transformation avoided producing any substantial results (Andō 2013).

However, a counterargument can be raised against the argument that Japanese citizens had shut themselves away in their personal lives while social movements consistently stagnated. The 1995 Great Hanshin-Awaji Earthquake Disaster triggered an increasing focus on volunteers, and expectations regarding 'citizens' activities' resulted in the establishment of the NPO Law in 1998. This has given weight to the view that denies the suggestion of weakness in Japanese citizens' attitudes towards participation in social activity.

Conversely, citizens' activities and NPOs that advocate such things as 'cooperation with the authorities' and an 'equal partnership with the administration' are sometimes characterized as having 'lost leftist leanings' (Higashi 2004). In Japan, where there is a weak culture of philanthropy, the source of revenue for NPOs is fragile, and their reliance upon government grants and commissions for projects has tended to increase. There is also the risk that citizens' activities will be harnessed by the authorities for their own uses. In this respect, the Japanese administration, which has only limited resources due to its small government, has looked externally to make up for the shortfall (Muramatsu 1994), making citizens' energetic activity very convenient for the government. On the other hand, the increasing invisibility of more political social movements antagonistic to the government spawned a discourse on the decline of social movements in general.

However, even in the period of so-called 'stagnation', a new current of social movements has arisen, and continuity with the anti-poverty movement, the Freeter movement and so forth that appeared in the 1990s is evident in movements since the 2000s. From the 1990s into the 2000s, social movements such as Amateur Revolt and Dame-ren (The Association of the Pathetic), with new ideas far removed from conventional common practice, began a variety of initiatives (Watanabe

2012; Cassegård 2013; see also Chapter Two of this volume). Mōri Yoshitaka says of the movements that have diffused among young people since the 2000s that 'it is impossible get a clear sense of where they originated':

> If they were union movements, the participants would be union members, and more than that, they would be employees of some company. With the left-wing movement, in many cases [...] they were divided into blocks centering on a political party. Even students, who were called 'nonsectarian' (*nonsekuto*), belonged to some sort of student council or group, or at least to a university. [...] Most movements nowadays are, in contrast, composed of people affiliated neither with an organization or faction, nor a company or university. [...] just as the labor market has become fluid, people's sense of belonging, too, has become fluid, and the places where they belong have also multiplied. (Mōri 2009: 183–184)

Among such movements, there are also elements of methods and style that have been inherited by subsequent movements, like the 'sound demonstrations' that attracted attention in the 2003 movement in opposition to the Iraq War. It is not rare for protest action in recent years to try to move away from the conventional style of movements by incorporating music, dancing and fashion. The spread of social movements after 3.11 did not emerge out of nowhere – there was certainly continuity with some aspects of prior social movements (see Chapter Two).

It has been suggested that the post-1990s movements which featured a festive atmosphere contributed to overcoming the nationwide trauma that resulted from the social movements associated with violence and danger (Cassegård 2013). In one respect, the anti-nuclear power movement, which also followed the tradition of festivity, emphasized ease of participation. For example, Hattori Norimichi, who later took part in Hangenren, says of the 'energy shift' parade in which he participated in April 2011, 'because demonstrations have had the image that they are hard for ordinary people to participate in, it was described as a parade, not a demonstration. It was a parade with a cheerful atmosphere in which many parents and their children participated together. I thought, "If this is what it is, I can do it, too. I shall help [in creating] a space for turning anger into action and raising our voices'" (Hattori 2016: 57). The word 'parade', which has a festive connotation, was frequently employed instead of 'demonstration' from the 2000s onwards.

However, festivity and antagonism are not necessarily incompatible. SEALDs' rap-like chants also often include phrases that convey aggression, such as 'Abe, quit!' (*Abe wa yamero*), and 'Don't arbitrarily decide' (*Katte ni kimen na*). As in the case of the 'Angry drummers' (*Ikari no doramu tai*), music can also be used to express anger.

Despite the developments described above, the image that social movements in Japan had stagnated was stubbornly entrenched. At the time of the Iraq War, protest actions involving hundreds of thousands of participants were held in the world's major cities, but Japanese participants were vastly lower in number. The anti-war demonstrations in New York and London were reported to have involved hundreds of thousands of people, while in Japan, the organizer of the 'Peace Walk' against the Iraq War said that 'the limit on mobilization in Japan is twenty to thirty thousand participants... Unfortunately, that is [the state of] Japanese citizen power at the present time' (Kobayashi 2003).

As such, in the 2010s, protest actions involving numerous participants emerged one after another in Japanese society where it had long been believed that social movements were in decline. What kinds of people participate in these movements? We turn to this question in the next section.

What kinds of people have participated?

Next, let us consider what kinds of people brought about the first upsurge in social movements in several decades.

News coverage of both demonstrations for denuclearization and those opposing the National Security Legislation was frequent, which was unusual for the Japanese media that was normally apathetic towards social movements in general. Certainly, their scale was quite large, but another major factor was that the participants departed markedly from the conventional image of demonstrators. News media on the anti-nuclear demonstrations reported that participants were 'ordinary people'. Their clear divergence from the traditional 'activist' image was often emphasized, many being of the younger generation, with numerous women and those accompanied by their children also participating. Television news particularly favored such aspects, and the camera was often directed at participants who had taken their children along (Hōsō o kataru kai monitā gurūpu, 2012).[7] 'Ordinary people without a labor union flag' were particularly favored in mass media coverage (Noma 2012: 160–162).

On the topic of participants in demonstrations against nuclear power generation, Itō Masaaki points out that the white-collar businesspeople who, under normal circumstances, would often be seen in the center of the metropolis on a Friday evening were relatively absent. This accords with our own observations. Itō broadly classifies the central participants in these demonstrations into the following three categories. The first were seniors mainly comprising people from the so-called Japanese baby-boom generation (*dankai no sedai*), mostly born between 1947 and 1949. The second were aged from their twenties to thirties and were young people who did not seem to be salaried workers, but instead 'free spirits'. They were members of the so-called 'lost generation',[8] different from students, and males were in the majority. The third category comprised housewives accompanied by their children, young couples and groups of women and students (Itō 2012: 119–122).

Oguma Eiji, who focuses on the second group, says that the people who were conspicuous at the anti-nuclear demonstrations were 'freely-dressed men and women in their thirties to forties, and unaccompanied by children' (Oguma 2012a: 142–143). This stratum, which is assumed to have 'high intelligence, and probably a high average level of education' from the way they discuss the issue of nuclear power generation and the way they call attention to it, would in former times have been 'working at a company, wearing a suit, or housewives busy with child-rearing', and would be expected to be a stratum most unconnected with demonstrations, aside from those mobilized by unions. As a result of the structural transformations in Japanese society, such as the 'increase in workers in non-regular employment, including those with a high education, and single-person households', the number of people able to take part in demonstrations has grown (Oguma 2012a: 142–143).

According to a survey of participants in demonstrations on 11 June and 11 September 2011, 40% of participants were in their twenties or thirties (Hirabayashi 2013). However, as we continued to commute to protest actions, we witnessed the proportion of young people gradually dwindle, and that of people in their sixties and above rise. According to a large-scale public-opinion poll targeting the general voting public in Tokyo conducted in 2017, several years after the movement's heyday, participation by people in their sixties to seventies was markedly large (Satō et al. 2018). Furthermore, although they were far fewer by comparison, participants in their late thirties to early forties were the mainstay of Shibakitai (Noma 2018: 76).

In Oguma's analysis of a survey conducted on fifty-five key activists, the major fields of occupation of core members organizing the movement against nuclear power generation which first appeared after 3.11 included the music industry, information technology, design, construction design, editing, translation and so on (nineteen out of fifty-five). Following Antonio Negri and others, Oguma calls these people in unstable employment the 'cognitive precariat'. Other key activists worked in healthcare and the like, and regular employees of major firms numbered only three, two of whom worked for foreign-owned companies (Oguma 2016). According to Hangenren's Misao Redwolf, 'Hangenren is a group of about twenty people, but among these there are only four or five with experience of being company employees' (Okuda, Oguma and Redwolf 2016: 36). Hangenren's activities, which have involved ongoing protest action every Friday for more than eight years, have been sustained by such people whose time is comparatively flexible.

In the aforementioned large-scale public-opinion poll, the rate of participation by the self-employed, freelancers and the unemployed was high, and that of students and people in non-regular employment was low. This is not the kind of simple schema that directly links the economic hardship of non-regular employment with participation in demonstrations. On the other hand, among the self-employed and freelancers, the participation rate of persons in occupations such as clerical work, sales and service was low, while that of professionals was high (Satō et al. 2018). It is not easy to interpret whether this point can be explained in terms of the cognitive precariat discourse, or whether time limitations might be involved.

Rather, we might say that social movements today have some characteristics that cannot be reduced to those of a particular social class or stratum. At least, it is getting more and more difficult to name the working class or university students as the main bearers of social movements. This situation reflects the social change that we call the 'amorphization of society' in this book.

Structure of this book

This volume adopts the following structure in order to unpack the characteristics of today's social movements from a range of perspectives.

In Chapter One, we define the character of contemporary social movements as being amorphous and present the hypothesis that this has been generated in response to the broader amorphization of society. In addition, we conduct an investigation into what kind of condition the concept of 'amorphous' indicates, taking into account its usage in the natural sciences; moreover, we show that it can also be applied to explain society and social movements. In order to elucidate the sequential burgeoning of social movements that are not expected to readily arise in an amorphized society, we explain the impact of the nuclear reactor accident and the chain reaction mechanism whereby one movement calls forth others.

Chapters Two to Six comprise a series of monographs on social movements in contemporary Japanese society. In Chapter Two, while discussing such movements as those against nuclear power generation, National Security Legislation and racism, Kinoshita Chigaya educes the characteristics of current movements while simultaneously considering what they have changed. In Chapter Three, Horie Takashi explores the political aspects of today's social movements, analyzing what participants advocate in the anti-nuclear power generation and anti-National Security Legislation movements. In Chapter Four, Tanaka Hikaru sheds light upon the aspect of resistance against integration into the system through a detailed examination of the practices of an extremely unique movement called Shirōto no ran (Amateur Revolt). In Chapter Five, Toriyama Atsushi highlights the geopolitical significance of the region called Okinawa through a historical delineation of the vicissitudes of the movement against the unwelcome, unilateral anchoring in Okinawa of U.S. military bases which have life-or-death implications for the Japan-U.S. security setup that has arguably enabled the viability of the current regime. Finally, in Chapter Six, Tanno Kiyoto examines not only the circumstances that gave rise to a resistance movement against hate speech directed at Japan-residing Koreans, but also those which brought about changes in the logic of 'society' that opposes hate speech, framing this as the amorphization of social recognition.

1 Amorphous Dissent – a Conceptualization

Horie Takashi, Tanaka Hiraku and Tanno Kiyoto

Theme of this chapter

As outlined in the Introduction, a huge upswell of social movements was seen in post-3.11 Japanese society, arguably for the first time in several decades, with markedly different characteristics than previous social movements. Among those that had formerly flourished in Japanese society, some developed as 'national (*kokumin*) movements' within the seemingly self-evident boundaries of 'the Japanese', and some were based upon the interpersonal links forged in workplaces, universities or local communities.

However, later transformations in Japanese society undermined the foundations underpinning the emergence of social movements. This book calls this shift the 'amorphization of society', and the new social movements that differ from their antecedents in a number of ways have arisen in the context of an 'amorphous society'.

In this chapter, we explain in a more theoretical manner the properties of the present-day social movements outlined in the Introduction, as follows. Firstly, we paint a picture of the amorphization of society and discuss how it arose in concrete terms; next, going back to its original usage in the natural sciences, we examine the actual term 'amorphous' which we have employed in a figurative sense, so to speak, and explain the reasons behind our usage of this concept. Continuing on, in response to the question of why social movements that attract large numbers of people have come to arise so frequently in spite of fluctuations in the conditions that once enabled the birth of social movements (see Introduction), we look at the changes in Japanese society and its people triggered by the accident at the nuclear power plant in Fukushima. Subsequently, we elucidate the mechanism by which social movements arise in a chain reaction – as one movement provides the momentum for others – in an amorphous society where connections between individuals are considered to have deteriorated. Finally, we probe the strengths and weaknesses of the social movements of today that have arisen in this way.

The amorphization of Japanese society

The disorganization of society

Underpinning the decline in or transformation of social movements is the social change that generates them. In this book, we conceptualize this as the 'amorphization of society'.

Advanced capitalist societies that achieved rapid economic development after World War II are sometimes explained from the perspective of organization (cf. Offe 1985; Lash and Urry 1987). Capitalism in post-war developed societies was organized with various mutually interlinked elements, including the following: Fordism, which centered on manufacturing in which the role of the working public as consumers was expected; systems of labor-management reconciliation; the welfare state; embedded liberalism as the international environment; and the nuclear family/male-breadwinner model. A typical social movement that responded to such a social structure was the labor movement. In exchange for labor suppressing its combativeness and choosing to cooperate with capital, workers obtained a family wage to support their wives and children and enhanced their consumer lifestyle. For corporations, guaranteeing the purchasing power of the workers who served as consumers meant that they had a huge domestic market, and so this system had merit for both labor and management.

However, all of the problems that we face in social life became difficult to grasp as issues of 'labor' and 'socioeconomic class' due to the onset of multiple social changes – such as the end of economic growth, changes in the industrial structure, the intensification of globalization and the denationalization of the economy and society, the transformation of family and gender relations and so forth – and the labor movement lost its privileged status among social movements.

The rate of unionization in Japan has fallen since its 1949 peak of 55.8%, but even so, it maintained a rate of over 30% until 1982. Since then, however, the unionization rate has continued to worsen, falling below 20% in 2003 and to 17% in 2018. Even if we look at actual figures, the number of union members, which had fluctuated around twelve million since 1974, had dropped below this figure in 1998, reaching just 10.07 million by 2018 (Kōseirōdōshō 2018).

Corporate society has also changed. It was once a commonly held view that in Japan, in the midst of the decline of traditional communities such as families and districts, companies had taken their place and functioned as new communities. However, after the bursting of the Japanese economic bubble in the early 1990s, Japanese corporations hastened to reduce labor costs in order to ride out the crisis, thus weakening their integrating function. The scaling-back of regular employees demonstrates a transformation in the Japanese-style business practice of 'looking after company employees'. While non-regular employment is on the rise (38.1% in 2018), a sense of belonging to the company has dwindled, as has the company's role as a community. Even company-specific labor unions have declined, and company-centric social integration has also deteriorated.

The declining trend is evident not only in labor unions and corporations, but manifests across all groups and organizations. Groups have weakened markedly, and 'all-embracing' mechanisms to mobilize people through existing groups and organizations in the 1950s and 1960s no longer function under this situation. People who were not members of any kind of group were in the tenth percentile in the 1980s, but since the 2000s, the number has reached the thirtieth percentile, and among the younger generation especially, disorganization has proliferated (Mori and Kubo 2016). Pressure groups linked to professional interests still exhibit a certain presence, but it is difficult to imagine them participating in political demonstrations in a comprehensive manner.

SEALDs drew attention towards student participation in politics for the first time in several decades, but their movement has had no basis in universities whatsoever. The Zenkyōtō movement which criticized 'Potsdam student councils' called itself the 'XX University Zenkyōtō', so its membership of universities was self-evident, so to speak. However, as Kinoshita Chigaya points out, the space called 'a university' is no longer worthy of being the base of a social movement (Kinoshita 2017; see also Chapter Two of this volume).

According to a survey of participants in the June 2011 anti-nuclear power demonstration, their means of finding out about the demonstration went in the following order: 1) 'The internet', 2) 'Twitter' and 3) 'From an acquaintance'. In a survey conducted in September in the same year, however, the order was 1) 'The internet', 2) 'From an acquaintance' and 3) 'Twitter'. In each case, these three options accounted for about 70% of the total (Hirabayashi 2013). According to a questionnaire survey carried out in the movement's heyday in front of the prime minister's official residence and in front of the Diet building in July 2012, responses to a question on where the participants had viewed material that had motivated them to protest in front of the prime minister's residence were: 1) 'Twitter' (39.3%), 2) 'Through the grapevine' (17.3%), 3) 'The internet' (11.6%), 4) 'Facebook' (6.7%), 5) 'Television' (6.5%), 6) 'Newspaper' (6.3%), 7) 'Group notification' (6.1%) and 8) 'Other' (6.1%) (Noma 2012: 162–163). These survey results can be read as evidence of the power of the internet, but they are also an expression of how existing groups barely function as routes for the dissemination of information about demonstrations.

The amorphization of identity

The disorganization and fragmentation of society also presses changes onto the identities of the people who participate in movements. Conversely, it could also be said that the amorphization of identity which complicates the formation of 'us', the agents who participate in the movements, underpins the stagnation of social movements. Once, the terms indicating the 'us' that assembled in social movements were, for example, 'workers', 'citizens' or 'nationals'.

The labor movement in post-war Japan has been an influential part of a broader movement engaged with the issues of democracy and peace, rather than simply aiming to achieve benefits for union members. The upsurge of the post-war democracy movement was enabled via the systematic participation of workers belonging to labor unions. Post-war democracy also aimed to overcome the village-like circumstances of Japanese society that brought about totalitarianism and the horrors of war, and looked towards a society composed of independent 'citizens'. Some advocates connected the establishment of civil society in Japan to citizens' spontaneous participation in the 1960 campaign against the US-Japan Security Treaty. Flyers distributed at Beheiren's first demonstration (in 1965) began with the words, 'We are ordinary citizens'.

The symbol of 'nationals' (*kokumin*) was also widely employed. The name 'Progressive nationals' movement' (Kakushin kokumin undō) was sometimes prefixed in the post-war democratic movement. The concept of 'nationals', which requires careful handling because it brings nationalism to mind, was long used without much question in the leftist camp as well (Oguma 2002). Equating the scope of 'us' with Japanese nationals has been ongoing, even while receiving no small amount of criticism. Nowadays, however, all of these words that are used to collectively designate people who participate in social movements have lost the power to represent them as a whole or give them a sense of 'we'.

Due to an improvement in living standards and the development of consumer society on the one hand, and the collapse of the socialist camp and the decline in Marxism's intellectual and moral authority on the other, the collective identity of 'workers' lost its power to encourage participation in movements. The once apparently self-evident homogeneity of 'workers' also came into question. Under the fiction of homogenous 'workers', questions of gender and ethnicity had long been subordinated as issues of socioeconomic class, and that, in part, brought about the rise of new social movements since the 1980s. In addition, the labor union movement, which had centered upon regularly-employed workers, came to have its legitimacy questioned due to the diversification of the workforce. There are not only large disparities between regular and non-regular employees of companies in terms of pay and working conditions, but in the sense that the jobs of regular employees are protected thanks to the flexibility that non-regular employees offer, their interests are in fact in conflict. The view that labor unions are organizations for the benefit of one group of privileged workers rather than of workers in their entirety became entrenched. One community union member says that even while being a worker, they feel uncomfortable with the term 'workers'. According to this union member, it is difficult to gain both rights as workers and a sense of collective identity as such: 'As I come face to face with different workers every day in the workplace, I never become friends with them [...] we workers, too, are presumed to be going to lose our jobs' (Hashiguchi 2011).

It does not follow that the identity of 'worker' was swapped for that of 'citizen', which does not rely upon socioeconomic class. In the 1990s, which saw the disintegration of the Soviet Union and Eastern European bloc, it was argued that there was a 'major historical change' comprising 'the rise of reappraisals of a snowball effect from a "logic of socioeconomic class" to a "logic of citizens"' within movements that aim for social reform (Watanabe 1996: 399). What is under discussion here is a decline in a 'logic of socioeconomic class' and a change in balance between it and a 'logic of citizens'. After that, we witnessed the transformation of 'citizens' with our own eyes. The neologism 'professional citizens' (*puro shimin*) which was born in the 1990s criticizes the participants in citizens' movements as being political professionals unconnected to the amateurism that had long been glorified. A political professional, in this case, implies a presence tinged with partisanship. The 1990s saw the appearance of a historical-revisionist grassroots conservative movement that deemed textbooks describing the aggressive action of the former Japanese military to be 'masochistic', but called themselves 'ordinary citizens' (Oguma and Ueno 2003). What is more, as noted above, a kind of racist exclusionist movement which arose in the 2000s that carried out hate speech against Koreans residing in Japan called itself the 'Citizens' Group that Will Not Forgive Special Privileges for Koreans in Japan' (Zaitokukai).

Among post-war social movements, the 'citizens' who projected a normative sparkle became the target of censure for being political 'professionals' tinged with partisanship; and they have had their title snatched away by exclusionist and discriminatory movements that are incompatible with the ideals of previous citizens' movements. Attention-drawing movements from recent years such as Hangenren and SEALDs do not call themselves 'citizens'.

These days, it is not possible to depend on the fiction of the homogeneity of 'nationals'. Criticism from within the movements against the new National Security Legislation has been leveled at the SEALDs' chant, 'Don't underestimate nationals' (*Kokumin namen na*). Participation in the demonstrations was not limited to Japanese people, and there were also many participants who baulked at the chant (Kasai and Noma 2016: 98). Increasing numbers of people feel it is hard to accept 'nationals' as the word that identifies the 'we' sharing responsibility for social movements.

In this way, today's social movements have become collections of people hard to envisage as 'workers' or 'citizens', or even as 'nationals'. They are a presence that cannot easily form a single crystallized identity. The situation whereby social movements in today's amorphized society have difficulty in finding a suitable word to identify 'us' is exemplified in the way SEALDs resorted to the term 'nationals'.

Formerly, Japanese society was characterized by such things as a high degree of homogeneity and an absence of conflict. The demythologization of such crystalline conceptualization of Japanese society and 'the Japanese' was a major subject for critical Japanologists (Sugimoto and Mouer 1995). Nowadays, however, the discourse of 'diversity' which deems the presence of minorities to be an agent of innovation and economic development rather than something hidden is employed by corporations and the government. There is a risk that the discourse of diversity, which has also become a convenient word for the system, will newly fulfill the function of privileging only the kind of diversity that contributes to economic growth.

Nevertheless, regardless of whether diversity is extolled or not, or whether it is somehow useful or not, Japanese society has increased its heterogeneity and become amorphous. For that reason, it has become difficult to rely upon a common identity and speak out on the basis of

Amorphous Dissent – a Conceptualization 33

such. Regarding the boundaries of the 'Japanese', Tanno Kiyoto points out that Japanese society which has long cherished its crystalline character is now forced to change the principle of its self-understanding through the introduction of hate-speech regulations. This can be interpreted through the lens of the amorphization of society caused by the fact that massive numbers of foreign workers have taken root in society, making the recognition of what constitutes society amorphous (see Chapter Six of this volume).

Denationalization

As a parallel problem to the difficulty Japanese society now faces in launching an 'us' that can be reduced to a single identity, our recognition of the extension of 'Japanese society' also becomes something amorphous.

Even though the post-war democracy movement was prescribed by the international environment comprising the US-Soviet Cold War structure, it is hard to deny that it was national in terms of its perspective. The ability of the identity called 'national' to be a worthy subject of the movement was one of its manifestations. Today's social movements, however, have intensified their character as movements that transcend national borders in several respects.

Firstly, thanks to the popularization of the internet, it is easy to communicate with overseas movements, and to learn from them. In addition to learning chants from the American Occupy movement, SEALDs interacted with Hong Kong's Umbrella Movement and Taiwan's Sunflower Movement. At Hangenren's Friday protests in front of the prime minister's official residence and the Diet building, overseas guests often take the microphone. In 2012, anti-nuclear demonstrations were called the 'Hydrangea Revolution', a nomenclature that referenced the 'Jasmine Revolution' in Tunisia.

Members of Amateur Revolt who planned the 'Stop nuclear power!!!!!' (*Genpatsu yamero!!!!!*) rally in Kōenji in April 2011 were strongly aware of the Arab Spring that had begun several months previously, especially the campaign in Egypt's Tahrir Square, but on the other hand, they themselves had become objects of imitation for movements overseas. In the Taiwanese anti-nuclear power movement, when the younger generation tried to hold a sound demonstration, the older generation's approval could not be obtained. When the latter were shown videos of Amateur Revolt's demonstrations, however, they too started to say 'This is good. We had better do this' (Matsumoto et al. 2012).

It is no longer unusual for movements that began in a certain country to spread internationally, such as the #MeToo movement and the 'Fridays for Future' movement started by Swedish high-school student Greta Thunberg to halt climate change, and for similar movements to arise in many countries. These are movements started by people spontaneously across the world who saw videos on the internet and who do not necessarily operate under an executive issuing directives to branches in each locality.

A kind of politics is being carried out that shifts the site for conflict over issues that were thought to be national to a local/regional/global stage. In Okinawa, although public opinion opposed to the construction of new US military bases has been voiced many times in national (and regional) elections, construction is progressing against local wishes. However, in 2019, a movement launched by young people achieved the holding of a prefectural referendum, while a Hawaiian resident with roots in Okinawa, Robert Kajiwara, set his eye on the provision that if 100,000 signatures were collected within thirty days of the initiation of a petition, the White House would have to reply. He started a petition movement seeking the cessation of construction, and signatures were gathered not only from Japanese people, but also internationally. If one were to view Japanese society as a uniform structure, only the central government which represents 'nationals' would be assumed to be the target of policy change. Amid the amorphization of the extension of 'society', however, the battle lines have also become multilayered.[1]

In March 2011, immediately after the Fukushima accident, a man who started a protest movement against the government and TEPCO says that he thought overseas media would take up the issue, as he knew that the Japanese media would not report on the movements (Sono 2011:

62). Moreover, only the South Korean media covered the activities of Shibakitai, while Japanese newspaper companies and television channels were completely absent. It was only after Arita Yoshifu, a Member of the House of Councillors, conducted an in-house meeting in March 2013 that the Japanese media began to gather (Kasai and Noma 2016: 147; Noma 2018: 143). Social movements today have to take overseas governments and mass media into account, not just their national counterparts. As a result, the relationship of national social movements vis-à-vis national politics is no longer valid.

Naturally, the idea of appealing to overseas public opinion is not completely new. Beheiren appealed to American public opinion by placing advertisements in *The New York Times* and *Washington Post*. The labor movement incorporated internationalism from the beginning, and one could also argue that the conception that social movements transcend national borders is not especially novel. However, this was largely an ideal, and at the time, when the extent of 'society' perhaps tended to be taken as equivalent to the nation-state, social movements were also in large part tethered to that entity. The propensity in present-day social movements to deviate from the nation-state differs in nature from the internationalism of the previous labor movement and international communist movement; they have neither organizational headquarters like Comintern (Communist International), nor branches in every country. Similar kinds of movements which have arisen in each country and each district have been started by local initiative, so to speak, and are not being run as representative of each country.

New social movements shared a similar tendency with the labor movement. Nancy Fraser points out that while on the one hand Western second-wave feminism repudiated the economism of state-managed capitalism, androcentrism and the state-managerialism that constituted the post-war social order, even while theoretically criticizing Westphalianism, on a practical level it sees each country as the destination for demands, and therefore it continued to be Westphalian (Fraser 2009).

Nowadays, however, the advance of globalization and the departure from the nation-state at various levels in society have encouraged social movements to transcend the nation-state. The accident at Chernobyl ought to have resulted in the wide recognition that radioactive contamination from accidents at nuclear power plants render national borders meaningless (Beck 1992), but the Fukushima accident again reminded us of that fact. After the Fukushima accident, Ikegami Yoshihiko, who spoke in Seoul about Japanese demonstrations for the abandonment of nuclear power generation, was reportedly asked, 'Will it be enough for Japan alone to cease generating nuclear power?', and was told, 'We want you to export the anti-nuclear power movement by all means' (Matsumoto et al. 2012). The expression 'export' still contains echoes that presuppose the nation-state, but if questions become global, not limited to nuclear power generation, movements will also be unable to afford to be swayed by the nation-state, and that tendency will likely be increasingly strengthened.

The scope of such stakeholders as 'us' as agents, the object of calls seeking empathy and assistance, adversaries, and the media that communicate these, is markedly undefined. Young people in Hong Kong who in 2019 opposed amendments to the Fugitive Offenders and Mutual Legal Assistance in Criminal Matters Legislation (Amendment) Bill that would enable the extradition of persons accused of a crime to the Chinese mainland similarly placed advertisements in overseas newspapers, covering the expense through crowd-funding. The potential for present-day movements to be able to seek resources from overseas is spreading more widely. Key members of Beheiren with rich international experience often invited renowned guests from overseas. By contrast, those who held the microphone at Hangenren's Friday protests in front of the prime minister's official residence and the Diet building, and the Taiwanese and Hong Kong students who interacted with SEALDs, were ordinary people who could not be called celebrities. The likelihood of the creation of solidarity that transcends national borders has heightened remarkably due to rapid changes in the conditions of air travel and communications. Circumstances which make it difficult to establish movements based on crystalline 'nationals' also constitute conditions that enable different types of movements.

What manner of condition is 'amorphousness'?

Amid the huge changes under way in the social structure that produced the social movements of the past, it is hard to understand at first glance why social movements have experienced a historical upsurge. In this book, however, we think of today's social movements as forming in accordance with different principles than in the past.

This book analyses the characteristics of the social movements of recent years in terms of their amorphous nature and addresses the amorphization of the current state of society. In general terms, 'amorphous' is used in the sense of being 'shapeless', 'unclassifiable', 'lacking organization or unity' or 'having no real or apparent crystalline form'.[2] More specifically, 'amorphous' has also been used to characterize the state of a society or social movements. For example, conditions in which politics and society are in confusion are sometimes referred to as 'amorphous' (Samalavičius 2008). Furthermore, according to Naomi Klein, social movements which have such features as 'rejecting identifiable leadership', 'eschewing programmatic demands' or having a 'fetish for structurelessness, the rebellion against any kind of institutionalization', possess 'amorphous structures' (2015: 158).

The term 'amorphous' was originally used in the domain of natural science, and is a concept that primarily expresses the condition of a substance in which various constituents combine in a random fashion to form a non-crystalline structure. In this sense, one of the antonyms of amorphous is 'crystalline'.

A crystalline substance has certain numerical values called 'material constants', including specific gravity, specific heat, hardness, conductivity, permeability and so forth, and it is possible to show the properties of the substance by means of those numerical values. An amorphous substance, however, has no set material constants, and what it does have can change. Moreover, although crystalline substances are in a thermodynamically stable state, the conditions of amorphous substances readily change by means of an external energy supply, such as heating or irradiation by a beam of light (Tsukio 1991: 27–28). The crystalline substance, quartz, is a mineral in which silicon dioxide (SiO_2) is structured in a lattice-like fashion. Because such minerals are crystals, they are strong in relation to force from a particular direction, but weak in relation to force from another direction. In comparison to such crystals, amorphous substances which lack a crystalline structure are sometimes fragile, but they occasionally become far harder than pure crystals in terms of strength. Titanium exploits this nature, and when used for industrial products, it is transformed into an amorphous state when certain amounts of aluminium and so on are added.

In this book, we invoke this concept of 'amorphousness', which has been employed mainly in the natural sciences, in reference to social movements and the state of the societies that generate them. In other words, we will liken the organized structure of past social movements and societies to 'crystalline' entities, and refer to those societies and social movements which have taken shape in the wake of their structural collapse (or while they are in the process of collapsing) as 'amorphous' entities. Embedded in this 'amorphous' metaphor is an implication that transcends the general sense of the term – namely, due to the mixing in of miscellaneous elements, and depending on the arrangement of their atoms, they sometimes demonstrate some sort of robustness that is lacking in highly pure crystalline structures, even while this involves some degree of fragility.

Although it may seem unusual to invoke the concept of 'amorphous' in explaining societies and social movements, this sort of analogy is not unprecedented.[3] In his critical theory, sociologist Zygmunt Bauman uses the metaphor of 'liquefaction' for society that conventionally indicates the form of a substance. He argues that in 'liquid modernity', while the old order disintegrates, there is no clear-cut structure governing the formation of a new order. Moreover, the social groups that functioned as the basis for identities that existed in the previous solid modernity become redundant in liquid modernity (Bauman 2000). This way of understanding society is akin to what Ulrich Beck and others term 'individualization', and also shares problem-consciousness with this book which focuses upon the advancement of social disorganization and the fragmentation of individuals.

However, the revitalization of social movements cannot be explained by characterizing society in terms of 'liquefaction' or 'individualization'. Isolated individuals falling into anomie and causing disruption out of their distress constitute the classical image of collective action, but such a view of movements as irrational explosions was superseded by resource mobilization theory which has emphasized the rationality of social movements since the 1970s. Resource mobilization theory points out that people participate through existing networks, and isolated people tend to find it difficult to take part (Oberschall 1978). As such, how should we best explain the unexpected eruption of social movements in the midst of advancing structural decay and individualism and the liquefaction of society?

Up until now, sociologists have directed focus on the 'individual', surveyed the attributes and personal backgrounds of participants and endeavored to explain their participation (Satō et al. 2018; Tominaga 2017). However, merely clarifying what kinds of people take part does not answer the question as to why large demonstrations are occurring with great frequency in Japanese society where demonstrations were invisible for a long time. Such people ought to have been present since before the upsurge.

As a prerequisite for political participation, and especially for participation in costly direct action such as demonstrations, it is first necessary to motivate people to participate – in other words, their interest in politics must increase. Moreover, even if interested people find it in themselves to speak out, the systematic basis to connect scattered individuals has been lost. How do people who are hard to collectivize by means of such characteristics as 'student' or 'worker' mutually connect and participate in demonstrations?

In the following two sections, we respond to the above question. Firstly, in the next section, we will investigate the impact of the Fukushima nuclear power plant accident that sparked the awakening of many people in the context of post-3.11 Japanese society. Secondly, we review several patterns relating to how people connected amid the weakening of various social groups and communities that would once have formed the foundation for social movements.

The impact of the nuclear power plant accident

In thinking about the Japanese social movements of today, one cannot ignore the impact of the accident at the Fukushima nuclear power plant. This one event gave rise to many subsequent movements, not limited to those aiming for the abandonment of nuclear power generation. For example, many of the members of SEALDs cite the Great East Japan Earthquake disaster or the nuclear power plant accident as the impetus behind their newfound interest in politics and social issues (Tamura and Tamura 2016). Saigō Minako, who started Mama no Kai in 2015, was involved in the movement for the abandonment of nuclear power generation with her family (Saigō 2018), and reports that other members who gathered for the first time at a press conference upon the launch of Mama no Kai said that 3.11 had been their starting point, too (Komori et al. 2016: 49).

The accident at the nuclear power plant sparked fears about exposure to radiation over a wide area, giving rise to evacuations not only in Fukushima Prefecture but also all over eastern Japan, including Tokyo. After Chernobyl, too, a new movement in Japan against nuclear power generation called the 'new wave' entered the scene, but its scale and breadth of influence were no comparison to the social movement that rose up in the wake of Fukushima (which is natural, as this time the accident occurred within Japan). The number of first-time participants in action such as demonstrations was also greater by far after Fukushima.

According to a survey of participants at a demonstration on 11 June 2011, 48% reported that this was the first time they had taken part in a demonstration in their lives. In a survey conducted at a demonstration on 11 September in the same year, first-timers accounted for 35% of participants (Hirabayashi 2013). In demonstrations against the 2003 Iraq War, too, the 'sound demonstration' style and the like attracted attention and interest was aroused by its 'novelty', but according to a survey of participants, only 10.9% of respondents said that it was the first time they had taken part in this sort of activity (Yamamoto et al. 2004). Even given that the survey methods were different, the fact that 48% of participants in the 2011 demonstration calling for the abandonment of nuclear power generation were first-timers is an extremely high figure. Although not based on a proper survey, Matsumoto Hajime from Amateur Revolt, who organized the 'Quit nuclear power generation!!!!!' demonstration in Kōenji in April 2011, says that out of the 15,000 participants, perhaps some 90~95% were first-timers (Yamamoto and Matsumoto 2012: 53; Matsumoto et al. 2012: 17). In 2012, when the scale of the movement had grown beyond all comparison to that of 2011, the number of people taking part in a demonstration for the first time is estimated to have been even larger. Moreover, in a survey conducted in July 2013, a year after the peak, 15% of participants were reportedly joining a demonstration for the first time (Oguma 2013: 246).

The Fukushima accident was the incident that prompted such large numbers of people to head to their first demonstration, but in terms of influence on social movements, the following two points are probably more critical than the actual damage caused by the accident. The first was that the nuclear power plant accident implanted serious misgivings in many people towards not only Tokyo Electric Power Company (TEPCO), which ran the Fukushima nuclear power plant, and the government of the day, but also towards the system as a whole. The second was that the hurdles against political participation were lowered, with the movement opposing nuclear power generation as the starting point, and demonstrations about other issues began to occur frequently after that.

The first impact of the nuclear power plant accident was its arousal of deep distrust towards organizations and institutions that supported the existing system, such as the government and mass media, or science and technology. The term 'nuclear village' (*genshiryoku mura*) was coined to refer to the nuclear power generation promotion system which, while causing an accident on an unprecedented scale, tried to evade responsibility by underplaying the damage, and showed enthusiasm only for restarting the reactor. This system included even the mass media and scientists, in addition to TEPCO and related enterprises, the government and political parties and so on. Misgivings began to be harbored about the systems that support society in general.

Photo 1.1: Fukushima nuclear power plant after the accident of 2011. Source: TEPCO.

Oguma Eiji estimates that in excess of ten million people have been involved in conducting some form of data collection aside from the government's official announcements, such as measuring the amount of radioactivity (Oguma 2013: 250). A website called 'De-nuke now. De-nuke-related event calendar' (*Datsu genpatsu nau. Datsu,' denpatsu-kei ibento karendā*) carrying information about denuclearization events which was established on 3 April 2011 had been accessed more than 100,000 times by the end of that year (Hirabayashi 2013: 169). As of December 2019, hits had exceeded 220,000 (http://datugeninfo.web.fc2.com/). In Japan, where the voting rate is low, the rampancy of a 'leave-it-up-to-them democracy' is often cited, but after the nuclear plant accident, people with a problem-consciousness that leaving things up to the government was unacceptable emerged to a certain extent.

Matsumoto, who organized the April 2011 demonstration, recounted as follows: 'I'm not sure, but there are not many people who are particularly opposed, and nothing but fake-sounding news has started to circulate, like that the accident has also settled down. I thought, "This is no joke". [...] And I thought that unless we strike a blow through a demonstration or something, this kind of accident happening and our having experienced such a dangerous situation, it would be intolerable if nuclear power generation comfortably remains as it is now; and demonstrations happened because we absolutely had to do something'. He continued: 'There were loads of people who had been affected by the disaster, and I thought it probably hadn't come to that situation yet, but then in two or three weeks the news came in sort of saying that things had calmed down, and I thought that kind of vagueness was the most frightening, and that I had to demonstrate' (Matsumoto 2012b: 12; Takahashi and Matsumoto 2012: 49–50).

While gathering information from the internet in the wake of the nuclear power plant accident, Echigo Kaori, from ACT March 11th Japan, one of the action groups that made up Hangenren, said that she felt, 'Both the government and TEPCO are dodgy, untrustworthy, and the mass media are hiding something, too'. Having continuously watched Ustream broadcasts from CNIC (Citizens' Nuclear Information Center), which were critical of nuclear power generation, as well as TEPCO press conferences, Echigo says she thought, 'This is absolutely unacceptable' (Tamura and Tamura 2016: 39). Although misinformation is rife on the internet, and it is sometimes referred to as a hotbed of anti-intellectualism, it was where people unable to believe government announcements and mainstream news media at the time sought information about radioactive contamination. In response, individuals and groups continued to transmit information online that the government and mainstream mass media did not talk about. In one particular survey, in relation to the question 'Do you know when the [Fukushima Nuclear Power Plant] Unit One meltdown occurred?', answers from people for whom television was their principal source of information were divided into roughly equal thirds: 'Correct' (36%), 'Incorrect' (31%) and 'Don't know [either way]' (33%). Those for whom the internet was their principal source of information replied: 'Correct' (55%), 'Incorrect' (13%) and 'Don't know [either way]' (32%) (Shiraishi 2011: 24).

Yamada Nodoka, who later became a member of SEALDs, experienced 3.11 as a Year Ten student, and felt increasing distrust towards the government after hearing Chief Cabinet Secretary Edano Yukio claim at a press conference that radiation does 'no immediate harm to the human body or to health' (Tamura and Tamura 2016: 183). This line, which Edano reiterated, became a buzzword, but according to a survey carried out by a social psychologist, many people understood the phrase to mean that radiation would trigger serious problems in the future, contrary to the government's intention (Kawamoto 2013). The words issued in order to prevent panic caused a proliferation of feelings of distrust towards the government. Rather than the accident itself, the post-accident response awakened many people's interest in politics.

According to a large-scale survey, the percentage of people who 'started to feel anxiety at Japan's future' as a result of 'the impact of the Great East Japan Earthquake Disaster' was 63.3% (the combined total of 'Agree' and 'Somewhat agree': the same applies hereafter); 52.3% of people 'intensified [their] distrust of the government'; and 41.9% of people replied that their 'life-view was altered' (Satō et al. 2018). In a survey on citizens' groups working on nuclear-energy related activities, responses to the question on 'motivation for engaging in activities after the earthquake disaster' (multiple answers were permitted) were: 'I felt that policies on nuclear power generation and disaster countermeasures were insufficient' (67.8%), with the next most frequent (48.7%) being, 'Because I felt doubtful about the state of Japanese politics and corporate governance' (Machimura and Satō 2016).

Oguma Eiji pointed out that 'Anti-restart' was identified as expressing opposition to the 'restart' of the Japan that existed prior to the accident as well as to the restart of the nuclear reactor (Kan and Oguma 2013: 182; stated by Oguma in an interview he conducted with Kan). The changelessness of Japanese politics and society in the aftermath of historical catastrophes was strikingly apparent.

Of course, this does not mean that distrust of existing systems will automatically give rise to social movements. In the next section, we consider how people who appear to have become disconnected have come to connect in the present day, when the systematic basis for inducing participation in movements has weakened.

How people connect to form amorphous social movements

The second identifiable impact of the nuclear power plant accident upon social movements today is that it brought about a chain of connections whereby one movement called forth another, with the anti-nuclear power movement as the starting point. As previously mentioned, many who were participating in a demonstration for the first time came forth; and there would have been no small number who, while not going so far as to take part, did develop a feeling of familiarity with demonstrations. The anti-nuclear power movement is thus also important in the sense that it served as an example that was used to advantage in issues other than nuclear power generation.

Although people became critical of the government and mainstream mass media and attempted to throw off the 'leave-it-up-to-them' attitude and raise their voices, in an amorphous society it is difficult to connect at schools and workplaces, which formed the launchpads of previous movements.

At the time of the Anpo protests of 1960, Sōhyō (the General Council of Trade Unions of Japan), which was the national center of labor unions, made the Socialist Party and Communist Party cooperate, and 134 groups under its umbrella created the People's Council to Stop the Revised Security Treaty (Anpo kaitei soshi kokumin kaigi). Each of the groups mobilized members of their organizations to assemble in front of the Diet. At the time of its launch in April 1965, Beheiren, which is seen as a collection of individuals, was called the Citizen's League of *Cultural Groups* for Peace in Vietnam. In October of that same year, it adopted a new name: the Citizen's League for Peace in Vietnam (Betonamu ni heiwa o! Shimin rengō). In Beheiren, along with individuals, several groups included their names on a list calling for participants. Takahashi Taketomo, who took part in most of the preparation meetings in the lead-up to the launch, says that the issue of nomenclature was not debated at the meetings he attended; but he speculates that 'there was flow-on from the past, too, and there was probably the feeling that [Beheiren] would not be able to manage well unless it borrowed the power of [other] groups' (Takakusagi 2016: 30).

Nowadays, as groups no longer have such power, movements have to make the individual their basic unit. Those involved in soliciting participation in demonstrations do not think it possible to gather significant numbers of participants through reliance on organizations such as XX University or XX Labor Union, or via socioeconomic class identity such as 'workers'. Among the thirteen action groups that formed Hangenren, those such as TwitNoNukes (hereafter, TNN) and Hangenpatsu Suginami (Denuclearization Suginami), which came into being after 3.11, started from rallying calls via Twitter and the like. In the case of Shibakitai, when Noma Yasumichi announced via the internet in January 2013 that it was recruiting members, it had more than fifty applicants in one week (Kasai and Noma 2016: 143). The motivation for Takatsuka Mao to begin her 'I hate war so much it makes me shiver' (*Sensō shitakunakute furueru*) activity in Sapporo, which trended all over Japan, was viewing a video made by young people in the Kansai area of an anti-National Security Legislation gathering. When Takatsuka said to an acquaintance, 'I wish there would be a meeting of young people in Sapporo, as well', she was told, 'You should start one'. Takatsuka, who up until then had 'thought that ignorant people like me "mustn't talk"', decided to demonstrate: she set up accounts on every platform on the internet able to be used for publicity, including Facebook, Twitter, Instagram, a home page and so on, and also made flyers, and over a nine-day preparation period gathered 700 supporters (Takatsuka 2015: 24–25). Unquestionably, the internet has become a critical medium to attract participation.

There were many student members of SASPL~SEALDs that either participated in, or observed, the anti-nuclear power movement. The impetus for the creation of the forerunner of SASPL was reportedly excursions by Okuda Aki and some others in June 2012 to watch anti-nuclear power rallies in front of the prime minister's official residence (Takahashi and SEALDs 2015: 30–31). Okuda, who frequented anti-nuclear power demonstrations, recounts, 'I think it was precisely because I used to watch at that time that I am now protesting in front of the Diet building' (*Asahi Shimbun* 2015). Motoyama Jinshirō, who later joined SEALDs and SEALDs RYŪKYŪ and instigated a prefectural referendum in Okinawa in 2019, saw an anti-nuclear power demonstration through the window of a bus passing through Kōenji, and thought, 'Oh, we can raise our voices this way' (Tamura and Tamura 2016: 210). We authors have heard it said on several occasions that if there had been no anti-nuclear power rallies, there probably would not have been such an uprising against the Act on the Protection of Specially Designated Secrets or in response to the National Security Legislation. It is hard to deny that the anti-nuclear power movement had a decisive influence on successive movements. At the very least, the anti-nuclear power movement sowed the seeds for later movements.

Interconnections between action groups arise between movements that share the theme of opposition to nuclear power, and also transcend issue-based boundaries. TNN, which began from Hirano Taichi's tweets, was not connected to any existing organizations, nor did it have a celebrity representative, but it put together beautifully-designed demonstrations and even published a book that packaged the know-how behind demonstrations, entitled *Let's go to a rally! If we raise our voices, the world will change; if we walk through the town, we will be able to see society* (TNN 2011). Demonstrations bearing the TNN name, such as TNN Osaka and TNN Kyūshū, spread to Shiga, Gunma, Nara, the Chūgoku region, Hamamatsu, Aomori, Wakayama, Kyoto and Tochigi (Tamura and Tamura 2016: 26–27).

Hangenren, which TNN was involved in organizing, is an alliance launched for the sake of harmonization by different groups that previously held separate demonstrations without coordinating their schedules (Redwolf 2013: 4). Hangenren was formed by a combination of thirteen action groups of miscellaneous origins, including those that had been active since the 1980s like Tanpoposha (No Nukes Plaza Tokyo), those active since the 2000s like No Nukes More Hearts, and action groups like TNN, newly-born post-3.11. Moreover, the alliance demonstrates a kind of robustness that is rare in the world, having continued its protests every Friday since March 2012 for a period that now spans more than eight years.

Not only did demonstrations draw large crowds, but social movements spread visibly in the form of regional versions popping up all over the country as if in response to the launch of a particular movement. On Friday nights, when Hangenren held its weekly protest action, demonstrations for the abandonment of nuclear power generation started to be held at a variety of places nationwide. These were not begun by affiliates of Hangenren or the like, but were initiated spontaneously, so to speak, in each location. More than 150 university supporters' groups were established across Japan via collaboration with academics' associations around opposition to the National Security Legislation. In addition, regional versions of SEALDs came into being, such as SEALDs KANSAI, SEALDs TŌHOKU, SEALDs RYŪKYŪ and SEALDs TŌKAI; young people's action groups that did not use the SEALDs name were formed, such as Kumamoto's WDW (We Disagree with War), Fukuoka's FYM (Fukuoka Youth Movement) and Osaka's SADL (Small Axe for Democracy and Life), as well as ones in Tottori and Kōchi; and T-ns SOWL (Teens Stand Up To Oppose War Law), organized by high-school students, also came into being. Members of regional action groups and SEALDs in Tokyo connected via Facebook and other social networking sites (Takahashi and SEALDs 2015: 96). In the three months after Shibakitai appeared in Tokyo, counter-action spread to the various areas of Kanagawa, Kyoto and Osaka (Noma 2018: 147). Further, Mama no Kai groups opposed to the National Security Legislation were formed in more than 100 locations.

A chain of influence is identifiable in the way SEALDs, which was influenced by Hangenren, in turn gave rise to successive movements. Mama no Kai was started by postgraduate student and mother of three Saigō Minako on 4 July 2015, when the National Security Legislation was being debated in the Diet. Saigō's motivation for forming Mama no Kai was a speech given by a SEALDs student in front of the Diet building. Saigō says that she listened to the speech from immediately

Photo 1.2: Demonstration against the National Security Legislation in front of the National Diet building on 30 August 2015: people with drums and a megaphone. Source: mkimpo.

behind the speaker, and 'a feeling that "I want to do it too!" surged up' (Saigō 2015: 140). One week later, she launched 'Mama no Kai' on Facebook, and on 13 July, she held a press conference with mothers she had connected with on the site. That day was the first time Mama no Kai members who had connected via the internet met face-to-face (Komori et al. 2016). After the press conference, there was a flood of messages from mothers everywhere, saying they wanted to start up a Mama no Kai group immediately (Saigō 2015: 142).

Just as Noma Yasumichi, who began Shibakitai, was a central member of Hangenren, there have occasionally been personal connections among fellow action groups. Hirano, the initiator of TNN, was also close to members of Amateur Revolt (Tamura and Tamura 2016: 29).

The 'Angry drummers', which made an appearance in the movements opposed to nuclear power, hate speech, the Act on the Protection of Specially Designated Secrets and the National Security Legislation, have continued activities that straddle different issues.

While on the one hand a movement was started with acquaintances who were fellow mothers (Anpo kanren hō ni hantai suru mama-no-Kai@Osaka 2016), on the other hand, people without any ties to existing networks have attended rallies with people they got to know via Twitter (Tamura and Tamura 2016: 62). Many who started going to rallies on their own later became acquainted with members of SASPL or SEALDs, and began to take part in their actions (Takahashi and SEALDs 2015: 118–121). Sometimes, movements that arise in various areas establish connections through social networking sites, and then start to meet in person. There are also numerous people making speeches in front of the Diet building at Friday protest actions who usually engage in activities in other districts. As many as 29.6% of participants (the total of 'Strongly agree' and 'Agree') cite 'making new acquaintances' as personal changes that happened through participation in demonstrations (Satō et al. 2018).

Unlike the previous student movement, today's movements do not conduct systematic recruitment drives at universities. Okuda says he has 'seldom' invited university friends to participate. Fellow SEALDs member Shibata Mana also says that she does not ask people along herself (Takahashi and SEALDs 2015: 99–100). One of the reasons for not soliciting participants at university is that today's young people dislike talking about politics and 'sticking out from their peers' (Tominaga 2017), but this might also be a consequence of the change in meaning of universities which no longer function as students' base for living or as a site for building solidarity (see Chapter Two of this volume).

Apart from the internet, people sometimes link up at sites of protest action. For example, when the Act on the Protection of Specially Designated Secrets was passed on 6 December 2013, Okuda recounts what happened in front of the Diet building, as follows: 'I spoke to every young person I found. And so I missed the last train, and talked with everyone until morning [...] and on the momentum of drunkenness, I proposed, "Let's hold a rally"' (Okuda and Inose 2015: 48–49). After the formation of SEALDs, new members were attracted 'kind of by calling out "Anyone who wants to join!" after Friday protest actions, assembling them beside the stage, talking to them and becoming friends, and exchanging LINE IDs' (Takahashi and SEALDs 2015: 87). From the beginning, priority was given to connecting with interested people via the internet or at the rally site rather than to enticing non-political classmates.

In this way, on the huge impetus of the nuclear power plant accident, people who thought it unsatisfactory to 'leave-it-all' to the government and mainstream media headed to demonstrations, all the while gaining information from the internet and so on, and the connections that developed from the encounters at the rallies sometimes gave rise to new action groups.

However, even if interaction has burgeoned in the above manner, amorphous movements linked by weak ties do not develop into tight organizations. On the day before the 30 August 2015 protest rally against the National Security Legislation, in addition to the Tokyo SEALDs, T-ns SOWL and various district versions of SEALDs, thirteen other young people's action groups hailing from Okinawa to Tōhoku that opposed the National Security Legislation gathered in one hall. Okuda says of the event, 'Most of the people who gathered there were ones I was meeting for the first time' (Tamura and Tamura 2016: 169). In 1969, the Zenkyōtō movement begun at each university across the country formed the nationwide Zenkyōtō, but SEALDs and Hangenren did not create such nationwide structure.

Sometimes, connections made on the internet among people who do not personally attend meetings and actions function as social movements (see Chapter Three), and these sometimes give rise to 'real' movements. It was K-POP fans, including many teenage girls, who first fought back against the anti-Korean Zaitokukai. They directed fiery criticism at the Twitter account of Zaitokukai's leader, Sakurai Makoto, berating, admonishing and lecturing him. Inspired by their drive, Noma formed Shibakitai, explaining, 'K-POP fans' righteousness communicated itself through the screen of my smartphone' (Noma 2018: 343).

The strengths and weaknesses of amorphous movements

In the labor movements that were typical of social movements in a crystalline society, the homogeneity of their membership was their strength (Korpi 1978). The perspective taken in this book, however, is that even while amorphous social movements harbored various weaknesses due to the diversity of their membership, they may have strengths that a crystalline structure cannot offer.

For example, precisely because the homogeneity that came from being employees of the same company was the basis for connection in the general company-specific labor unions in Japan, these unions have been unable to respond to situations in which companies demerge or outsource, or utilize non-regular employment. For that reason, when society de-crystallized, and people started spilling over and falling from the structure it offered, many labor unions which had their foundations in the community, such as the Freeter Labor Union, came into being in order to respond to this shift.

Unlike in conventional labor unions in which employees automatically become union members when they join the company, in the case of such new labor unions, people who face some kind of problem join as individuals. As the issues that they encounter are various, and their negotiating partners are also different, participants do not have even the fact of being employees of the same company in common. The Freeter Labor Union has become an anchor for those workers that existing labor unions cannot include, rather than on a platform of conducting activities based on the freeter identity. Some unions even extend membership to people who are not in paid employment (Hashiguchi 2011). It is paradoxical to have people who are not workers participate in a labor movement, but here, too, we can identify the amorphous nature of today's society and social movements; Mama no Kai also has members who are not mothers (Anpo kanren hō ni hantai suru mama-no-Kai@ Osaka 2016: 5).

In contrast to the way that company-specific unions with their crystalline structure have excluded non-regular employees, amorphous movements which have had a high level of diversity from the start have the advantage of including minorities. They also have the advantage of being collections of unconstrained individuals. The 'nuclear village' has established a powerful community of interests that also involves the mainstream mass media and academia, in addition to politicians, business leaders and bureaucrats, and labor unions occupy one corner as well. As labor unions from the electric power generation and electric machine sector call for the restart of the reactors, Rengō, the national center of Japan's labor unions, is unable to embark upon denuclearization. As a result, the LDP, which has promoted nuclear power for many years, and the Democratic Party, which was also in power at the time, faced big obstacles to commence the abandonment of nuclear power generation demanded in public-opinion polls because the Democratic Party had many parliamentarians that relied upon Rengō's support. For that reason, it ought to have been difficult to organize a broad-ranging anti-nuclear power movement if it were drawn into the orbit of political parties or labor unions, as had happened previously. However, in the post-Fukushima anti-nuclear power movement, diversely scattered individuals came together on the single issue of opposition to the resumption of nuclear power generation. An absence of structure deprives a movement of the basis for mobilization, but it also entails freedom from ties of obligation.

In the present day, when university student councils have become obsolete, the role played by student dormitories and groups in fostering solidarity has declined and universities are no longer adequate hubs for social movements, it is hard to gather a sufficient number of participants at a single university. The SEALDs movement consists of students from diverse universities, and it does not have a specific university as its base. In a way, this has been forced upon it by young people's disaffection with politics which has resulted in student movements today being unable to gather sufficient numbers of participants at a single university. The SEALDs example demonstrates that a student can start a movement even if they cannot find like-minded individuals at their university.

Alone, a student cannot launch XX University Student Council or XX University Zenkyōtō, but they can participate in SEALDs TŌKAI and SEALDs KANSAI in the same way as they take part in community unions in the area in which they live.

The impetus for SEALDs TŌHOKU's Sugawara Hikari to raise her voice was reportedly her participation in an SASPL rally in February 2014: 'Even though I had feelings of dissatisfaction and negativity towards society and politics, I didn't know where and how I could express them'. Sugawara says, after seeing a tweet from SASPL:

> [A]lthough I had never taken part in a demonstration, and while it seemed quite far from Sendai, where I lived, I was charmed by the image of university students the same as me trying to raise their voices, and I jumped onto a night bus.
>
> While of course the experience of demonstrating was memorable, too, I will never forget the evening when we gathered at a joint nearby and talked together after the rally. (SEALDs 2015: 116)

Miyazaki Sayaka, the organizer of 'Fridays for Future Tokyo' in response to the Fridays For Future movement, read about Greta Thunberg in a newspaper and tried to mount an action at Rikkyo University where she was enrolled, but the response was sparse. She says, 'In the midst of participating in events external to the university, having felt isolated for some time and not knowing where on earth I could go to share this awareness of the issue, I finally arrived at the student strike that endorsed Greta's actions' (Miyazaki 2019).

Amorphous movements which include diversity also have the advantage of being able to serve as mediators between organizations with different standpoints and opinions because they are the antithesis of crystalline in terms of structure. Factional antagonism arising from an intensification of theoretical purity dogged the previous left-wing movement, but this situation has now utterly changed. This is in part due to the reduced space that the left occupies, to the extent that there is no longer any room for internal leadership struggles, and in part related to the nature of social movements today. Amorphous movements have the ability to link unrelated elements that have a crystalline structure, such as the joint events accomplished by Gensuikin and Gensuikyō facilitated by Hangenren acting as a bridge.[4] After the establishment of the National Security Legislation, supporters of other groups who had opposed the bill, such as Gakusha no Kai, SEALDs and Mama no Kai, created the Civil Alliance Calling for Peace and Constitutionalism (Anpo hōsei no haishi to rikkenshugi no kaifuku o motomeru shimin rengō; hereafter, Shimin rengō), and have become intermediaries in the opposition parties' joint struggle (see Chapter Three).

When SEALDs was in the spotlight in the 2015 anti-National Security Legislation movement, it was sometimes referred to as a young people's movement. For that reason, SEALDs has faced derision to the tune that it is not necessarily widely supported by the younger generation, and tends rather to appeal to middle-aged and older people.[5] In fact, even in the aforementioned large-scale survey, there were many rally participants in their sixties or older (Satō et al. 2018), and in spite of SEALDs receiving a lot of media exposure, the majority of the younger generation in Japan still have a low level of interest in politics.

From the perspective of its role as an intermediary between diverse elements, there are some aspects of SEALDs that can be positively appraised. Even if its impact on people of the same generation was limited, SEALDs energized the middle-aged and seniors, and motivated many people to attend a rally for the first time in several decades (Kobayashi 2016). Attracting the participation of elderly people is not something for which it should be derided. As SEALDs was not a crystalline action group that relied on such attributes as 'young people' or 'university students', it was able to connect with people across a wide spectrum of ages, including people as elderly as their grandparents. Speeches by SEALDs members often recounted extremely personal feelings that aroused the empathy of a broad range of people because their words were not specific to 'university students' or 'the working class'. Behind this lies the fact that the 'young person' identity is no longer self-evident in contemporary Japanese society (cf. Kawasaki and Asano 2016).

In spite of all the advantages discussed above, the fact that Japan is an amorphous society where it is hard to make connections still means that it is disadvantageous to the formation of movements. Even if diverse individuals from different backgrounds sometimes connect, there are various limitations such as the connections being only weak or short-term. Compared to labor unions that collect membership fees and compulsory student councils which collect ample membership fees, movements in which people gather after seeing information on social networking sites are weak in terms of resources. Staff carrying donation bags are always walking around in front of the Diet building.

Even if like-minded individuals who connected through social networking sites and so forth form a loosely-bound action group, it would be hard for that group to make decisions to organize all of its members. Saigō says, 'Because Mama no Kai is an association to which anyone may give their name, it has no collective will as an association' (Komori et al. 2016: 139). Ushida Yoshimasa from SASPL~SEALDs cites the day in February 2014 when he was asked by a newspaper for 'an opinion as [a spokesperson for] SASPL' as being 'the day that we decided on the cornerstone of SASPL's thought'. He explains that he discussed with two other key members whether there was such a thing as an 'SASPL opinion', and says that they concluded that 'individuals simply come of their own volition, and it doesn't have the feeling of a group or an organization, right?' and 'There are no opinions as SASPL, only my opinions as an individual'. For this reason, everyone states their own name at the end of their SEALDs speech, because there are no collective opinions as SEALDs as a group, only individuals' opinions (Takahashi and SEALDs 2015: 48–49).

Movements which are loose connections of various individuals who speak their opinions as individuals in this way have the advantage of being able to attract a lot of people through broad goals (opposition to the restarting of nuclear power generation, opposition to the National Security Legislation, stopping hate speech), and all kinds of differences tend to be shelved. Shibakitai, which is a single-issue movement, 'did not pretend to have a collective view on issues where opinion was divided. Even in regard to the waiver of fees at North Korean schools and the regulation of hate speech, they only said extremely ambiguous things at the initial stage' (Noma 2018: 291).

Furthermore, while from 10% to 30% of people who participated in a survey targeting the European general voting public answered that they had participated in a demonstration at the time of the post-Lehman Shock economic crisis, in surveys of the general Japanese voting public, those who had demonstrated against nuclear power generation and the National Security Legislation accounted for no more than about 1.5% of the population (Satō et al. 2018). Even though participant numbers have increased since 3.11, in international comparison participation in demonstrations in Japan is still well below the norm. The fact that the society which produces social movements has amorphized entails all kinds of disadvantages in terms of the shaping of movements, resulting in the appearance of undefined and weakly-connected amorphous movements as the only form of social movement possible in this context.

An 'Occupy Tokyo' movement that problematized such issues as economic disparity arose in 2011 in response to the Occupy Wall Street movement, but it was small, and drew little public attention. The Fridays for Future movement spread to Japan, as noted above, but the number of participants was again extremely small in comparison with Europe. Even though overseas movements have become familiar through the internet, the way they are received remains typically Japanese.

Nevertheless, Japanese social movements that had stagnated for several decades attracted many participants that systematic mobilization had failed to draw, and Hangenren has continued the kind of protest action over the long term that previous crystalline movements were unable to achieve. A multitude of people took part in demonstrations for the first time after 3.11, and the number of 'experienced demonstrators' increased markedly, signifying that the hurdles to participation had lowered.

On some impetus, these people might stand in front of the Diet building next time for the sake of a subject that is different from nuclear power generation or the National Security Legislation. On that occasion, those standing next to them will probably be neither fellow university students nor workmates, nor members of the same labor union. Apart from the reason why they turned up, maybe those gathered will have few points in common. In the following chapters, let us look more deeply into how such people connect and into what they produce as a result of their collective action.

2 What Have Post-3.11 Social Movements Changed?

KINOSHITA *Chigaya*

Nine years have passed since 3.11. During this period, a variety of types of social movements not previously seen in Japanese society have emerged. Most notable were the large-scale demonstrations and rallies that initiated the movements opposed to nuclear power and against the 2015 National Security Legislation. They were accompanied by mobilization on the streets against racism. Women's movements such as exemplified in the #MeToo Movement were also conspicuous, as were mass movements for LGBT rights. A number of European countries and the United States have, to a large extent, already tackled most of the issues motivating these social movements, but, while a section of the intellectual class in Japan had some awareness of these issues, the prolonged period of stagnation experienced by Japanese social movements meant that popular action to address them had been scarce. Although the trigger for the emergence of the post-3.11 social movements was the Fukushima nuclear power plant accident, their revolutionary nature lies in the way in which they have turned a variety of issues that have emerged concomitant with changes in Japanese society into mass movements.

What has been the source of the motivation behind people's participation in these social movements?

It is easy to imagine that social movements exist in order to 'bring about change in society because it is not changing'. In reality, however, social movements are strongly characterized by a sense of 'bringing about change because society has changed'. Japan's post-war social movements emerged in the midst of the dramatic social changes that accompanied the country's defeat and rapid economic growth, and the structural changes they underwent kept pace with ensuing social change. In the case of the 1960 campaign against the US-Japan Security Treaty, the central issue that prompted the spread of the movement was, in fact, a backlash by people who had adopted post-war democratic values against the pre-war reactionary policies of the Kishi government, rather than the rights and wrongs of the treaty. Thus, we see the emergence of large-scale, new social movements when there is popular opposition to attempts by political or corporate power, 'reactionary power', to check changes that have already begun to occur in society.[1] The post-3.11 social movements highlighted shifts that had already been instigated in Japanese society.

The people who actively participated in the post-3.11 movements were drawn to do so by a feeling of 'I have to do this, here and now'; they leaped into an uncertain future. Their motivation came about as a result of the immense shift occurring around them at the time; change that threw into confusion what had been their 'unchanging everyday'. This sort of external shock that shakes one's daily life and transforms normal social relationships can be termed a 'crisis'.

What is a crisis and what are its effects? Naomi Klein and Rebecca Solnit provide possible answers to these questions. Klein (2007) deals with an abundance of examples of disasters – including despotic South American regimes, the terrorist attacks of 9.11, the Afghan and Iraqi Wars, Hurricane Katrina and the Sumatra Earthquake, and also events in China, South Africa and Israel as well as other wars and coups d'état. Klein highlights how capitalism and the state have historically taken advantage of the 'shock' accompanying these natural disasters as well as military and economic crises and used heavy-handed means to construct an environment that is advantageous to capital. 'I call these orchestrated raids on the public sphere in the wake of catastrophic events, combined with the treatment of disasters as exciting market opportunities, "disaster capitalism"'. In other words, the neoliberal doctrine of seeking to reduce the role of the state to a minimum, under the banner of the free market, is nothing more than an official stance in reality, and the practice of using crises to clear a path to the free market via undemocratic and violent means will continue (Klein 2007: 5–6). In Japan, a series of government measures such as the granting of public works projects, creation of special free economic zones and development of policies for opening up possibilities for the free market as part of the disaster reconstruction process, against the will of residents, all make it clear that the 'crises' that accompanied the great earthquake and nuclear power plant accident of 3.11 represented an opportunity for capitalism.

What of the people, then? Are they just powerless and passive beings who, full of anxiety, panic in the face of capital taking advantage of disasters? Rebecca Solnit stresses the fact that the disintegration of social relationships as a result of disasters has provided people with the 'opportunity' to spontaneously construct new forms of solidarity. Through an examination of a number of historical disasters – including the Great San Francisco Earthquake, the London Blitz, the Mexico City Earthquake, the 9.11 terror attacks and Hurricane Katrina – Solnit argues that it was the police and the military, that is, government authorities, who either carried out or incited criminal and aberrant acts, while ordinary people set about creating a new order through cooperation driven by volunteerism. This kind of 'utopia' is undoubtedly fleeting; however, it has sometimes been connected with large-scale political change – for example, in the case of the link between the Chernobyl nuclear power plant accident and the collapse of the Soviet Union (Solnit 2010).

The word 'crisis', thus, contains within it two seemingly contradictory meanings: danger and opportunity – the 'danger' which brings about the collapse of the existing system simultaneously presents an 'opportunity' to construct a new world. The appearance of the 3.11 crisis at a time when Japanese society was becoming increasingly amorphous, as discussed in the Introduction, lent a new quality to Japan's social movements. The disintegration of the post-war democracy movement occurred in tandem with this progressively amorphous aspect of Japanese society; new social movements were formed in reaction to emergent crises such as those related to disasters and the great depression. In order to clarify the relationship between this increasingly amorphous nature of Japanese society and the establishment of new social movements, as well as their character, we first need to go back to the 1980s – the period which saw the demise of post-war social movements in Japan.

The demise of post-war social movements

The full-scale disintegration of Japan's social movements dating from the period following the end of World War II occurred in the 1980s, when the state and corporate actors had honed their systems for controlling Japanese society. There had been a sharp decrease in labor strikes, the Japan National Railways labor movement, which had been the mainstay of the post-war labor movement, had been dissolved and progressive political parties were not doing well.[2] The student movement, which reached its peak during the campus strife of 1968, had also declined dramatically; this coincided with both the greater cohesiveness of universities and the weakening of group identity among students. On the one hand, the decline of the student movement can be understood in terms of the relocation of universities to the suburbs and 'legal forces' such as the strengthening of university management as well as control over violence within student groups; however, the main reason lies in the progressive changes to student lifestyles throughout the 1980s. Up until the 1970s, university students paid low tuition fees and had low living expenses, and community life tended to be on campus, which became the basis of the student movement. Today, however, the subsequent steep rise in tuition fees has meant that university students face the stress of finding employment, work, a reduction in time on campus and pressure over tuition fees and stipends. This need for greater employment flexibility in conjunction with students' impoverishment has acted to turn them into a labor force. The former pattern of life in which students experienced campus life dissolved under this 'subsumption by capital' which undermined the earlier student lifestyle and group identity.

This is an example of how the expansion of consumer culture – through its encouragement of individualization and diversification – came to replace the waning role of social movements with workers and students at their core. Consumer culture continued to deconstruct group identity which had been the foundation of social movements until that time.

The expansion of the entertainment industry, the ongoing pressure provided by speculative and large-scale redevelopment to turn urban spaces into service areas and the growth of dedicated consumer areas are resulting in the diminishment of spaces for demonstrations and rallies on the streets. In the pre-war period, it was the power of the state that suppressed social movements, but in the post-war period this has been achieved by people's willingness to believe in the myth of the 'affluent society'.

The dominant group identity of the late 1980s and early 1990s in Japan was the 'company', having transcended those of 'worker 'and 'student'.[3] However, unlike the communities based on homogeneity and solidarity that had existed previously, this shift has been accompanied by fierce competition and division. People living within a corporate-centered society see contributing to the company's performance as being integral to improving their own lives, even though this requires them to make considerable sacrifices in terms of their daily lives, and this triggers ongoing competition. The labor unions in large private enterprises collaborate in restructuring efforts; in 1990, Japan's annual average of 2,200 work hours was 30% greater than the figure for Europe.[4]

As workers and students dropped out of social movements during this period, their places were taken by 'housewives and the elderly'. Japan's first urban anti-nuclear movement sprang up following the 1986 Chernobyl nuclear power plant accident. The central figures who took on responsibility for this movement were highly educated housewives from urban areas in their late thirties to early forties (Oguma 2012b: 166–167). Employment discrimination against women was even more extreme in this period than it is now, and considerable numbers of women were unable to find suitable employment even when they had graduated from university with excellent grades. These housewives poured their abilities into social movements that dealt with matters such as neighborhood issues and food safety. It was the wives of employees of large companies who formed the core of the 'Movement against the Construction of US Military Housing in the Ikego Forest' in Zushi City, Kanagawa Prefecture, a battle fought throughout the 1980s.[5] The relative time-use flexibility possessed by the elderly and housewives, compared to workers driven by fierce competition, was one of the reasons why they were able to take the lead in activism during this period. While smaller-scale social movements did exist in this period, there were no mass social movements in which the majority of society participated.

The increasingly amorphous nature of Japanese society

With the arrival of the 1990s the bubble economy collapsed, and Japan entered a phase of zero growth. In 1993, one-party rule by the Liberal Democratic Party (LDP) ended, ushering in the period of coalition government. Since then, the LDP's membership has decreased sharply from 3,600,000 at the beginning of the 1990s to the current level of around one million.[6] There has also been an ongoing steady dissolution of the community that had supported the LDP government until that time – groups such as conservative farmers and shopkeepers. The progressive side of politics also went into decline, with the organization rate for labor unions slumping to 17% (*Asahi Shimbun* 2018). The Socialist Party of Japan, which had been the basis of the labor movement and also representative of post-war democratic politics, was dissolved in 1996 leaving only the Communist Party and the Social Democratic Party to uphold the ideals of the Constitution. Collectively, the parties won just forty-one seats at the 1996 election, meaning that the parties upholding the ideals of opposing constitutional reform comprised less than 10% of the Diet. At the same time, the post-war democratic consciousness that had been established in the 1950s was becoming diluted. Responses to public opinion polls that agreed with the statement, 'It would be best not to alter the Japanese Constitution' had exceeded 50% at the start of the 1980s. However, by the end of the 1990s, this number had dropped to 40%, and further to 30% by the mid-2000s. With the passing of the generation that had personal experience of war, hawkish arguments were again tolerated (*Asahi Shimbun* 2017).

'Places of work, study and living' have undergone significant change. With the deregulation of the labor market, irregular employment is becoming the norm. Despite an improvement in women's ability to participate in the labor market and climb the career ladder, the failure to build a social environment that is suited to this development has resulted in a steady decline in the birthrate as childbirth and childcare have become a heavy burden. As for students, they are constrained by spending all their free time working because of steep rises in tuition fees and the need for a stipend; thus, students have been incorporated into society not as 'people who study' but as a 'labor force'. Japan's external environment has also changed – it is no longer the only economic powerhouse in Asia, as China, South Korea and Taiwan have also experienced significant economic growth. China's GDP has swollen to three times that of Japan's, and South Korea, which half a century ago had a weaker economy than that of North Korea, now has a minimum wage approaching that of Japan.[7]

Referred to as the 'lost quarter century', the period in Japan after the 1990s saw the weakening of all of the bases that had sustained Japanese society and politics: there was a disintegration not only of the communities that had sustained the post-war social movements, but also of those that had supported conservative politics and, ultimately, even the corporate community. Initially, there were hopes that the 'political realignment' of 1993 would create a new citizen's politics. Around 1995, the spotlight was on developments such as the volunteer movements following the Great Hanshin Earthquake and the 'HIV-tainted blood issue' as opportunities for citizens and students to actively participate in social movements. However, these movements were not accompanied by the revival of grassroots communities and did not lead to the birth of new political forces. Rather, this period brought to the fore far-right social movements. From the beginning of the 2000s, when public opinion in Japan was engulfed in a tide of nativism, largely in response to the North Korean kidnapping issue, the existence of 'online right-wingers' became noticeable and they began to exert an influence on politics and the press that could not be ignored. Hate speech, which was touched on in the Introduction to this book, did not appear suddenly, but only emerged after some ten years of activity that established the far-right community (Higuchi 2016).

In this period, Japan entered an era marked by the fundamental dissolution of the post-war democratic communities that had configured post-war politics and society. Meanwhile, there were also signs of the emergence of social movements opposed to the contradictions brought about by globalization and neoliberalism.

Towards 'post-3.11'

In the 2000s, Japanese society has witnessed a dizzying array of events: participation in the Iraq War, neoliberal reforms, the global financial crisis known as the 'Lehman Shock' and the assumption of political power by the Democratic Party. This process saw the sprouting of new types of social movements that embodied features that went on to configure the post-3.11 social movements and opposition politics.

The 'Article Nine Association' was launched in 2004 following a call by nine scholars, intellectuals and artists with personal experience of war.[8] At its height, this movement was a national organization with 7,500 associations in workplaces and regions throughout Japan but, lacking central leadership, it remains a loose network constructed around the aim of 'Protecting Article Nine of the Constitution' as its only point of agreement and each association tackles this as it sees fit. This network-type of movement uses as its springboard the social movement communities of the post-war generations that were established in the period of high economic growth. However, a point of difference is that considerable numbers of conservative intellectuals and residents took part in movements in the former period. Participation in the Iraq War and neoliberal reforms under the Koizumi government tore down the existing consensus – that Japan had had enough of war and that the goal should be a society that is as equitable and stable as possible – that had been established at the time of the Security Treaty struggles of the 1960s and had endured among conservatives and progressives. The sense of crisis surrounding the sorts of changes seen in this period spurred the establishment of new regional communities that went beyond the conservative–progressive axis of confrontation. In this period, former senior leaders of the LDP, such as Nonaka Hiromu, and conservative politicians who had in the past thoroughly censured reformist local governments, both now advocated the importance of Article Nine of the Constitution and rang alarm bells about the increasingly stratified nature of society. The abandonment of the provinces under neoliberal reforms had driven hostility toward conservative politics in rural communities. In the same way, the appearance of the Article Nine Association presented an opportunity for post-war democratic generations, who had moved beyond conservative/progressive divisions, to unite.[9]

The Iraq War, which began in 2003, sparked worldwide anti-war movements. In Japan, it inspired the first anti-war street demonstrations since the anti-Vietnam War movement. The people in their twenties and thirties who participated in this movement introduced the culture of the 'anti-globalization movement' which emerged around the world at that time, thus attempting to construct a culture of street movements that departed from the status quo. The generation that experienced this anti-Iraq War movement – also central members of Amateur Revolt discussed by Tanaka Hikaru in Chapter Four – would go on to construct the first model of street action that featured in post-3.11 social movements.

Amongst all these social movements, the anti-poverty movement had the greatest impact on politics. The worldwide upheaval that stemmed from the 2008 sub-prime mortgage crisis (the Lehman Shock) in the US inflicted the greatest damage on Japan's economy since its wartime defeat. Overseas exports instantly fell by more than half and the manufacturing industry laid off large numbers of workers in response to severe financial pressure. In the middle of 2009, the unemployment rate worsened to 5.5% and the number of people looking for work after having fallen victim to 'downsizing by laying off part-time and jobless people including temporary workers' reached 400,000 (*Asahi Shimbun* 2009). Up until this point, Japan's business community had won the loyalty of its employees and managed, however imperfectly, to stabilize society by committing 'to avoiding layoffs as far as possible' as collateral against fierce competition and division. 'Downsizing by laying off part-time and temporary workers' dealt a blow to the myth of the stability of Japanese society, and words such as 'unemployment' and 'poverty' that had long faded from use regained prominence.

At the end of 2008, NPOs and labor unions set up life counselling and emergency food stations as well as housing for the homeless in Tokyo's Hibiya Park. The movement 'occupied' Hibiya Park with this 'New Year's Eve Temporary Employee Village' and early in the new year they opened up a large hall nearby that belonged to the ministry of health, labor and welfare and 'occupied' it on behalf of those who had lost their jobs. In the summer of 2011, the Occupy Wall Street movement broke out in the US and activists filled New York's Central Park calling for equitable economic policies. The movement's slogan, 'We are the 99%', swept across the world at the time, but, in reality, the movement in Japan eighteen months earlier had already taken this initiative. The Japanese movement developed into an 'anti-poverty movement' and spread to every part of the country, transcending existing differences and conflicts between labor unions and opposition parties and managing to encourage agreement and cooperation between them on the issue of poverty. The first area of cooperation was built between the three big national unions – the Japanese Trade Union Confederation, National Confederation of Trade Unions and National Trade Union Council – with all opposition parties, from the Democratic to the Communist parties, lending their support (*Asahi Shimbun* 2008). This anti-poverty movement provided the basis for the form and actions of post-3.11 social movements; for example, in terms of winning popular backing and prompting opposition parties and labor unions to overcome their internal divisions and collaborate. This movement had the political power to check further neoliberal employment reforms proposed by the Koizumi government with only a quarter century of experience and realized the goal of 'changing politics via social movements'.

In the general election held six months after the establishment of the 'New Year's Eve Temporary Employee Village', the LDP suffered a historic crushing defeat and the Democratic Party won government. A national sense of unease about neoliberalism was undoubtedly responsible for this shift.

The Democratic Party government under Hatoyama rose to power thanks to the tailwind provided by the anti-poverty movement; it entered government touting 'brotherhood politics' and its cabinet boasted an initial support rating of 70%. However, this support dropped sharply as a result of the government's failure to carry out its campaign pledge to relocate the Henoko US military base in Okinawa and, in less than a year, it was forced to resign. The Naoto Kan government which followed also suffered a crushing defeat due to its pledge in the House of Councillors election to increase the consumption tax, thus losing its majority in that chamber. The ruling party was resoundingly defeated in the nationwide local elections in the Spring of 2011, and it was anticipated that this would spell the end of Kan's government. Thus, at the start of 2011, hopes regarding politics in Japan turned into despair. Meanwhile, new social movements were coming to the fore in other countries. In January 2011, a demonstration sparked by the self-immolation of an impoverished young man in Tunisia grew, eventually resulting in the collapse of the country's dictatorship. Large-scale democratization movements against Mubarak's dictatorial regime broke out in neighboring Egypt, sparked by the Jasmine Revolution. Tahrir Square, in front of the president's office, was 'occupied' by more than a million protesters (*Asahi Shimbun* 2011a). These democratization movements saw the first full-scale use by social movements of social networking sites (SNS) such as Facebook and Twitter which were spreading rapidly at the time (Sōmushō 2012). These uprisings were broadcast around the world in live transmissions, providing unprecedented opportunities for people around the world to experience, in a virtual sense, democratization movements in other countries and sparking social movements in various parts of the world. President Mubarak announced his resignation on 11 February 2011, exactly one month before the Great East Japan Earthquake, and the joyous voices of the one million citizens who had gathered in Tahrir Square were instantly circulated around the world via SNS.

Post-3.11 expansion of the anti-nuclear power movement

The Great East Japan Earthquake and the Fukushima nuclear power plant accident, which occurred on 11 March 2011, were – particularly for those living in the affected area – a time when people coped as best they could with a succession of incidents such as the accident itself, aftershocks and planned power outages. People's responses varied and there were many instances of conflict in homes and workplaces. Disputes and conflicts arose over fears about evacuations from the Tokyo area and the disaster areas as well as about the radioactive contamination of food and water.[10] Although distrust in politics swelled rapidly in the midst of uncertainty about just how far the impact of the nuclear power plant accident would spread, it remained unclear as to how this would translate into demands and which methods would be employed to meet them. This is unsurprising given that there were no prospects of reconstruction during this period and people could see no way out. It took around one month for a vague outline of a course of action to be formulated.[11]

Those for whom the earthquake and nuclear power plant accident brought on a sense of crisis included some who had never previously participated in social movements. They were eager to find a place to express their mistrust of and anger towards the political establishment. On 27 March, a demonstration against nuclear fuel reprocessing in Rokkasho Village was held in the Ginza area of Tokyo. The monthly demonstrations on the issue that had been taking place for many years usually attracted around thirty participants, but on this particular day 1,200 people took part. It was reported that the organizers of this movement were deeply moved by this dramatic increase in numbers and shed tears, and that some participants became involved 'after having searched the internet desperately thinking that there must be a demonstration somewhere'. Two other demonstrations were held on 3 April – one in Nagoya against the Hamaoka Nuclear Power Plant drew 450 participants and a 'Cherry Blossom Viewing Rally' in Chūō Park in Shinjuku was attended by hundreds of people. Cultural figures called the latter a protest against appeals made by Ishihara, the Governor of Tokyo, that people exercise self-restraint in their cherry viewing because of the earthquake (Tomisama 2011; 'Stop Hamaoka nuclear plant' blog 2011; *Mainichi Shimbun* 2020). It is not necessarily the case that most of the participants in these demonstrations and rallies endorsed the appeals, demands or styles of the organizers. People were instead looking for an 'opportunity' to express the feelings of hopelessness that had enveloped Japanese society following the earthquake and the nuclear power plant accident and to find others with whom to share their distress and pain.

Two demonstrations were held in Tokyo around one month after the earthquake, on 10 April. The demonstrations and rallies in Shiba Park were attended by 2,500 people, with veterans of citizens' groups forming their core (*Nihon Keizai Shimbun* 2011). In contrast, around 15,000 people assembled for the 'Stop nuclear power!!!' demonstration held in the Kōenji area. This demonstration, in which I participated and worked in the legal team, was largely made up of relatively young people participating in a demonstration for the first time who had obtained information about it via SNS. The actual number of people who turned up on the day was thirty times the anticipated number (500 people) given in the application to hold a demonstration, and the resultant inadequate police presence led to participants spreading out to fill the available free spaces rather than being assembled in orderly columns. This Kōenji demonstration contributed considerably to changing the existing image of street demonstrations in Japan because the varied nature of the movement rendered it 'visible' to wider society: it created free spaces, individuals participated spontaneously of their own free will, shouting their own slogans as they pleased and the movement freed up public access to the streets. In fact, the participants in this demonstration went on to attend later rallies held in the Tokyo area in significant numbers. The success of this demonstration laid down a 'pattern' for the subsequent anti-nuclear power movement. The Kōenji demonstration proved its overwhelming superiority over existing forms of organization at other demonstrations in terms of numbers and unifying force. As a result, this style of demonstration also had a considerable influence on the format of existing citizen's movements and the rapidly growing regional movements for abandoning nuclear power generation.

In the first half of 2011, the group favoring the abandonment of nuclear power generation was still a minority and Japanese society's feelings of antipathy towards direct action, fostered over many decades, still held sway. In the Kōenji 'Stop nuclear power!!!' demonstration, a minority group movement displayed a methodology that opened up a 'path for participation with the aim of becoming a majority'. The 'Goodbye nuclear power' rally of 19 September 2011, drew 60,000 participants; on 16 July 2012, it attracted 170,000 (*Shimbun Akahata* 2012).

This Kōenji type of demonstration was in part triggered by the worldwide trend in activism evident in 2011. The third 'Stop nuclear power!!!' demonstration, held on 11 June 2011, saw 20,000 people occupy the square in front of the Shinjuku ALTA building[12] (*Our Planet TV*, 2011). This vision that involved giving a movement visibility by packing a public square to capacity with a crowd and occupying that space was adopted from the Tahrir Square demonstration in the Egyptian Revolution, and it was also the form of protest later used in the US by the expanding Occupy Movement. The occupation of public spaces is not the only feature shared by the demonstrations in Tahrir Square, the Shinjuku ALTA Square and Zuccotti Park in the Occupy Movement: the absence of any leadership groups or organizations engendered unfalteringly friendly relations between participants in these movements. The 2011 movement for abandoning nuclear power generation, which had this kind of format, can be seen as part of a worldwide trend in social movements. Although there were diverse causes and motives behind these movements around the world, they had a democratic longing as their common cause: the attempted reform of existing political, social and organizational authority.

The anti-nuclear demonstrations, which expanded from Tokyo at their core, gradually became both national and localized. In April 2011, demonstrations began to spread throughout the country, and on 11 June were held in hundreds of places around Japan in a synchronized national action. It was not necessarily greater metropolitan areas or prefectures with nuclear power plants that saw the biggest demonstrations. Gunma, Tochigi and Nagano, all examples of places that fitted into neither of these categories, had rallies attended by more than 2,000 protestors. Two-and-a-half years after the earthquake, all of Japan's prefectures had experienced at least one anti-nuclear power demonstration. However, all were diverse and uneven in terms of style, each being significantly influenced by the particular strength of each region's existing social movements.[13]

Photo 2.1: *Anti-nuclear demonstration in Osaka on 15 June 2011.
Source: A. Gotō.*

From around the end of 2011, participants in the 'Stop nuclear power!!!' demonstration that had taken place in Kōenji began to strengthen their ties with the residents and residents' movement of Suginami Ward in Tokyo, going on to establish 'Datsu-genpatsu Suginami' (Denuclearization Suginami). This group planned to hold a 5,000-strong regional demonstration in February 2012 with residents of Suginami Ward at its core. It adopted a style that emphasized a consensus-building type of participation – reminiscent of the Occupy Movement in the US – in which anyone could participate. The agendas of meetings were posted online, and decisions were taken on the spot after people had voiced their opinions and debated each issue. There were usually around 100 participants at the executive committee meetings that I attended, and they were places where democracy was actually put into effect.

Thus, individualistic and diverse ways of making connections were developed in the process of planning demonstrations at the regional level. People interacted via SNS and at demonstrations in Tokyo, such as at 'Friday protests in front of the prime minister's official residence', strengthening their networks in multilayered and interactive ways. As a result of the establishment of this kind of network-type of group, no organizational body is formed to give consistent direction to the movement. Movements that emerge in response to a particular 'situation' and then disappear lay out innumerable routes which open up opportunities for greater mass participation as participants engage with and inspire each other.[14]

The anti-nuclear power demonstrations reached their peak, in terms of scale, in July 2012. The total number of participants in demonstrations around the country during this month reached more than one million. This July movement was symbolized by the 'Friday protests in front of the prime minister's official residence', rallies which had been held there every Friday since March 2012. However, the Metropolitan Coalition Against Nukes (Shutoken Hangenpatsu Rengō; hereafter, Hangenren) which organized these protests, in complete contradistinction to the US-Japan Security Treaty Joint Struggle Council (Anpo Kyōtō Kaigi) in 1960, had neither the power to command the national movements nor did it issue any mobilization orders. Quite to the contrary, Hangenren did not even issue calls for 'Friday protests throughout Japan'. And yet, the 'Friday protests' broke out spontaneously in close to one hundred locations throughout Japan. People who had previously taken part in demonstrations and those who had been thinking of taking part identified 'protest points' in their own prefectures and regions and sent out calls to action themselves. From the time of the 3.11 disaster until the middle of 2012, the nationwide anti-nuclear power movement, aside from sometimes taking up particular local issues, basically held demonstrations in concert with other simultaneous actions on the 'anniversary' of 3.11 or various related issues. These movements, at a stroke, and, moreover, without any orders from anyone, put together simultaneous nationwide actions in response to the political situation. Naturally, the sense of danger regarding the resumption of nuclear power generation was one of the factors motivating this transition. The fact that the media finally began to discuss the demonstrations in this period also sparked their intensification. Equally important, however, had been the development of solid regional movements via national networks rather than by relying on mass media and the use of this strength to *effect* a change of opinion regarding nuclear power generation that, in the course of a year, saw a majority of people become opposed to it. In short, it is important to note that the movement already felt a real sense of having the power to change public opinion. On 26 December 2011, six months before the 'Friday protests in front of the prime minister's official residence' became large-scale, 'yes' responses to a public opinion poll in the *Asahi Shimbun* on the question, 'Do demonstrations have the power to influence politics?', reached 44%, the highest figure in recent years (*Asahi Shimbun* 2011b).

Thus, the 'crisis' of 3.11 became an opportunity for the rebirth, in a new form, of Japanese social movements that had disintegrated in the 1980s. It is likely that other new social movements raising a variety of issues will continue to emerge from within this newly expanded action space.

The anti-racism movement and experiences of struggle

The emergence in the twenty-first century of nativist 'movements' in Japan was a sign of the unrest vis-à-vis Japanese identity that had first appeared during the process of high economic growth. The rise of democratization and social movements in the various countries of East Asia from the 1980s on, and the economic growth seen throughout Asia in this period, has completely transformed the Cold War era map of the region. Having lost its unique position in East Asia as 'the economically rich and advanced democratic nation', Japan is being engulfed by a wave of East Asian globalization. The far-right nativist movement is a backlash against, and stimulated by, this crisis in Japan.

At the start of 2013, racist groups commenced action aimed at obstructing businesses in Shin-Ōkubo in Tokyo's Shinjuku Ward, where large numbers of Zainichi (Korean residents) live and run businesses. There was a flood of angry comments on the internet in response to this, largely from K-Pop fans (young fans of Korean pop idols). Participants in social movements, who sympathized with these online opinions, began to counter this racism through street action. The number of participants spontaneously attending the actions to counter the racist demonstrations occurring in Shin-Ōkubo increased rapidly; the counter action, which was now several thousand strong, had become a showdown with the racist demonstrators (Noma 2018).

In Shin-Ōkubo, on 8 September 2013, several hundred people seemed to materialize out of nowhere onto the streets to prevent the departure of a racist street march and carried out a sit-in that blocked the road. Even though they were pulled roughly off the road by the riot squad, the anti-racism protestors repeatedly flung themselves back onto it. Most of those who took part in the sit-in had participated in the anti-nuclear power movement. This sort of mass sit-in in a public space had not been seen in Japan for decades. However, it subsequently came to be used in the movement against military bases in Henoko and also in that against the 2015 National Security Legislation.

In this way, the social movements that followed 3.11 built up people's 'struggle experience'. Countless demonstrations and rallies have taken place in the intervening nine years. As a result of the accumulation of these experiences, when public concern is ignited it has now become established practice to gather in front of the Diet or in front of the prime minister's residence. On 27 July 2018, 5,000 people protested in front of the LDP headquarters in objection to discriminatory remarks about LGBT people made by Sugita Mio, a far-right Diet member from the LDP, and published in an article in the magazine *Shinchō Yonjūgo*. This demonstration was only announced via SNS, and most of the participants were young people who had probably never taken part in demonstrations before (*Mainichi Shimbun* 2018).

The countless protest actions – beginning with the anti-nuclear power movement – that had taken place over the past decade helped these people to find a place to protest where they could voice their anger and dissatisfaction and have an opportunity to directly engage with each other. Just as a path will appear as the result of many people taking the same route across a deserted plain, the accumulated *struggle experience* discussed above opened up a path along which people wanting to participate in social movements can walk from now on.

Viewed historically, large-scale mass gatherings, such as revolutions and social movements, do not go on for months. Moreover, when social movements swell in size to a scale of several hundreds of thousands, those taking part are no longer necessarily only the organizers and people sympathetic to the movement's stated goals. As sociologist Higuchi Naoto has clearly shown through surveys, the ranks of participants in the 2012 anti-nuclear power movement and in the 2015 movement against the National Security Legislation contained 'unsympathetic elements'; in other words, a considerable proportion of attendees were not necessarily sympathetic to the sponsoring group or the demonstration.[15] If we broadly label these people 'curious onlookers', when social movements attain their highest level of 'magnetic attraction as a place' – when they make ordinary people want to become 'curious onlookers' – participant numbers can swell as high as the hundreds of thousands. The strength of social movements' magnetism is restricted by political, social and economic conditions. The 'struggle experiences' cultivated there are not lost; the scale of this accumulation serves to increase the magnetism of the social movements that rise up in response to the next phase of crises and changes.

Conclusion

The answer to the question, 'What have the post-3.11 social movements changed?' is tucked away inside the respective struggles of the millions of people who responded to the various 'crises' that have occurred over the past nine years and in their shared experiences. These experiences come about in a broad variety of ways: from directly participating, being on the footpath next to a street demonstration and thinking it is unacceptable, to becoming curious about what is happening when viewed remotely on a mobile phone screen. In the midst of the maelstrom brought about by widespread changes, the path for reform is created as these actions and reactions produce countless scattered reflections. This path is, however, amorphous; just as one thinks that it opened up because of certain conditions, it may also, in the twinkling of an eye, appear to have crumbled due to these same conditions. Consequently, there is no firm idea regarding the goals that ought to lie at the end of this path or even when they might be achieved. Quite to the contrary, the more extreme the changes, the more obscure the vision one has even about what might happen tomorrow. Below are the characteristics that underpin the amorphous nature of the social movements that responded to the amorphous nature of Japanese society.

The political background

The post-Cold War period saw the waning of the 'authority' of both the conservatives and the reformists who had constructed the post-war order. By this time, the post-war reformist forces lacked the 'authority' to even develop a large-scale mass movement. Current social movements emerged from the vacuum in which neither political nor social authorities were able to take the leadership initiative.

The movements' organizers

Neoliberal reforms put an end to the stable governing of Japanese society and gave rise to a mass of new classes. These new classes include those in irregular employment and casual laborers who, with the considerable gap in cultural capital and social status between them and the established classes of those in regular employment and freed from the Fordism-type work rules, ran the social movements as a new 'intelligent political body'.

The movements' antagonistic nature

The establishment of clear 'enemies' – such as 'Nuclear village' (*Genshiryoku mura*) and 'racists' – led to a heightening of the cohesive power of social movements. In these movements, there was no setting of goals or platforms for total social reform; instead, they adopted a pragmatic approach which aligned methods with aims.

Group formation and spontaneity

No individuals or organizations emerged from the post-3.11 social movements wielding leadership: there was no scope for charisma. The process by which these movements functioned involves the creation and development of a network via the very disputes and arguments already being engaged in – either on SNS or at meetings. Appeals by the movements were not made via the previous approach of vertical mobilization but instead spread horizontally, and when these intersected with political or social situations, thousands to tens of thousands of people mobilized.

The accumulation of this kind of practice produced spaces which generated even more social movements, and these led to the emergence of other movements addressing a variety of issues.[16]

Consequently, unlike previous social movements, these new social movements with their increasingly amorphous nature have not been 'constructed'. In other words, they do not adopt the modern style of forming an organization with the aim of grabbing hold of power by basing themselves on workers' or farmers' identities, expanding membership and then building a sustainable organizational base. As a result, the fluctuations in the power of these movements will be bewildering, but it will not be accidental or negotiated. Accordingly, we will not see here a repetition of the construction of a political bloc of the sort produced by socialist and social democratic parties during the modernization process. Amorphous movements in an amorphous society have a high level of affinity with populism, and, in the political sphere, new responsible actors will emerge who are likely to bring about reforms and instability simultaneously.

Post-3.11 social movements have replaced the post-war type of social movement formed in the period of high economic growth and have constructed a movement style and experience that is compatible with changing modern society.[17] Hereafter, Japanese society will resolutely confront a range of structural crises in various areas such as disasters, population, industry and the democratic system. When new social movements appear, what kinds of ideas and issues, one wonders, will they focus on in response to these crises? The seemingly endless democracy struggles in Hong Kong, which began in earnest in 2019, may well foreshadow the route for social struggles in Japan, which coexist inside a political vacuum in an East Asia experiencing a period of great change.

3 Post-3.11 Social Movements and Politics

Horie Takashi

Introduction – overview of the issues

This chapter considers the relationship between post-3.11 social movements and politics. In recent years, it has become increasingly common in Japanese society to see large-scale demonstrations and rallies. Theorists who see Japanese social movements as having entered a new cycle of protest cite five factors as causes for this phenomenon, namely: changes to the geopolitical context in the East Asia/Pacific region; economic stagnation and a society with widening social disparity; a new political agenda, and the style of the conservative ruling class; opposition to nuclear power; and new opportunities for mobilization, namely through social media (Chiavacci and Obinger 2018). These are the structural factors that form the backdrop for the emergence of the movements. We might also regard attention to the cognitive precariat touched upon in the introductory chapter and analyses of the characteristics of movement participants as attempts to identify the social foundation of the movements (Oguma 2016; Satō et al. 2018).

By contrast, in this chapter I directly focus on the political dimensions of the movements, rather than upon the structural background and social conditions that have facilitated mobilization, specifically analyzing the distinguishing features of post-3.11 social movements by firstly directing attention to their claims. I will then consider the kinds of influence that the contemporary social movements could bring to bear on politics in the future.

Given the all-too-obvious opposition to nuclear power (and reactor restarts) and to the National Security Legislation, prior analyses are thought to have eschewed probing their demands in favor of looking towards such social background issues as the expansion of non-regular employment and how difficult it is for young people to live. However, the young people who actually experience those difficulties rarely take part in demonstrations, and the rate of participation of non-regular workers is also low (Satō et al. 2018). While still being constrained by structural factors, the people involved in activism have done so in pursuit of some kind of political outcome, and so there is ample scope to explore the specific characteristics of their demands. The political consequences of the movements themselves should also be examined, but I wish to consider not only such short-term outcomes as the movements' failure to stop reactor restarts or to prevent the passing in 2015 of the National Security Legislation, but also to ponder the movements' significance from a longer-term perspective. This is bound to lead to an understanding of the movements' claims.

Post-3.11 movements through the features of their demands

Post-3.11 demonstrations have often been noted as embodying the emergence of a new type of participant that differs from the conventional 'activist' stereotype. From around the time of demonstrations against the 2003 Iraq War, this new style, which included the creation of a festive atmosphere via so-called 'parades' as well as 'sound demonstrations' accompanied by loud music, first attracted notice as something that symbolized a break from previous movements.

Even within the markedly larger-scale post-3.11 movements, attention was drawn to their campaign style, such as the use of social media, speeches read from the screens of mobile phones, rap-inspired chants and stylish flyers, and to the attributes of their participants, namely, young people, women and families accompanied by children, all of whom were considered unlikely to have taken part in demonstrations in the past.

Yet, were the demands they made really novel? This chapter will analyze the nature of the claims made by post-3.11 social movements, focusing on two representative activist groups: the Metropolitan Coalition Against Nukes (Hangenren), and the student collective known as SEALDs (Students Emergency Action for Liberal Democracy / Jiyū to minshushugi no tame no gakusei kinkyū kōdō).

Direct target and scope

In the wording of its calls for participation and its websites, and also at the sites of its protest action, Hangenren has appealed to participants to refrain from speeches, banners and placards on topics not related to nuclear power. This strict single-issue principle has been deemed necessary in order to attract a broad range of participants, including conservatives. One member explained: 'In order to make our voice heard ever more loudly, we have to be aware of the general public, and secure their diversity'. For this reason, 'We stick to a single issue. We lower the threshold for participation. We try not to be a movement that attracts only a narrowly-defined group of people. If we brought in issues of poverty, national security, or the Constitution, as well, opinion would be divided', and so 'we ask people not to touch on matters apart from nuclear energy [...]. There are rightists and leftists, conservatives and radicals, too, opposed to nuclear power. We have ensured diversity by transcending all ideologies, moving forward as a popular movement that opposes the use of nuclear power' (Hattori 2016: 59–60).

What is inextricably linked to such a single-issue principle is the absence of a systematic ideology such as Marxism. Spokesperson Misao Redwolf laughingly says of the weekly Hangenren meetings, '[we] always discuss practical matters, and there's no time to talk about things like ideology' (Ide et al. 2013: 15). Oguma Eiji, who used to take part in preparatory meetings for 'Stop nuclear power!!!!' (*Genpatsu yamero !!!!*) demonstrations that predated the formation of Hangenren, states: 'The people who gathered probably had diverse ideological inclinations, and wouldn't have had anything in common except denuclearization' (Oguma 2013: 206).

SEALDs, on the other hand, is known as a movement that opposed the National Security Legislation, but that was not its sole focus. The parent body from which SEALDs emerged, the activist group SASPL (Students Against the Secret Protection Law / Tokutei himitsu hogohō ni hantai suru gakusei yūshi no kai) which opposed the State Secrecy Law (officially the Act on the Protection of Specially Designated Secrets (SDS) / *Tokutei himitsu hogo hō*), was formed in December 2013 by a group of university students who had observed anti-nuclear power demonstrations and held events at clubs which doubled as study meetings. They had therefore been engaged in activism even prior to the emergence of the National Security Legislation issue. Many cite the Great East Japan Earthquake and tsunami and the Fukushima nuclear reactor disaster as factors that motivated their involvement (Tamura and Tamura 2016). The SEALDs founding statement on its English website reads as follows: 'In order to protect our Constitution of Japan which is currently in danger, we state a clear vision with focus on Constitutionalism, Social Security, and National Security' (http://sealdseng.mystrikingly.com/#statement). However, according to one member, Suwahara Takeshi, 'As well as democracy, the things that have really become the mainstay of SEALDs [activities] are social security, national security and constitutionalism', but once 'the National Security Legislation came to prominence, that grew too big'. So, 'although we were originally supposed to frame ourselves in terms of defending "freedom and democracy", we ended up being seen as a group opposed to the National Security Legislation' (SEALDs 2016: 32–33). As will later become evident, rather than relying on a specific ideology, its advocacy of 'freedom and democracy' was one with considerable scope and flexibility.

The problems of 'collective language' and individual speech

The absence of a systematic ideology is related to the practice of members each talking about their 'personal issues'. Takahashi Gen'ichirō (b. 1951) notes that in the student movement in which he participated circa 1970, individuals had no 'words of their own'. According to Takahashi, at the time of the 1960 Anpo movement against the Treaty of Mutual Cooperation and Security between the US and Japan, 'there were still probably many who believed in a "collective language". Although few believed in this anymore by our time, there was no custom at political events of speaking on our own terms, nor did we actually know how to do it'. Therefore, Takahashi laughingly continued, 'we said things that we ourselves didn't really think'. It was for this reason that he 'felt dazzled' as he watched SEALDs members reading speeches from mobile phones written in their own words (Takahashi and SEALDs 2015: 50–51). Prominent feminist scholar Ueno Chizuko (b. 1948), who had similarly experienced the student movement at around the same time, is impressed by SEALDs, noting that in the movement in her day there were set chants and expressions akin to 'What do we want? No Anpo! When do we want it? Now!' (*Wareware wa, ANPO o...!*), and mostly, only male students gave speeches. 'But now', Ueno continued, 'girls, too, both lead the chants and mount the rostrum. That feels really natural' (Ueno 2015: 42). Komori Yōichi (b. 1953) points out that at political gatherings in the 1960s and 70s, the grammatical subject was always 'we' (*wareware wa...*). In contrast, SEALDs member Motoyama Jinshirō remarks that in their movement, 'there was increasingly really widespread use of the first-person pronoun, "I"' (*watashi*). Motoyama further notes that 'not only has the use of the pronoun "I" become common among people of our generation, but it seems that Mama no Kai [Anti-National Security Legislation Mothers Against War], lawyers and scholars also express themselves in the first person' (Komori et al. 2016: 34, 41, 61). At Hangenren's regular Friday evening anti-nuclear power demonstrations, too, many speakers address the crowd in their own words.

From a different perspective, this also means that it is hard for a viable 'collective language' that appeals to the full cross-section of society to develop in a society that has become more amorphous. Given that most people who experienced the war have now gone, and most people do not have a sense of the reality of the term 'exploitation', it is difficult to put together a discourse that embraces a collective identity. That is why there is no alternative to speaking personally, using 'I'. Moreover, even if there were a unified ideology, it would be impossible for an amorphous movement which is completely antithetical to a top-down organisation to make that ideology permeate to every corner.

Photo 3.1: Demonstration against the National Security Legislation in front the National Diet building on 30 August 2015: many people gathering. Source: mkimpo.

The SEALDs proclamation states:

We uphold the tradition of freedom and democracy in Japan that has been built for the past 70 years after the [sic] World War II. Our principal aim is to protect the Constitution of Japan which is fundamental to this tradition. (SEALDs English website: http://sealdseng.mystrikingly.com/#statement)

While crowned with the Japanese words for 'liberty' and 'democracy', SEALDs' name, 'Students Emergency Action for Liberal Democracy' (Jiyū to minshushugi no tame no gakusei kinkyū kōdō), has an element of 'having a sly dig' at the party in power – namely, the Liberal Democratic Party (Jiyū minshu tō) – which dismisses those tenets (Okuda, cited in Takahashi and SEALDs 2015: 104), but their demands certainly fit into this frame.[1] Unlike the requesting of 'post-war democracy' implemented by the Zenkyōtō (Zengaku kyōtō kaigi / All Campus Joint Struggle Committee) student movement that operated at the end of the 1960s, SEALDs' assertions are moderate, generally operating within the parameters of post-war democracy. In fact, spokesperson Okuda Aki was advocating for the 'reactivation of post-war democracy' (Tamura and Tamura 2016: 172).

The legacy of the past and anti-anti-intellectualism

SEALDs members often mention social movements of the past. Okuda observes that, listening to speeches made by his fellow activists, he 'realizes that they are trying to spin them from somewhere such as the words of our historical predecessors. It is as if we have inherited that language in an unbroken tradition from those who went before us' (SEALDs 2015: 108). Ueno Chizuko, who experienced 'generational conflict' in the student movement, states:

> [Y]oung people today pay proper respect to their elders; and they say things in their speeches that bring tears to my eyes, too, such as: "For seventy years, it has been the activists who have gone before us that protected Article 9 [of the Constitution], neither killing nor being killed". They themselves are very aware of this succession. In contrast to the oppositional relationship that I experienced, they maintain continuity with preceding generations. (Ueno and Kitada 2015: 16)

Okuda, too, expresses acknowledgement that there is 'intergenerational cooperation on the part of the activists' (SEALDs 2015: 132).

At rallies conducted in conjunction with the Association of Scholars Opposed to National Security Legislation (Anpo hōsei ni hantai suru gakusha no kai, known as Gakusha no Kai), SEALDs students openly demonstrate respect for academics. While there may be a strategic element to their words, it is strange to see student movements being regarded as equating to intergenerational conflict.

Resistance to the anti-intellectualism of the Abe Shinzō administration, which insisted on supporting constitutional reinterpretation that a majority of constitutional scholars argued was unconstitutional, is thought to underpin SEALDs' approach to the scholars. Okuda points out that previous student movements had included 'types that were determined to create a schema in which young people were set against faculty members, and whose aim was to ridicule scholarly endeavor and to make a whole lot of ruckus' (Takahashi and SEALDs 2015: 108). SEALDs, on the other hand, conducted a selected readings project, drawing up a list of recommended books that the group requested be placed in libraries. While there is no doubt that many of these works are relatively light, this arguably demonstrates a thirst for knowledge in this day and age, when it has long been said that university students have stopped reading books. Noting that 'SEALDs' concept is not especially new', Okuda observed that they said 'very similar things' both to the Article Ninety-Six Association (96 jō no kai) and Save Constitutional Democracy Japan (Rikken demokurashii no kai), most of whose press briefings he saw. He further stated that 'what we do fundamentally is something like translating the sorts of things that are published in the Iwanami journal, *Sekai*' (The World) (Okuda, Kuramochi and Fukuyama 2015: 21).[2]

Post-3.11 movements and democracy

As its pride of place in the SEALDs name suggests, democracy is clearly an important issue for its members. Okuda, however, is rather exceptional, as the democracy apprehended by the majority of students who participated was a little more flexible than what was specified as 'post-war democracy'.

Democracy – merely in the sense of demanding of a regime that forces through legislation to which many have objections that one's voice is heard – has been widely shared not only by SEALDs, but also by participants in the anti-National Security Legislation movement and those opposed to the restarting of reactors at nuclear power plants. Both in the case of the Noda administration's restarting of the Ōi nuclear power plant, and the Abe regime's forcing-through of the National Security Legislation, the indecent haste with which they attempted to act, ignoring the voices of dissent, led to a swelling of movement participation.

Within SEALDs, there was also an understanding that Japan was currently at a critical crossroads where the choice was between democracy and dictatorship (Okuda and Inose 2015: 51; SEALDs 2015: 93). While the phrase 'democracy or dictatorship' is well-known to have been expressed at the time of the 1960 Anpo crisis by China scholar Takeuchi Yoshimi (1910–1977), it cannot be argued that there was any similarly widespread sense of crisis in 2015. That is to say, there was no general awareness that the kind of democracy under discussion here is a matter connected with a choice of political system.

However, rather than opposition to reactor restarts or the National Security Legislation *per se*, what constituted the driving force behind the movement was anger towards the forcing-through of policies that lacked majority support on dubious pretexts, in the absence of any proper explanations and in disregard of dissenting voices. Democracy was one of the main themes of the movements in that sense. Okuda pointed out that information about the dangers of nuclear power generation was concealed, it being deemed 'best to leave things to the experts', and that, too, was what he 'felt was the biggest problem' with the Special Secrecy Law. In other words, Okuda continued, 'It was as if they thought that stupid ordinary people didn't need to know, and it would be fine to conceal information that they didn't want known. In my opinion, it was a bill that demonstrated that sort of mentality'. He further explained how 'among members, there was widespread disgust with that structure', noting that the 'anger at being treated with contempt and at continually being given explanations which did not seem to be explanations at all, no matter how many times we heard them', applied similarly to the National Security Legislation. Pointing out the existence of the chant, 'We are the ones with the power to rule' (*jibuntachi ga shukensha da*), Misao Redwolf said that this feeling was also shared by the anti-nuclear power generation movement (Okuda, Oguma and Redwolf 2016: 39). Moreover, SEALDs often employed the chant, 'Make no more selfish decisions!' (*Katte ni kimen na*). Thus, democracy in this sense was a theme shared by movements opposing reactor restarts and the National Security Legislation.

Conservatism and majority awareness

This kind of 'democracy' is something that is located purely within the current system. Rather than being a denial of parliamentary democracy or party politics, direct action such as demonstrations is a defense of or a call for their revival. While being opposed to National Security Legislation that enables the exercise of 'the right to collective self-defense', that is, the mass overseas deployment of the Self-Defense Forces, these groups have not suggested that the Anpo Treaty be rescinded, and neither do they raise the issue of 'American imperialism'. And although they call for constitutionalism to be protected, the SEALDs foundation statement features a sentence that reads: 'We do not mean to deny the possibility of constitutional amendment itself'. As constitutional reform concerning such issues as the 'rights of sexual minority [sic] and different lifestyles' needs to occur in a context in which these matters are 'publicly discussed and practiced' (SEALDs English website: http://sealdseng.mystrikingly.com/#statement), while SEALDs as an organization does not advocate for the revision of Article Nine, there are members who favor changing it (Takahashi and SEALDs 2015: 56). Similarly, there are members who have 'absolutely no interest' in the 'Cross out the national flag!' (*Hinomaru ni batten*) campaign (SEALDs 2016: 76). This would seem conservative from the perspective of the former leftist movement, with its arguably self-evident stance of protecting the Constitution and opposing the Hinomaru flag (only legalized as the national flag in 1999) that was utilized in the war of aggression.

Although sometimes misunderstood from their passionate chants and the like, the calls made by Hangenren, which aims purely at denuclearization, and by SEALDs, which seeks to preserve the freedom and democracy sustained since the post-war era, are both extremely moderate. While the style adopted by post-3.11 movements seems solely to have attracted interest, the moderate – one might even say conservative – nature of their assertions has also played a part in attracting participants. As Uchida Tatsuru (b. 1950) points out: 'The student movement of the past generally argued for "change!". They had to change the system. [...] This was common sense to those in the student movement. But rather than saying, "[We demand] change!", SEALDs says: "Don't change!"' (SEALDs 2016: 158). A frequently used SEALDs chant was 'Protect Japan from Abe Shinzō!'. Here, rather than the formula of social movements = anti-system, they claim it was Abe Shinzō himself who was demolishing the order of things.

Considering this from a different perspective, while on the one hand it is easy to initiate a movement as a *reactive* response to an offensive mounted by an administration (such as opposition to reactor restarts, opposition to the Special Secrecy Law or opposition to the National Security Legislation as a means of protecting constitutionalism), *proactive* campaigns – such as those calling for the expansion of renewable energy or for Japan to become a signatory to the Treaty on the Prohibition of Nuclear Weapons – have more difficulty attracting large numbers of participants.

Henmi Yō (b. 1944), who experienced the 1960s student movement, notes that, in contrast to the fact that Western demonstrations against G8 or G20 summits were 'opposed to the very operation of capitalism', resistance by SEALDs was 'probably aimed at preventing the Abe administration from making the current situation even worse', and states, 'But I feel that they are in some aspects typically Japanese, and are hoping, rather, for maintenance of the status quo' (Henmi 2016). Henmi's observation is correct. Many of the young people who participated in movements such as SEALDs that were opposed to the Abe administration were in fact demanding that things would not become any worse than they already were. There is no doubt that, compared to the revival of a capitalist critique among Western social movements (Della Porta 2015), support for such a view is weak in Japanese social movements.

Yet, rather than being beholden at all to 'vested interests', this sort of conservatism takes an opposite approach. Okuda explains as follows:

> I think the idea that this society has come to an end is one shared by all. [For] those of us who were born after the collapse of the bubble economy, it is like, "When was Japan ever in a good situation? [we have never experienced it]". It is for that very reason that [we] are conservative, as well; and we want [the government] to preserve the current situation, anyhow, and not to make things any worse than they are now. We have no thought of making a revolution to overthrow society (laughter). (Okuda, Oguma and Redwolf 2016: 40)

This sort of perception is widely shared. Motoyama, for example, has said, 'The bubble economy had long ago collapsed by the time we were born […] and it is those now in their teens and twenties that grew up in the midst of a derelict society where the economy, too, was getting steadily worse' (Komori et al. 2016: 97). Ushida Yoshimasa, in turn, commented that 'There was a sort of atmosphere that this society had come to an end', and 'there was a sense that Japanese society itself was finished from the start, or that everything came to a complete end with 3.11, and so we kind of had no alternative but to take action' (SEALDs 2015: 103). Ōno Itaru notes, 'It's not that we have something like a [vision of] a shared utopia. There isn't a way that we aspire to be. It's just that we have a kind of shared desire for a society in which at least this much is preserved, and it feels as if we have gathered in support of that shared view' (SEALDs 2016: 148). As Ōsawa Mami explained,

> I feel that the young people who take part in the movement now have shared internal urges: a change in values due the accident at the nuclear power plant (loss of faith in existing authority, and rediscovery of the necessity – the imperative, even – of social movements) and a survivalist attitude to human life for living through a stagnant age in which tomorrow will not be any better than today. (Ōsawa 2015: 53)

In other words, rather than making a revolution for a better society, the common denominator here is a desire to preserve the status quo in order to somehow endure in a 'finished' society. The kind of conservatism which seeks to prevent things from becoming worse than the current situation is also something that has generated high levels of support for the Abe administration among the younger generation. Put another way, the movement by young people opposing the Abe regime has sprung from the same breeding ground as that of the young people from the majority who more or less support Abe's government.

The themes of movements and recipients of the messages

What were these young people demanding, in order to prevent things from becoming worse than they already were?

SEALDs member Honma Nobukazu explains,

> Ever since the time that the Special Secrecy Law became an issue, we have been discussing freedom and democracy, and all along in our speeches we have been talking about things like our own sense of insecurity and dissatisfaction in our everyday lives, the struggle to live and our feeling of being suffocated. I don't think we could limit what we want to say to one issue or anything. (SEALDS 2016: 34)

Since the 2000s, the expression 'the struggle to live' (*ikizurasa*) has been one of the keywords when discussing the young in Japan, but it can encompass a variety of elements. If it is a question that can be rephrased in such terms as 'employment insecurity', 'poverty' and 'social stratification', then it can become the driver for the movement. According to Okuda, around half of all SEALDs members had a student loan debt of as much as several million yen, with some not even able to take part as much as they wished in the group's activities because they could not afford the several hundred yen for transport (Okuda and Inose 2015: 50; Furuya and Okuda 2015: 132). This could constitute a point of contact with the anti-poverty movement. Some SEALDs members later became active in AEQUITAS, an organization demanding a 1,500-yen minimum hourly wage. On the other hand, though, if the nature of the community of young people today – where they are expected by their peers to read each other's mood and behave 'to avoid sticking out' – were rooted in that 'struggle to live', then this probably would instead be an impediment to the success of future activist movements.

In fact, what prompted large numbers of people to participate were themes that could even seem old-fashioned by comparison, with 'opposition to war' and 'protecting the Constitution' appealing to more than one specific age-group. The likely reasons behind the movement's ability to draw large numbers of people in their sixties and seventies (see Introduction) are both that they have free time and experience in the previous student movement, and also that a message that resonated with this age group could be emitted as a result of the focus being limited to the National Security Legislation.

In reality, questions of the Constitution and peace *are* connected to the problems encountered by the young in their daily lives, and this is well reflected in SEALDs members' frequent references to 'economic conscription' (*keizai chōheisei*). Mentioning a friend who, driven by student debt repayments, had an abortion, and the problem of poverty among the young, Osawa also deftly connects this to the broader picture, saying:

> How could she have been responsible for a social structure that created such a daily struggle (*ikizurasa*) for single mothers, or for having grown up in a poverty-stricken household that had no option but to depend on a student loan? ... The kind of politics that did not permit her to give birth to and raise even one child is now attempting to establish a security-related bill. The world that surrounds us is no longer safe, thus we cannot ingenuously approve a bill that a regime which has already left countless lives for dead extolls as the "guaranteeing" of "security". (2015: 52–53)

However, while SEALDs gave the impression of being an activist group that specialized in the National Security Legislation, it was not necessarily successful in presenting this in relation to problems of daily life and the economy. What had pervasive ability in SEALDs' message were things linked to peace and the Constitution, but while these got through to members' grandparents' generation (Kobayashi 2016), they could not arguably have been accepted by a majority of the members' generation. Of course, this was not only SEALDs' problem. For the very reason that these are not the kinds of difficulties that can simply be verbalized to the extent that they can connect to the circuit that constitutes a social movement, they are likely to be perceived as 'hard to survive' (*ikizurai*).

Achievements of the movements

In this section, I will consider the political influence of post-3.11 social movements that feature the particular elements outlined above. I will firstly explain how an amorphous movement was able to act as mediator both between political parties and between factions, some of which were not connected to political parties. Secondly, I will elaborate how it lowered the threshold for movement participation; and thirdly, how, as a consequence, it became easier for protest action to be mounted on topics other than nuclear power generation, the Constitution and peace.

Approaches to political parties and interfactional mediation

An unexpected development in the state of affairs emerged from around the time of the enactment of the National Security Legislation, namely, approaches to political parties by contemporary movements which had never been incorporated into any political alliance nor had backing from any existing political groups. In this, however, we can see evidence of the strength of the amorphous nature of today's social movements – especially in their political dealignment.

In the post-3.11 environment, Diet members from the various opposition parties had often made speeches at demonstrations and rallies opposing nuclear power, but it was through the anti-National Security Legislation movement that the relationship deepened markedly between social movements and political parties. During Diet debates, members of opposition parties would make reference to the protest movement outside the Diet, and it also became commonplace to see representatives from opposition parties making speeches at protest rallies, while rally participants watched Diet proceedings on YouTube during protests.

Democratic Party of Japan House of Councillors member Fukuyama Tetsurō offers the following explanation of the motivations of the opposition parties: 'It made us quite tense to know that there were people gathered outside the Diet building and who were watching us on social media'. He went on to say, 'Eyes outside the Diet were watching us, and so there was no point in being politicians if we disgraced ourselves during question time or by our general behavior' (Okuda, Kuramochi and Fukuyama 2015: 107). As Fukuyama declared to the House of Councillors full sitting, 'I have never experienced a time when the people of the nation and politics have been as connected inside and outside the Diet as this' (House of Councillors, Plenary Session 2015, 19 September). Moreover, Motoyama, who was one of the SEALDs members chanting outside the Diet building, recounts, 'Looking at the live television broadcast, I really thought it was a moment when inside and outside the Diet were connected' (Komori et al. 2016: 37).

In the final stages of Diet deliberations over the bill, in addition to chants of 'Opposition parties unite to fight' (*Yatō wa kyōtō*), there were also chants of 'Opposition parties, do your best!' (*Yatō wa gambare*) and 'Let's go to the polls' (*Senkyō e ikō yo*). While these were certainly unusual demonstration chants, the appeal to the opposition parties to fight together with the protest movement continued even after the bill was enacted.

Political participation in Japan is overwhelmingly biased towards elections, but while enthusiasm for involvement in activities that require a strong commitment has been at a low ebb (Dalton 2014; Yamada 2016), it cannot be argued that there is much interest in electoral participation. Many even decline to cast a vote: even in national elections, the rate of voter turn-out hovers at around 50%.

In spite of the size of the crowds amassed outside the Diet and both the streaming of these scenes on the internet and their reporting in traditional media such as newspapers or television, it was hard for the strength of a social movement alone to stop a ruling party that held such a massive majority in the Diet. There was an understanding that 'politics will not change due to demonstrations alone' (Okuda, quoted in SEALDs 2016: 184). While the purpose of SEALDs' most famous call and response, 'Tell me what democracy looks like?'/'This is what democracy looks like!', was to demonstrate that democracy was not only about elections (spoken by Okuda, cited in Okuda, Oguma and Redwolf 2016: 45), protestors were nonetheless aware that participation in elections was also a crucial aspect of democracy.

Given this chain of events, the passing of the National Security Legislation led to the formation of an alliance between the Association of Scholars Opposed to the National Security Legislation (Anzen hoshō kanren-hō ni hantai suru gakusha no kai), SEALDs, the Anti-National Security Legislation Mothers Against War (Anpo kanren-hō ni hantai suru mama no kai) and interested persons from other groups that had opposed the legislation. Known as the Civil Alliance for Peace and Constitutionalism (Anpo hōsei no haishi to rikkenshugi no kaifuku o motomeru shimin rengō), or Civil Alliance (Shimin rengō) for short, this group worked upon opposition parties to make them cooperate against the ruling LDP.

Following the lower house election of 2012 that saw the Liberal Democratic Party and the New Clean Government Party (Kōmeitō) return to power, both parties remained victorious through the 2013 upper house and the 2014 lower house elections. Often referred to as 'Abe's power surge' (*Abe ikkyō*), these elections saw no gains in support for the opposition parties, but in spite of the fact that the lower house electoral system focuses on single-member constituencies while the key to success in the upper house is the one-person district, the government benefited from several opposition parties splitting the overall opposition vote by nominating candidates against each other in various electorates. Had the opposition parties collectively nominated only one candidate per electorate, such a disparity in the number of seats probably would not have arisen, but the majority opposition party, the Democratic Party of Japan, was cautious about aligning with the Communist Party, fearing a backlash from conservative voters. At a rally held in May 2015, attention was drawn to the fact that Nagatsuma Akira, the acting leader of the Democratic Party of Japan, refused to join hands on the podium with Communist Party Committee Chair Shi'i Kazuo. This led to a deliberate SEALDs campaign to force Diet representatives from the various opposition parties to physically join hands (Komori et al. 2016: 31, 126). That campaign was the genesis of the chant calling for the opposition parties to unite and fight.

After lengthy consultation, the opposition parties accepted a proposal from the Civil Alliance regarding single opposition candidates, and they were successful in eleven of the thirty-two one-person districts in which this streamlining strategy was deployed in the 2016 upper house elections. This contrasted with the previous upper house elections in 2013, when the various opposition parties had run their own candidates in thirty-one seats but won only two seats. As this unified approach continued, there were also growing instances of the head of the Communist Party grasping the hands of the leaders of other opposition parties.

While these outcomes were not solely due to the efforts of the Civil Alliance, they would not have been possible without the collaborative approach between the protest movement and the opposition during the anti-National Security Legislation campaign. Concerning the Communist Party's change of policy direction in terms of working in tandem with other opposition parties, Deputy Committee Chair Koike Akira commented as follows:

> Why could the Communist Party shift its position? All those members of SEALDs and their supporters surrounded the Diet building and tens of thousands of people raised their voices. […] A political party that did not respond to these voices would be meaningless, wouldn't it? The Communist Party has shed its skin, too. We were forced to shed our skins! (Yokota 2016: 123)

In this case, a de-affiliated social movement had fulfilled the role of mediator between political parties. Furthermore, as they lacked firsthand knowledge of the historical circumstances of the hostility and antagonism between the various opposition parties, SEALDs members were able to urge opposition members of the house to 'join hands' (Komori et al. 2016: 132).

The event called 'NO NUKES DAY', which began in 2013, brought about a triadic symbiosis in which the anti-nuclear Hangenren movement was flanked by two organizations – the Goodbye Nuclear Power Ten Million People's Action (Sayōnara genpatsu 1000 man-nin akushon), which was associated with the Japan Congress Against Atomic and Hydrogen Bombs (Gensuikin), and the National Liaison Council for the Elimination of Nuclear Power (Genpatsu o nakusu zenkoku renraku-kai) associated with the Japan Council Against Atomic and Hydrogen Bombs (Gensuikyō) (Hattori 2016: 60) – and the three groups began to hold regular meetings. As mentioned in the Introduction of this book, the Japanese anti-nuclear weapons movements have worked separately since 1965 when Gensuikin (closely related to the Socialist Party) split from Gensuikyō (closely related to the Communist Party). Moreover, the achievement of co-organization on constitutional issues by the three groups – the Socialist Party, Communist Party and the independent citizen's movements – is attributed to the existence of NO NUKES DAY, and that action further evolved into the All-Out Action Implementation Committee (Sensō sasenai: kyūjō kowasu na! Sōgakari kōdō jikkō iinkai; known as 'Sōgakari kōdō') which opposed the National Security Legislation (Redwolf 2015: 65). Amorphous movements without overt political affiliation, therefore, can play the role of go-between among hardcore organizations such as political parties.

Although SEALDs claims not to support a particular political party, it nevertheless deems that it is necessary to marshal the power of those opposition parties founded on liberal values in order to counter the politics of the current administration. It points out that although at the time of the 2014 lower house election the LDP captured only 20% of votes from the total electorate, it won 80% of seats. Noting, moreover, that the sum total of votes cast for the opposition parties was greater than the number of votes received by the LDP, SEALDs expressed a 'strong hope' for the 'emergence of an inclusive platform for the different types of liberals' (SEALDs English website: http://sealdseng.mystrikingly.com/#statement).

Hangenren also talks about new initiatives, saying, 'We thought that if we did not topple the Abe administration, nuclear power generation would not cease. No matter the issue, the main culprit has been the Abe administration'. Accordingly, in 2014, Hangenren says it called upon groups that were engaged in a range of issues and launched the 'Executive Committee for NO to the Abe Administration' (*Abe seiken NO: jikkō Iinkai*) (Hattori 2016: 65).

The advance of the joint struggle, which overlooked small differences between groups, was due to their pulling-back of the battlefront, as it were, in their opposition to the reactionary Abe administration. As SEALDs member Honma observed, 'With the critical situation created by the dangerous policies of the current administration, moves by the opposition parties in their joint struggle have progressed' (SEALDs 2016: 60). Although Oguma has pointed out that 'we little imagined that even in 2015 we would gather supporters with a chant urging them to "Protect the Constitution!"' (Okuda, Oguma, Redwolf 2016: 34), the entity to be defended under the Abe regime was scaled back from the existing Constitution to the more general notion of constitutionalism. Although the word 'constitutionalism' (*rikkenshugi*) had hitherto been relatively unknown to a majority of people, it can be seen from the following table that its use rapidly became widespread following the Abe administration's ascension to power in December 2012.

In contrast to how attention was drawn to novelty in such aspects as music, fashion or the use of social media, campaigns nowadays have been waged on old-fashioned points of concern, and there has also been a reconsideration of the value of elections and political parties. Moreover, due to the redrawing of battle lines, joint struggle on positions which was difficult in the past has progressed, and an amorphous movement new to the scene has played a mediating role among the various stakeholders.

The visibility of demonstrations and their significance

Next, I will consider the effect of the visibility of demonstrations. The activism of social movements is by no means confined to

Table 3.1: The number of articles in the Asahi Shimbun featuring the term 'constitutionalism'

1990–1999	2000–2009	2010	2011	2012	2013	2014	2015	2016	2017	2018	2019
31	93	3	4	3	139	367	522	636	367	91	102

demonstrations. The anti-nuclear power movement, for example, undertakes various activities that include providing support to disaster-affected areas and evacuees, measuring radiation levels and collecting petition signatures for municipal plebiscites (Kinoshita 2013a: 49; Satō et al. 2018: 40). In addition to their Friday evening protests, Hangenren conducts what are known as 'quiet demonstrations' (*shizuka na demo*), by issuing leaflets in batches of several hundred thousand that argue, for example, the dangers of nuclear power generation (Redwolf 2013; Hattori 2016: 62). There is an even more comprehensive diffusion of information through the internet. As such, counting the numbers of participants in street-based protest demonstrations is merely one measure of a movement's momentum.

Nevertheless, considering the situation in the past, crowds exceeding 100,000 people gathered in the vicinity of the Diet building is in itself a phenomenon that demands our attention. Compared with other movement activities, demonstrations readily become visible even to non-participants and, in effect, convey the message of a movement's existence.

After the 1960 Anpo struggle, when 330,000 people gathered around the Diet Building, hardly any rally or demonstration had attracted more than 10,000 participants (Hasegawa 2018: 123). According to Oguma, protest movements in the latter half of the 1960s in which young people were the standard-bearers had fewer participants than in 2012, and the largest student movement gathering at the time – the occupation of the University of Tokyo's Yasuda Hall in November 1968 – attracted 20,000 participants, while rallies organized by the anti-Vietnam War collective, Beiheiren, peaked at 70,000 in June 1969 (Oguma 2016: 217). At the height of the 'New Wave' anti-nuclear power movement that followed the Chernobyl disaster, 20,000 people came together in 1988 (Suga 2012: 276). On the other hand, campaigns involving organized mobilization, such as those spearheaded by labor unions, have brought together considerably larger numbers of participants, while anti-war and peace movement events based in the labor movement – such as the 'one-day joint struggles' (*ichinichi kyōtō*) organized by the Socialist Party and the General Council of Trade Unions of Japan in concert with the Communist Party – held rallies in Tokyo alone that drew between one or two hundred thousand to several hundreds of thousands. Across the whole country, there were even instances of up to several million people taking part (Yui 2019).

Now, when these sorts of 'mobilized protests' are no longer occuring, Hangenren marshalled 200,000 people to gather in the environs of the Diet building, while 120,000 people attended an anti-National Security Legislation protest. Protest action, of course, was not confined to Tokyo: a survey conducted by SEALDs through the internet, newspapers and so on indicated that a cumulative total of 1.3 million people had participated in anti-National Security Legislation protests held more than several thousand times in over 2,000 different locations across Japan (statement by Okuda Aki, House of Councillors Special Committee Public Hearing, 15 September 2015).

Hangenren reports it was particularly focused on recording participant numbers as a means of putting pressure on the government (Redwolf 2013: 17), and circumstantial evidence suggests that some pressure was in fact exerted. Ishiba Shigeru, the then general secretary of the LDP, wrote in a blog that 'there is not much difference in essence [between the 2013 demonstrations opposing the Special Secrecy Law] and terrorist action', while in 2014, the LDP considered how to regulate hate speech and tried to regulate propaganda activities on the streets in the vicinity of the Diet building altogether. In 2015, the former governor of Tokyo, Ishihara Shintarō, criticized demonstrations as 'seeming to have absolutely no meaning whatsoever. Demonstrations themselves are just hot air' (*kūki no kesshō*: 'crystals of air') (http://www.sankei.com/politics/news/150910/plt1509100037-n1.html). Osaka City Mayor Hashimoto Tōru urged, 'You people who spend your time protesting – put your efforts into elections! Should circumstances permit, form a political party yourselves' (Hashimoto 2015). This kind of hostility shown by the ruling party and influential conservative politicians towards demonstrations and their claims of their ineffectualness could, on the contrary, be interpreted as demonstrating their impact.

In addition to how the demonstrations attracted large numbers of participants and achieved visibility, it is also important to note that as a result, demonstrations stopped being something special, and the bar for participation was lowered.

Before 3.11, in Japan, demonstrations were the exclusive province of particular groups, but a survey in 2013 of environmental and energy protest organizations indicated that 23.1% of respondent groups held demonstrations or street propaganda events, while participation in such events climbed to 47.4% of groups. Although it is difficult to make a simple comparison, a 2006 'Survey of citizen activist groups in the Tokyo area' (*Shutoken no shimin katsudō dantai ni kansuru chōsa*) indicated that 'participation in and implementation of street action (such as demonstrations)' was 11.9% (Machimura and Satō 2016: 27).

SEALDs member Ushida notes as follows:

> I think it is a really big deal for Japanese society that demonstrations have become comparatively normalized, or for them to have become a regular thing almost to the point that it seems uncool to say that "Demonstrations have no power to influence people" or to question whether they have any meaning. So, I really feel that the discourse related to demonstrations has changed. It has become a normal thing for people to say, "Let's demonstrate". (BLOGOS Henshūbu 2015)

Okuda and Katō Yūji, also, showed an awareness that the bar for demonstration attendance had lowered (Furuya and Okuda 2015: 235; SEALDs 2015: 63). Nevertheless, as stated above, demonstration participants had begun to realize that it was also necessary to win elections.

The police, too, began to implement a 'soft security approach' that involved designating a protest area along the pavement, then steering foot traffic through it rather than unnecessarily ejecting demonstrators. The head of the Tokyo Metropolitan Police Department is on record as saying, 'We aim to not create a pattern of conflict of "police versus citizens", in order to avoid injuries arising from unforeseen incidents' (*Asahi Shimbun* 2013). Hangenren commended this move, with Misao Redwolf saying, 'one of our successes was bringing about a change in police attitudes towards the movement' (cited in Okuda, Oguma and Redwolf 2016: 44). The results of one large-scale survey indicated that a total of 62% of respondents either 'agreed' or were 'likely to agree' that through having taken part in demonstrations, they 'valued demonstrations and rallies more than in the past' (Satō et al. 2018). These figures also have significant implications for subsequent movements.

One commentator, who thinks that the violent image of the previous student movement resulted in something akin to trauma in Japanese society, points out that this negative image was successfully dispelled by movement activity between the 1990s and 2000s (Cassegård 2013). Even among Hangenren and SEALDs members, many attest that they had previously thought of demonstrations as dangerous activities in which certain radical elements took part (see, for example, Oguma and Kinoshita (eds.) 2013; Tamura and Tamura 2016; Tominaga 2017). Police countermeasures against the 'radical factions' from the 1970s onwards had successfully marginalized movements (Andō 2013). Nevertheless, as a result of movements during the 2010s, it became increasingly difficult to regard demonstration participants as members of radical factions. The fact that there was a decline in the numbers of people who regard demonstrations as something to be feared is of great significance.

Breadth that transcends a single issue

Today, as a result of the lowering of the bar for demonstration participation, demonstrations and protests are held on a range of topics apart from the traditional Constitution or peace, or nuclear power generation, which attracted interest post-3.11. After demonstrations calling for a phasing-out of nuclear power, it became normal to regard the public space outside the prime minister's official residence (*shushō kantei*; hereafter, the PM's residence) and the Diet building as sites of protest. For that reason, both those protesting new issues and the media covering these events headed for the Diet building.

In 2016 Diet proceedings, for example, an opposition member took up the case of an anonymous blogger, a mother whose child's application for nursery school entrance had been unsuccessful. The blogger had written, 'We flunked the nursery school entrance exam. I hope you die, Japan!!!' (*Hoikuen ochita. Nihon shine!!!*). In response, the prime minister remarked, 'Given that it is anonymous, there is no way to know if it actually happened', and ruling-party members' heckled, such as, 'Who wrote that stuff?'. People angry at their responses used social media to call for support for a gathering to be held outside the Diet where people held placards that read, 'I am the one whose child failed nursery school entry'. When in 2017 the Abe administration brought the draft Anti-Conspiracy Law before the house, protests were held outside the Diet building at the same time as deliberations concerning the bill were taking place inside. Many other demonstrations addressing a range of topics and themes continue to be held in that location. The point has been made that it is a 'huge outcome' for Japanese society that there is now a shared consciousness of the fact that, 'if something is not right in society, then let's go to the Diet building!' (Yoshida 2016: 103). Yet, as SEALDs member Okuda observes, 'the very idea of firstly going to see a demonstration outside the Diet building if you are interested in [a social issue] was unimaginable before the earthquake and tsunami disaster' (SEALDs 2015: 111).

The Facebook page belonging to the 'We flunked nursery school' blog registered 47,000 'likes' in a little over a month, even though, according to a newspaper report, only thirty people gathered to protest outside the Diet (*Asahi Shimbun* 2016). Still, the fact that reporters attended to cover this event further demonstrates that there was now an awareness of 'outside the Diet building' as a place of protest.

According to a search of newspaper articles (see Table 2.2), in 2012 there was a huge rise in references to 'outside the PM's residence'. The fact that there had been no change in the frequency of the use of this term in 2011, the year of the nuclear accident, confirms that this style of activism had not been established up to that point. While references to 'outside the PM's official residence' diminished after 2012, in 2015 the term 'outside the Diet building' became a feature of many articles. While references to both have settled down now, there

Table 3.2: The numbers of articles in the Asahi Shimbun that contain the term 'outside the PM's official residence' (kantei mae) or 'outside the Diet building' (kokkai mae)

	2005	2006	2007	2008	2009	2010	2011	2012	2013	2014	2015	2016	2017	2018	2019
Outside the PM's residence	8	3	9	8	5	20	5	244	91	101	57	20	19	28	26
Outside the Diet building	24	20	21	38	38	24	36	41	66	53	399	199	91	65	38

still remains an awareness of 'outside the Diet building' as a site of protest. It is envisioned that in the future, too, those who protest on various topics and the media covering these events will both continue to gather in that location.

On that point, it is of huge significance that Hangenren has continued its activities and preserved its protest sites. In one way, as conducting protest action outside the PM's residence and the Diet building was something that was started and developed over time into a fait accompli, if Hangenren were to discontinue the weekly protests, then permission for use of the sites could be withdrawn. As Misao Redwolf explains, 'We of course continue the protests with the aim of bringing nuclear power generation to an end. But Hangenren members were unanimously of the view also that the sites would not be made off-limits as long as we continued [to demonstrate there]' (Okuda, Oguma and Redwolf 2016: 45–48).[3]

Naturally, it is true that not all movements aspire to assemble outside the Diet building. In 2019, newly-emerging movements including the 'flower demonstrations' against sexual violence and the movement protesting changes to the university entrance examination system drew attention, the former expanding to more than thirty sites across the entire country (and overseas), with gatherings held outside Tokyo Station in Tokyo. The latter group protested outside the offices of the Monbukagakushō (MEXT: Ministry of Education, Sports, Science, Culture and Technology) in Central Tokyo.

Generally speaking, in a society in which social movements are ubiquitous, various factors lower the cost of initiating a movement around a new issue (Meyer and Tarrow 1998). The existence of a role-model type of precursor movement is not insignificant. SEALDs members, for example, looked to the activities of Hangenren for inspiration and became, in turn, a reference point for many later movements. As long as media coverage of protest activities continues, even without demonstrations involving several tens of thousands or several hundreds of thousands of demonstrators at a time, this chain is likely to continue.

The uncertain permanence of an unstructured movement

Finally, I will consider whether it is possible to predict what the future holds for the sort of amorphous movement under discussion here. In the previous section, I examined what influence demonstrations might reasonably be expected to bring to bear on politics from this point forward, but in spite of a lowering of the threshold for participation, and in spite of the fact that demonstrations on various themes continue to occur, there have not been any large-scale gatherings to match the 2012 anti-nuclear power generation or the 2015 National Security Legislation events since then. I will now examine the significance of this from the perspective of the amorphous nature of movements.

In addition to the threshold for participation in demonstrations having fallen, today there is a way to lower the bar even further, in that people can view and comment upon an internet stream of an event, 'participating' in a virtual manner from a distance, so to speak, even without actually having to make their way physically to the demonstration site. We might include here the actual circulation of event information through social media. One demonstration participant argues that 'surely people watching on Ustream are also "participants"' (Hirabayashi 2013). This sort of external extension alone ensures that a movement will become more amorphous.

Among today's examples of protest action, there are some in which footage is uploaded onto YouTube and viewed by large numbers of people. For instance, while there were 12,000 participants in a 15 June 2012 demonstration, YouTube footage showing scenes from that day was replayed 100,000 times (Noma 2012: 104). There was also one demonstration with a mere twenty-six participants that in fact had 25,000 internet views (Kinoshita 2013c: 2). Although not a demonstration *per se*, an event entitled the 'World Conference for Abolishing Nuclear Power 2012 YOKOHAMA' (*Datsu genpatsu sekai kaigi 2012 YOKOHAMA*) had 11,500 attendees but was also watched live on the internet by approximately 100,000 people (Machimura and Satō 2016: 24). In addition to being viewed by 150,000 people on YouTube, the 'Prime Ministerial and Expert Advisor Open Colloquium'

(*Sōri yūshikisha ōpun kondankai*) event attracted 15,000 comments (Kan and Oguma 2013: 177–178).

Even in an amorphous society where existing networks are in decline, collective activities by people who have never met sometimes come about. The anonymous writer of the 'We flunked nursery school' blog, the people who made the placards and those who called for participation in holding placards were all different people, none of whom knew each other (Kasai and Noma 2016: 176). While it has become difficult to collect large numbers of petition signatures in workplaces or local areas, there are now sites such as Change.org where anyone can initiate signature collection through the internet. This, too, is a form of amorphous activity in which people who have never met initiate campaigns and collect signatures for their individual causes, one that operates without systematic organization or leadership and without any traditional chain of command, even though there might be one specific individual who creates the platform for the collection of signatures.

Certainly, these sorts of connections have limits in the sense that they were never more than weak links from the start. Participation via the internet is characterized by an absence of tight organization or the force of compulsion, much less a daily allowance in recompense for mobilization (trade unions sometimes mobilized members to attend demonstrations and rallies by paying an allowance to union members). The only thing that encourages people to participate is their own determination, but as that mechanism is particularly volatile, demonstration organizers have no means of predicting attendance numbers (Ide et al. 2013: 16).

Even assuming that there has been progress in the joint struggle by opposition parties, it is evident from the fall in party membership numbers that political parties organized on traditional hardcore lines have not been revitalized. The partnership established through the mediation of an amorphous social movement that transcends party factions has a strong character of having scraped together existing withering elements, and does not indicate that the brakes have been applied to the decline of tight organizations.

However, such a development is surely to be expected, given the liquefaction of contemporary society and the difficulty of the viability of a 'social language'. When participant numbers in denuclearization demonstrations, which peaked at 200,000, reduced in scale in 2013 to only several thousands, even newspapers sympathetic to the demonstrations reportedly began to only publish articles to the effect that attendee numbers had dropped (Redwolf 2013: 53–54). However, rather than several hundred thousand people gathering to protest in the Diet building environs, would not the sporadic occurrence of small-scale demonstrations and rallies on disconnected issues be a more appropriate format for movements in an amorphous society?

It might be argued that the seeds for this were sown by the fact that in 2012 and 2015, many people experienced demonstrations, and even more became aware of demonstrations' existence. Moreover, the weak connections arising from certain movements have the capacity to form the basis for activism relating to other issues.

The movement known as 'Datsu-genpatsu Suginami' (Denuclearization Suginami), which later participated in Hangenren, for example, began from the following call on Twitter and other media: 'People from Suginami Ward who want to take action in order to halt nuclear power, let's get together!'. However, one core member remarks, 'We don't regard [Datsu-genpatsu Suginami] as an "organization" that should continue doing activities', and:

> It is like a big receptacle that came into being in the locality, one where people could meet lots of others they could call upon to do something together when they wanted to hold any kind of event. Rather than being an organization that would last forever, it is an assembly of people who have become loosely associated locally; and we think that when everyone's desire to speak out in the local area arises again, that would be the time to act. (Nakamura 2013: 78–79)

The Osaka mother's group, Mama no Kai, was initiated to oppose the National Security Legislation, but when the women in this group gathered together, they realized that 'in spite of the fact that although the mothers were thinking about a huge number of things', including caring for children, superannuation, education, nuclear energy and food, 'there was no space where they could discuss them solidly. [We] think everything is a political issue. Society won't change, either, unless [we] make politics shift'. They began to think, 'We want to advocate for various matters more widely. I wonder if we could expand the target of our activities so that, as Mama no Kai, we would be able to hold study meetings on a broader scale, too' (Anpo kanren-hō ni hantai suru mama no kai @ Ōsaka 2016: 3).

Among other Mama no Kai assemblies in various areas, there were also some that started to hold study meetings on different topics with invited expert speakers. There were also some associations of university scholars established to oppose the National Security Legislation that continue to hold a range of classes and symposiums that involve regional communities.

Not only the kind of connections where members can see each other's faces – ones that have come into being through opposition to nuclear power generation and the National Security Legislation – but also those mediated by social media, might arise in the future, as Saigō Minako, the founder of Mama no Kai, points out. After Saigō launched her group on Facebook, she received approximately 20,000 messages in a little more than a month. Upon reading them, Saigō said, 'Looking at these, I think that even though I do not have a direct individual connection with each of these mothers, these women are all over the country and, if in the future it again comes time for constitutional reform, they will again put up their hands as if to say, of course, let's work together once more' (Saigō 2018: 16).

SEALDs members recount that the kind of thing they wanted to do was to 'become a vessel', to 'create a space for expressing [our] will' (SEALDs 2016: 54), while Hangenren protected their spaces in a physical sense, namely, outside the Diet building and outside the PM's residence. There is no doubt that the enduring impact left by this kind of idea to transcend a specific issue has given rise to the chain of movements such as those discussed above. The terms 'spaces' and 'vessels' signify the maintaining of loose links even when a movement appears not to be active on a particular issue. Such connections are likely to have arisen from amongst even the small-scale movements addressing new issues that appear one after another. This means, does it not, that even in times when huge demonstrations are not occurring, movements have continued to endure in amorphous form.

4 Amateur Revolt: The Amorphous Social Movement Resisting the System

TANAKA Hikaru

Introduction

This chapter case-studies the street activist and lifestyle group, Amateur Revolt (Shirōto no ran),[1] with a view to investigating factors contributing to the new ties that since 2011 have brought participants together in activist groups such as the anti-nuclear power movement (see the Introduction and Chapter Two by Kinoshita). While 'Amateur Revolt' is the name of a collective of businesses such as recycling shops that have operated since 2005 in the Kōenji district of Tokyo's Suginami Ward, the term is used here to refer to the name of the network and movement that formed around the individuals connected with those stores. Although focused on the stores and individual store-holders, the movement expanded as a loose and non-hierarchical collective. The aim of key movement members was the creation of a community lifestyle based on the ideal of the 'here and now' that resisted conventional organizational norms and that avoided reliance on existing ideologies or activist movements. Key members also shared antagonism towards existing political, economic and social systems. Accordingly, the shops and similar businesses operated by Amateur Revolt functioned as spaces that facilitated the creation of alternate value systems and mindsets that rejected the controlling norms and values of Japanese society and that enabled group members to initiate intermittent events such as street demonstrations.

Amateur Revolt is not a social movement in the classic sense. It does, however, have features in common with European movements such as the squatter movement, sometimes known as the autonomous movement, which seeks to occupy empty houses (Obinger 2015: 65).

The squatter movement, too, when analyzed merely in terms of its advocacy for the right to residence through illegal occupation, might be rejected as a movement and instead viewed as a group seeking social reform. If, however, we focus on the actual occupation of the buildings and the activities that occur within as core elements of that group, it becomes apparent that we are witnessing the emergence of a new type of social movement that functions as a 'submerged network' within the fabric of everyday life (Melucci 1989: 70; van der Steen, Katzeff and van Hoogenhuijze 2014). I argue that Amateur Revolt, too, displays the characteristics of this new kind of social movement.

From the time of its formation, Amateur Revolt drew interest both for the nature of its street demonstrations and the lifestyle promoted by its members. There was also considerable press coverage of Matsumoto Hajime as the group's central member. However, Amateur Revolt really came to the attention of the public from April 2011 following its involvement in the organization of large scale antinuclear demonstrations. Since its early years, the group has been a subject of interest for researchers and commentators both inside and outside Japan. Cassegård (2013: 104–113), for example, considers the group to be an example of the 'freeter activism' involving young people in irregular employment that emerged during the 1990s. Obinger (2015: 61–73, 130–134) views Amateur Revolt as a networkstyle movement in which the formation of a collective identity depended on a range of key elements, each arising from a small scale experiential base. She further notes many shared similarities with the squatter movement in Europe. Brown (2018: 78–95) makes the point that demonstrations and various similar activities were the result of shared values and ideals within the Amateur Revolt network.

Existing research, however, focuses on similarities in factors such as the experiences and values of Amateur Revolt members. Obinger's interviews with twenty-eight people associated with Amateur Revolt, for example, led to the following findings. Interviewees were largely born from the second half of the 1970s until the late 1980s to families with middle-class backgrounds. Most, excluding a small number of either full-time or self-employed workers, were in casual or irregular employment. Childhood, adolescence or young adulthood experience of the recession that followed the collapse of the bubble economy made the majority of people involved in the movement antagonistic towards their parents' ideal life-course of full-time employment with a single company until retirement. Instead, interviewees sought a lifestyle that rejected both economic prosperity and hyper-consumption (Obinger 2015: 61–62, 85–86). The value system advocated by the group is perhaps encapsulated in Matsumoto Hajime's declaration that all part-time and full-time workers are 'model slaves' (*yūshū na dorei*) (Matsumoto 2008a: 9).

Notwithstanding these similarities, there are also differences in both thinking and experience between members of the group, which is comprised of different types of individuals. While they participate as equals, they do so from widely divergent motivations. It is possibly this variety that gives the group the impetus to undergo continual renewal. Given this diversity, it is apparent that Amateur Revolt can be understood as an amorphous movement. The analysis below begins by highlighting the different backgrounds of the two central personalities involved in Amateur Revolt, Matsumoto Hajime and Yamashita Hikaru, while considering how the new kinds of street demonstrations and gatherings or assemblies promoted by this pair drew increasingly diverse groups of people to the movement. I then consider the factors that saw Amateur Revolt emerge as an amorphous movement in which individual participants with different backgrounds melded together. These factors include the bonds of a 'hidden network' of the everyday, the creation of a range of alternative spaces, the operation of the principle of 'autonomy' (*jichi*) in those spaces, the physical experience of being part of 'a gathering of people' (*atsumari*) and the desire to initiate demonstrations that were 'fun'. It will be argued that these factors worked to ensure that a diverse range of people with a broad range of motivations came into the group, through which they often acquired a new set of values.

The amorphous circumstances of constitutive members

Matsumoto Hajime: Making a different social movement

Having grown up in the downtown area (*shitamachi*) of eastern Tokyo, Matsumoto Hajime entered Hōsei University in 1994. Here, he saw how student opposition to campus redevelopment delayed the demolition of university buildings. Experiencing a major transformation of his personal values, he too joined that campaign (Matsumoto 2008b: 27–29). This was just at the time of the disintegration of student activism and Matsumoto regarded the existing movement as one in which students acted out of self-interest to impose their ideas on others (*BeFlat: 10 dai no jinken jōhō nettowāku* 2009).

Matsumoto had meanwhile joined a student club known as 'The Outdoor Sleeping Appreciation Society'. While sleeping out in the open in minus thirty-degree temperatures, he discovered that the average student enjoyed taking part in 'silly' or 'frivolous' (*kudaranai*) activities. As a result, in 1996 he formed the 'Society to Preserve the Run-down Feel of Hōsei University' (Hōsei no binbō-kusasa o mamoru kai) as a movement to advocate for 'a sense of the ridiculous' (*bakabakashii sensu*). This use of the term 'run-down feel' was, in fact, a means of expressing theoretical resistance to developments such as the commercialization of the university and the systematization of job-search processes for students, credentialism as a means to secure employment and the 'consumerist ethic' and 'desire for wealth accumulation' that operated well beyond the confines of the university's walls (Matsumoto 2008b: 30–39; Matsumoto and Futatsugi 2008: 30–32).

By 1995/1996, when Matsumoto began the society, the collapse of the bubble economy and stagflation of the entire Japanese economy had seen a steady rise in the rate of relative poverty from 12% in 1985 to 14.6% in 1997 (Kōseirōdōshō 2017). However, this was a time when the term 'poor' had a negative connotation that portrayed those in straitened circumstances as deserving contempt and when young people who chose a freeter lifestyle were made individually responsible for the poverty they experienced. In other words, it was a time when it was difficult to present poverty as a social problem. Nevertheless, Matsumoto successfully campaigned using this word in a way that made activists of his own generation admire his highly incisive sense of reality (Matsumoto 2008a: 162).

The aim of the Society to Preserve the Run-down Feel of Hōsei University was to defend traditions associated with autonomy. These included valorizing 'the university as community', reclaiming 'society' within the university, creating a 'place' and having students make decisions about their own institutions (Matsumoto 2008b: 46–47; Matsumoto and Futatsugi 2008: 52–53). Becoming aware of plans to demolish old university structures on campus to make way for highrise buildings, the group set out to disrupt construction by setting up large footpath signs (*tatekan*) that read 'Hōsei University is run-down!' (*Hōsei Daigaku wa binbō-kusai daigaku da!*) and distributing flyers declaring, 'We don't need no luxury buildings!' (*kanemochi biru iranē*) (Matsumoto 2008a: 95; Matsumoto 2008b: 38–39).

In 1997, in response to planned price rises of university refectory food, Matsumoto again mobilized students, this time to attend a protest meeting after which those gathered stormed the refectory (Matsumoto 2008b: 39–43). When the event resulted in a rise in the society's membership numbers, Matsumoto organized a 'curry struggle' (*karē tōsō*) where members sold curry for 100 yen which they had made in front of the refectory (Matsumoto 2008b: 44), a '*kotatsu* struggle' (*kotatsu tōsō*) where members served dinner on *kotatsu* (small tables with heaters beneath the surface) that were placed around campus and a 'hot-pot struggle' (*nabe tōsō*) where low dining tables were set up and members served hot-pot food (Matsumoto 2008b: 47). As a result, he clashed violently with university authorities and was eventually suspended (Matsumoto 2008b: 50). While all this was happening, Matsumoto and his colleagues were also publishing 'News for the Poor' (*Binbōnin Shimbun*) with print runs of 2,000, a sizeable student readership (Matsumoto 2008b: 52–53). After graduating in 2001, Matsumoto left the Student Clubs and Activities Building (Gakusei Kaikan), in which he had actually lived for two years while a student, and moved into an apartment in Shin-Ōkubo (Matsumoto 2008b: 65, 69). After taking up part-time work in a recycling shop, Matsumoto launched the 'Poor People's Great Rebellion Collective' (Binbōnin daihanran shūdan) (Matsumoto 2008b: 88–89).

In September 2001, corporate chairmen and the presidents of Tokyo's larger and more prestigious private universities gathered for a symposium on university-business collaboration in one of the high-rise buildings newly constructed on the Hōsei campus. A younger colleague informed Matsumoto that students were 'going to wreak havoc' at the meeting and invited him to take part. On the day, total chaos erupted when about twenty people, including Matsumoto, emptied fire extinguishers, threw paint-filled balloons, overturned desks and tables and threw paint at the assembled university presidents. As a result, Matsumoto was incarcerated for five months from January 2002 on charges of breaking and entering and forcible obstruction of business. The experience made him keenly aware that, rather than the lower-ranked police officers who worked where he was detained, 'it was the state and those in power' that were the problem (Matsumoto 2008b: 72–84).

Upon his release, Matsumoto began to hold sidewalk 'hot-pot parties' with other members of the Poor People's Great Rebellion Collective. There, he had the chance to talk with the homeless, salarymen, young people struggling to survive after coming to Tokyo from provincial areas and sex-workers. These conversations made him realize angrily that the government and corporations had set out to revive the economy by sacrificing those in the lower echelons of society (Matsumoto 2008b: 88–90). Then, in 2003, there were news reports of a man who, outraged at his employer's refusal to pay his wages, locked himself in the company building where he set himself alight. However, the fierce ignition intensity of the vaporized gasoline used by the victim to self-immolate led to the press reporting the death as '*bakushi*', death or suicide by explosion. Shocked at the man's fate, Matsumoto and his colleagues set out to use the Poor People's Great Rebellion Collective to make it known that 'many people face similar struggles and it will be a pretty major thing if they can cause an uproar'. Matsumoto himself had no intention of 'living like some slave of the rich guys' (Matsumoto 2008b: 92).

When the publication and distribution of 'News for the Poor' saw more and more people join Matsumoto's cause, he and his colleagues rented a shed on the rooftop of a building in Shin-Ōkubo to use as the movement's base (Matsumoto 2008b: 94–95; Matsumoto 2016: 20–25). Matsumoto felt uneasy, however, at the lack of connection between the movement's activities, the people involved and 'everyday life'. He also rejected the idea that 'the bloke who got a movement going should act as its boss' (Matsumoto and Futatsugi 2008: 50–51).

Continuing to work part-time throughout, even after his release from detention, Matsumoto realized that not only did a job in a recycling shop suit him personally, this was a place where community bonds were formed. He also felt strong contempt for the 'excesses of the throw-away consumer society'. Thinking that he might start his own recycling business, he looked for a location along inner Tokyo's Chūō Line. It was during that time that he met Yamashita Hikaru (b. 1977) and Ogasawara Keita (b. 1977) in Kōenji (Matsumoto 2008b: 106–110; Matsumoto and Futatsugi 2008: 42–44). Below, I will examine the background of the former. Although Yamashita's Amateur Revolt activities are relatively well-known, I will focus on his life prior to meeting Matsumoto in order to profile the differences between the two men.

Yamashita Hikaru: Experiencing Kōenji's subculture scene

Yamashita Hikaru was born in Kagoshima. From primary school, he had a strong interest in punk music and fashion. While visiting Kōenji during high school and making contact with the punk scene there, he came across people whose norm seemed to be 'going around in things never seen in ordinary society, things you couldn't buy in shops and wearing everything that they had made themselves' (Toyama 2010a). This prompted Yamashita to make his way to Tokyo after graduating from high school and to live in Kōenji while attending fashion college at night. With punk as the point of contact, Yamashita made many friends in the several months following his arrival in Tokyo (Matsumoto and Futatsugi 2008: 18).

From the 1970s, Kōenji had been a place where young people had gathered to live. By the 1980s, there were growing numbers of 'livehouses' – relatively small venues dedicated to playing live music. By the mid-1990s when Yamashita arrived, more and more second-hand clothing outlets were being opened in empty shops. Opposition by residents to redevelopment meant that these old shops were still standing, making it possible for young people to use the corner of an empty shop to set up a small-scale business. In 2000, there were 200 or so second-hand clothing shops in Kōenji and, although this number fell to about half by 2011, they remain a distinguishing feature of the Kōenji area (Konomachi Ākaibuzu 2017; Narumi 2019a; Narumi 2019b; Shimomura 2011).

Around 1995 and 1996, when Yamashita first lived in Kōenji, the area was a 'punk town' with 'live houses' that hosted punk band performances, punk record shops and the editorial headquarters of punk music magazines. This also influenced Yamashita's decision to live in the area. As a result of regular attendance at live-house punk band performances during his early days in the district, he broadened his friendship circle by meeting individual members of the punk subculture who were hanging out on the streets. As the youngest among them and as a boy from the country, Yamashita was shocked by the behavior of punks who engaged in such practices as shoplifting to guarantee their access to food and alcohol. He nevertheless remained friends with this group (Matsumoto and Futatsugi 2008: 18; Toyama 2010b; Toyama 2010c).

Through part-time work, Yamashita met artists with whom he began to collaborate (Toyama 2010c). One of these was Ogasawara Keita, who was born and raised in Kōenji and with whom Yamashita formed a performance group around 2000. Rather than looking for conventional work after graduating from high school, Ogasawara had tried to support himself through performance-type activities. From 2001 to 2002, Ogasawara, Yamashita and several friends published 'NOPPIN News' (*NOPPIN Shimbun*), a hand-written daily newspaper.

The group began this 'newspaper', the name of which reads as the word 'Japan' (*Nippon*) in reverse, with 'a plan to overturn Japan and to destroy the internet' (Matsumoto and Futatsugi 2008: 19–24; Toyama 2010d; Toyama 2010e).

During this time, Yamashita briefly rented a corner of the floor in a shop at Kōenji Station South Exit where he opened a second-hand clothing store. Directly after this, a member of the Poor People's Great Rebellion Collective asked if they could sell t-shirts in Yamashita's retail space. Familiar with 'News for the Poor', Yamashita agreed. When Matsumoto heard this, he visited the shop and met Yamashita for the first time (Matsumoto and Futatsugi 2008: 19–22). In November 2004, Matsumoto gave Yamashita his first demonstration experience by inviting his new acquaintance to participate in an event held to support an activist arrested for making 'graffiti' opposing the Iraq War (Toyama 2010f). Yamashita then attended a gathering of the Poor People's Great Rebellion Collective held from 31 December into the first day of the new year, remained awake throughout the night in front of the ALTA building[2] near the Shinjuku Station East Exit and participated in a performance that involved distributing *amazake* (warm, sweet sake) provided by the collective to passers-by and writing *kakizome* – the first calligraphy of the new year – on the street. It was here that Yamashita and Ogasawara first saw Matsumoto, after deliberately bumping into police officers who were keeping order in the same way that the police often harassed protesters by deliberately physically colliding with them, avoid arrest by pretending that the contact was the fault of police (Matsumoto and Futatsugi 2008: 36–37). They also saw that the 'movement' and the friends of Matsumoto who were connected to it were completely different to themselves. Thus, while Matsumoto was totally absorbed in activities aimed at expressing dissatisfaction with politics and society, Yamashita, having spent his twenties in the world of hobbies and play, was in fact conscious that he had previously taken absolutely 'no interest' in 'movements or revolution' (Matsumoto and Futatsugi 2008: 51). I therefore now look at the circumstances that led Yamashita and Ogasawara, who had such different experiences and backgrounds to those of Matsumoto, to form a single movement with the latter and his like-minded colleagues.

Amateur Revolt

In April 2005, Yamashita, followed by Ogasawara, began broadcasting on internet radio. Soon after, using a name that came from another source, Ogasawara called his program 'The Amateur Revolt' (Matsumoto and Futatsugi 2008: 39–40; Toyama 2010f). Around this time, Matsumoto asked Yamashita if he knew of somewhere he could open a recycling shop. Coincidentally, Yamashita was looking for a second-hand shop venue at the time and had planned to meet with the deputy chair of the North-Central Avenue shopping street situated near the north exit of Kōenji Station. The pair accordingly went together the following day to meet with and explain their ideas to the deputy chair. Although he was initially not too keen on giving them an empty shop, once he knew that Yamashita and Matsumoto were friends of local figure Ogasawara, he agreed to allow them to rent a space (Matsumoto and Futatsugi 2008: 43–44; Toyama 2010g). At that time, the viability of the shopping street was under threat with the closure of more and more North-Central Avenue shops. The deputy chair realized that this might just be the time to do business with the younger generation (Matsumoto 2008a: 59–60; Matsumoto 2008b: 109–110; Matsumoto and Futatsugi 2008: 45).

This was the background to the opening of a store that housed Matsumoto's recycling shop, Yamashita's second-hand clothing shop and Ogasawara's internet radio studio. While Matsumoto suggested that the store be named 'Peasant Revolt', Yamashita preferred 'NEET Spot'. Ogasawara's first choice, 'Amateurs', was seen as a problem by Matsumoto who thought that, in the case of a second-hand store, the term would give the impression of being unreliable (Matsumoto 2008b: 113; Matsumoto and Futatsugi 2008: 44, 84; Toyama 2010h). Ogasawara persisted, however, and his colleagues eventually agreed to 'Amateur Revolt'. Even these different opinions regarding the shop's name provide insights into the amorphous nature of the connection between Matsumoto, Yamashita and Ogasawara. Upon his move to

Kōenji, Matsumoto closed the rooftop base he had established for the Poor People's Great Rebellion Collective, and members now gathered in the new store, as they had in the past in Shin-Ōkubo, to hold events like hot-pot gatherings (Matsumoto 2008b: 117–118). Thus, there was a 'feeling of chaos' in this shop space where a continuous stream of people gathered to 'do whatever they liked' (Matsumoto and Futatsugi 2008: 50–51). Attention now turns to the various demonstrations and events which, notwithstanding the sense of 'chaos' that prevailed in the store, the group went on to organize.

New 'playful' demonstrations

'Give back my bike' and 'Three people' demonstrations

On 20 August 2005, almost immediately after forming Amateur Revolt, Matsumoto and Yamashita organized the 'Give back my bike' demonstration. After Yamashita said he wanted to demonstrate about something but before the application for permission was made, a number of the group's friends talked about having their bicycles impounded by the authorities, leading to the promotion of the slogan 'Give back my bike' (Matsumoto and Futatsugi 2008: 70). In an afterword (Matsumoto and Futatsugi 2008: 84), Matsumoto explained the demonstration's objective as follows. Those in power imposed laws that restricted activities in public spaces. In addition, there were growing numbers of areas in which people were permitted to do nothing more than walk down the road or spend money and consume. It was important, therefore, to wrest back the 'freedom of the streets'. With regard to impounded bicycles, rather than appeal to the government, it was better that people take matters into their own hands (Matsumoto 2008b: 143–146).

The name given on the application for permission to demonstrate was 'Kōenji NEET Union' (Matsumoto and Futatsugi 2008: 70–71). At the time, the group told the police that this was actually only a group of gamers and the demonstration would likely attract no more than ten people (Matsumoto 2008b: 140), but the flyer advertising the event

Photo 4.1: 'Give back my bike' demonstration in 2005. Source: mkimpo.

had been distributed all along the Chūō Line resulting in a gathering of 100 on the day. The parade was led down the street by a truck fitted out with a sound system which loudly blared out the music of the band and DJ on the tray. The police, who had prepared for a very small showing, were infuriated. In addition to the initial 100, many people joined the march from the roadside while, in order to slow things down, there were various performances which included Ogasawara and Yamashita deliberately falling to the ground and starting to fight each other (Matsumoto and Futatsugi 2008: 74–79).

In February the following year, 2006, Matsumoto and his two colleagues held the 'Three people' demonstration. Having angered the authorities with the previous event, they now 'pretended a vow of allegiance to the police'. They also thought that applying to hold a demonstration with a very small number of participants meant that they would not be inhibited by an excessive police presence. The police were initially unwilling to issue a permit because of what had occurred on the previous occasion. Eventually, however, they agreed to an event demanding 'free tissue paper in station toilets'. The application was for a four-person demonstration but, when one slept-in on the day, the number dropped to three. Expecting a gathering similar to the 'Give back my bike' demonstration, the police turned out in force with even the riot squad in tow. Once they realized that the event actually had only three participants, they looked completely bamboozled. The 'demonstration' was filmed by a filmmaker who happened to be present, while another activist made a film that was loaded onto YouTube (Matsumoto and Futatsugi 2008: 85–94; Oda 2006). The humor of the activist's clip, which included subtitles featuring fictional conversations between the police and Matsumoto and his colleagues, drew widespread attention. In this way, many people became aware of Amateur Revolt (Matsumoto 2008b: 149).

Anti-PSE Law and 'Make rent free' demonstrations

In March 2006, Amateur Revolt held an anti-PSE Law demonstration at Kōenji and a rally opposing the same law in front of the ALTA building. The PSE Law stipulated that no electronic goods or home appliances could be sold without having a so-called 'PSE mark' enabling identification. Set to come into force from April 2006, the bill was interpreted by the ministry of economic trade and industry as also applying to used and second-hand appliances. Once this position was made clear, people in the second-hand and recycling business and also those in the musical instrument business began to voice concern. Opposition came, too, from celebrated musicians such as Sakamoto Ryūichi (Matsumoto 2008a: 119). Matsumoto was angered by the fact that some in the recycling business had joined large-scale electrical appliance dealerships in preparing for the law's April introduction (Matsumoto and Futatsugi 2008: 104). The opposition movement nonetheless picked up pace nationwide, further gathering momentum once Matsumoto and his colleagues created unique hand-written newspapers and manga and uploaded these onto their homepages. The campaign culminated in March with a demonstration designed to 'selfishly make a bit of a fuss and appeal to public opinion', led by a truck with a fan fixed to the roof and the tray loaded with household appliances. The sound of a stereo mounted on the back of the truck caught the attention of passers-by, as did brandished placards that read, for example, 'Can't poor people use air-con?', 'Can't poor people listen to the radio?' and 'Can't poor people watch television?'. The event was even covered by NHK's 7 p.m. news and by the *Asahi Shimbun* (Matsumoto and Futatsugi 2008: 101–113; *Asahi Shimbun* 2006a; Inoue 2006). While talking and drinking together after the demonstration, Matsumoto and Yamashita decided to hold a Shinjuku rally the following week. Matsumoto immediately arranged a vehicle and also appealed to a lower house Communist Party member to take part (Matsumoto 2008b: 153–154; Matsumoto and Futatsugi 2008: 117–119). With only four days to prepare, the 'Kill off the PSE Law for good' rally eventually went ahead in Shinjuku accompanied by the endless beat of loud music. Responding to the fact that the PSE Law virtually decreed that 'people in the recycling business will not eat', Yamashita prepared a photograph of a cut-out headshot of punk rocker Machida Machizō (now known as Machida Kō), who sang the song, 'Don't eat food'. Calling on people in the street to put their faces into the cut-out space, he gave them bread to eat that was stamped with the letters 'PSE'. Since in Japanese the syllables *pan o kuu*, meaning 'to eat bread', sound like the word *panku*, meaning 'punk', this was a clever play on words that also enabled people attending the rally to participate in the action. Ogasawara climbed onto the roof of a sound truck to make a fake self-introduction in which he claimed, 'I became a NEET after leaving middle school and today I came to Shinjuku from Kōenji with the commuter ticket my mother uses to go to her part-time job'. He then gave a speech saying, 'Even I who have no learning nor money know enough to understand that this PSE law is evil' (Nakamura 2008). These performances were designed to capture the attention of passers-by. The rally, which also featured an auction of second-hand appliances

Photo 4.2: Cut-out headshot of punk rocker Machida Machizō. Source: documentary film Shirōto no ran *by Y. Nakamura.*

without PSE marks, resulted in a highly original activist streetscape that had little resemblance to other political protest actions. The rally was successful in the sense that revisions to the PSE Law meant that it was never retrospectively applied to electrical appliances made before the introduction of the PSE mark system (*Asahi Shimbun* 2006b).

Six months later, in September 2006, Amateur Revolt held a 'Make rent free' demonstration. Rather than being organized by Matsumoto and Yamashita, this event was planned by Matsumoto in conjunction with a group of art activists, RLL (Radical Laughter Left), who produced and distributed YouTube announcement videos and flyers (Matsumoto and Futatsugi 2008: 148–149). There was a huge response to the RLL video, which included clips of events unrelated to the 'Make rent free' campaign such as the October 1990 Nishinari Riot in Osaka and the 1972 soft-porn samurai drama directed by Suzuki Norifumi, *The erotomaniac daimyō* (*Tokugawa sekkusu kinshirei: Shikijō daimyō*, literally, 'A Tokugawa ban on sex: The lustful daimyo'). By the time the event had come to an end, a protest march that began with less than 100 people had swelled to 300. Participants carried placards with slogans such as 'Riot', 'It's our right to have sex in a large room', and, because many landlords did not allow tenants to affix posters and the like onto walls, 'It's our right to stick drawing pins into the wall'. There was also a performance that involved people charging into the crowd carrying a portable shrine on which was written 'Kōenji NEET Union'. Although this was a tactic designed to excite participants, the unexpected nature of the performance successfully confused the police (Matsumoto 2008b: 126–127; Matsumoto and Futatsugi 2008: 155–159). While the 'Make rent free' demand had emerged in the natural course of the group's discussions, the campaign carried force precisely because it gave a voice to real people suffering rent distress and to those unable to start the business of their choice because they had no money to pay a lease. This led to discussions around what being a renter actually entailed, a conversation that influenced the choice of demonstration slogans going forward (Matsumoto and Futatsugi 2008: 150–151).

'Kōenji riot', anti-nuclear power demonstrations, 'No Limit'

At the demonstration held by the General Freeter Union (Furītā zenpan rōdō kumiai, established in 2004) immediately before the 'Make rent free' rally, the people on the sound car had been arrested. Discussions thus began on how to broadcast sound during a demonstration without having a DJ on the back of a truck (Matsumoto and Futatsugi 2008: 149). It was apparent from these arrests, coupled with the heavy police presence at the 'Make rent free' rally, that the authorities were tightening the regulation of demonstrations. As a result, Matsumoto decided in the following year – 2007 – to run for the Suginami Ward Assembly to take advantage of the fact that police were unable to intervene in activities connected to a candidate's political campaign. Accordingly, Matsumoto set out 'legitimately and above board' as a candidate 'to make a huge uproar' by holding a 'one-week long, never-ending outdoor party'. The aim was to 'reclaim society by breaking down the management and suppression of the streets' and to create 'a liberation space' in front of Kōenji Station. The 'Kōenji Riot' was the name given to the successful live performances, talk shows and dance performances held in front of Kōenji Station at the time (Matsumoto and Futatsugi 2008: 170–200; Nakamura 2008).

From April 2011, Amateur Revolt organized anti-nuclear power demonstrations, each attended by crowds that ranged from several thousand to more than 10,000 (see the Introduction to this book). Prior to this, Matsumoto had made links with activists around the world by visiting the headquarters of movements in places such as Asia, Europe and the US. With the 2011 rise of the anti-nuclear power movement, the type of 'order' that was imposed by some movement leaders once more became a feature of demonstrations in Japan. Uneasy with this development, Matsumoto traveled back and forth to places like Korea, Taiwan and Hong Kong, giving rise to a cross-border 'underground culture' (Matsumoto 2018a). One outcome was the exchange that occurred between researchers, musicians, artists and activists at the 'No Limit Tokyo Autonomous Zone' and 'No Limit Seoul Autonomous Zone' events held in Tokyo in 2016 and in Seoul in 2017. For eight days in Tokyo and ten days in Seoul various sites hosted live music performances, demonstrations, talk shows and workshops (Matsumoto 2016a; 'No Limit Tokyo jichiku' 2016; Matsumoto 2017). At a demonstration opposing Kōenji redevelopment held in September 2018, young people from Hong Kong, Korea and Taiwan spoke on gentrification in their home countries (Matsumoto 2018b; Amamiya 2018). With the formation of this kind of 'underground culture', Kōenji became a gathering place for young activists from Asia who sympathized with Amateur Revolt's activities (Tahara 2019).

As noted above, Amateur Revolt is a group whose gatherings and demonstrations are characterized by an absence of predictable organization, clear objectives or ideological systems. Yet, even without following previous traditions, members such as Matsumoto and his colleagues were able to assert themselves politically, while those such as Yamashita developed protest actions involving music, art and performance. In addition, the group counts people from various places throughout Asia as its members. On this basis, I argue that Amateur Revolt is an amorphous collection of separate individuals with widely different characteristics. Below, I consider how shops such as the Irregular Rhythm Asylum (IRA), which is associated with the recycling shop network, and the demonstrations considered above connect the divergent people of Amateur Revolt.

Bonding amorphous individuals together

Free spaces creating alternative values and ideas

At the time of the joint opening of Amateur Revolt Shop No. One, Yamashita, as noted above, believed that he had 'no interest' whatsoever in 'activism or revolution'. This view was held in common with most of the people he knew. When friends of Matsumoto came to visit the shop, however, they repeatedly asked about his background in the protest movement and also about his opinions on political issues. Yamashita really had no idea how to respond. To use Ogasawara's words, 'It was weird how this pair did things together'. For example, one man known as NORANERO, who came from Nagasaki and who had worked in a clothing store, had formed a connection some time before with Yamashita through a shared interest in fashion and music. Upon meeting Matsumoto immediately after the opening of Amateur Revolt Shop No. One, NORANERO relocated to Kōenji. In September 2009, he opened a bar there that became Amateur Revolt Shop No. Nine (Matsumoto and Futatsugi 2008: 130–134). At first, he felt uncomfortable because he had absolutely no shared topic of conversation with Matsumoto and his activist friends. Further interaction, however, eventually bridged this gap (Toyama 2010h). Exchange among these sorts of very different people was promoted by the principle of 'chaos as connecting people' (*hito no tsunagari no kaosu*) that operated at Shop No. One. This principle refused hierarchical structures and excluded no-one (Matsumoto and Futatsugi 2008: 63–64).

A separate focal point connected to the Amateur Revolt network was the Shinjuku Infoshop IRA. The IRA, which like Amateur Revolt had operated from 2005, sold things such as books, posters and CDs that were exchanged between customers, including anarchists around the world. The IRA also held various events and workshops and played an important nodal role in the networks linked to Amateur Revolt. When the 2011 anti-nuclear power movement became active, those Amateur Revolt-IRA networks took on key information dissemination tasks including posting demonstration schedules on their webpages (Obinger 2015: 80–82; Brown 2018: 85–6). The IRA also ran events such as sewing workshops on hand or machine sewing. A woman who took part in these confirmed that, while she may have had no political consciousness prior to enrolling, her ideas and attitudes changed through her workshop participation (Obinger 2015: 198). Similar alternative spaces operated in places such as the Kiryūsha (Quiriusha) bookshop in Shimokitazawa, the Akane event space in Waseda and the Rabanderia (Lavanderia) café in Shinjuku (Brown 2018: 78–81). Along with the Kōenji Amateur Revolt shops, these businesses became event sites that marked the 'No Limit Tokyo Autonomous Zone' (Tokyo No Limit jichiku). Outside these spaces, it was the demonstrations that worked to bring people together ('No Limit Tokyo Autonomous Zone' 2016).

The demonstration as a site of play bridging different viewpoints

During 'Give back my bike' demonstrations, the key roles – over and above those of Matsumoto and his activist colleagues – were played by associates of Yamashita and Ogasawara. One friend of Yamashita and his circle from before the Amateur Revolt days who ran a music studio in front of Kōenji Station supplied the sound system and musical instruments for the band on the back of the truck that led the demonstrations. This same friend performed as the band's frontman. Ogasawara's cousin, from the same music studio, also took part (Matsumoto and Futatsugi 2008: 71–77). Mochizuki, who drove the truck leading the demonstration, had lived in Kōenji from before 2005 and had become friends with Yamashita and Ogasawara while moving between part-time jobs. He had also helped prepare for the opening of

Amateur Revolt Shop No. One, and in 2007 started work in Shop No. Eleven (Matsumoto and Futatsugi 2008: 58–59, 69). The demonstrations thus brought together two very different groups of people. One revolved around and had similar leisure activities and interests to Yamashita, while the other was comprised of Matsumoto and his activist colleagues. Below we will consider how these two groups came to be involved in the same demonstrations.

Prior to the formation of Amateur Revolt, Matsumoto had identified a consensus along the lines of 'we must hold a serious event' among participants in the demonstrations he attended. These people were angered by attempts to create a 'crazy uproar'. Matsumoto was totally opposed to the idea that a demonstration must be serious. He had even felt uncomfortable when participating in the Shibuya sound demonstrations held several years previously. While the events themselves might have created an 'uproar detached from reality', this was merely 'consumed' by participants who were then 'dragged back to their daily routines'. A mutual friend of Yamashita and Ogasawara named Itō, who had run a street stall in Shibuya, had a similar response to Matsumoto. Itō dismissed the sound demonstrations as the 'unseemly' product of a group of people who 'couldn't do anything by themselves'. However, the 'fun' he experienced during the 'Give back my bike' events changed his attitude toward demonstrations (Matsumoto and Futatsugi 2008: 80–83). Itō had been friends with Yamashita from before 2005 when both had been fans of the same punk rock band. Although his response to the Anti-Iraq War sound demos had been negative, he felt that the 'stupid uproar' of the 'Give back my bike' demonstration had been fun. Furthermore, he believed that the demonstration organizers who came from the local Kōenji community were certainly not the kind of people who 'couldn't do anything by themselves'. There was also perhaps the fact that the 'Give back my bike' demonstration demand related to the lived experience of participants. After 'Give back my bike', Itō collaborated with Ogasawara to create manga for the anti-PSE Law demonstration. The protagonist of the manga, which was distributed free to demonstration participants, was Amateur Revolt confronting the authorities who were about to implement the PSE Law (Matsumoto and Futatsugi 2008: 104). Thus, although previously critical of such events, Itō's participation in the 'Give back my bike' campaign saw him become active in a social movement that made political demands.

The emergence of a type of demonstration in which it was possible for participants to come from diametrically opposed groups, such as the apolitical people associated with Yamashita and Ogasawara and the Matsumoto activists, was largely a result of Matsumoto's desire to be part of a movement that valued play and fun. These elements became a feature of later Kōenji demonstrations and events. Furthermore, elements of '100% stupidity' that had no apparent connection to the demonstration – such as a DJ performing on the back of a truck or Gundam cosplayers – were completely acceptable (Matsumoto and Futatsugi 2008: 83). Each event also involved Ogasawara and his friends giving some sort of performance. These open and free carnivalesque acts of demonstration as 'uproar' drew a diverse range of people, each of whom experienced the demonstration as 'fun'. It is perhaps for this reason that people like Itō, who felt no affiliation with anti-Iraq War sound demonstrations, were attracted to Amateur Revolt activities; and, as Mōri Yoshitaka has pointed out, the 'fun' promoted by Amateur Revolt is surely diametrically opposed to the 'fun' stipulated for the people by the authorities (Mōri 2009: 21).

The several hundred people who gathered for the anti-PSE Law demonstration were apolitical in the sense that their affiliation with Amateur Revolt was possible because there was an absence of 'political discussion' at the post-demonstration party (Matsumoto and Futatsugi 2008: 114–116). These people became interested in demonstrations after finding out about Amateur Revolt from media such as flyers, magazines and the internet (Matsumoto 2008a: 120; Matsumoto and Futatsugi 2008: 104, 114). To them, rather than seeking to make a political statement, they were drawn to the carnivalesque atmosphere that was 'fun'.

In other words, Amateur Revolt demonstrations and gatherings did not follow the traditional demonstration style of participants marching and chanting slogans in unison. Rather, the loud band performances and DJs meant that these were street events in which individual people with no interest in politics could take part. For example, at the anti-

PSE Law demonstration held in front of Shinjuku ALTA, all of the events – including the address by a Communist Party Diet member, Yamashita's performance involving the cut-out headshot of a punk rock singer, Ogasawara's speech as a 'fake NEET middle school graduate' and the auction of used household appliances – took place against the blare of loud music. Since the format bore no resemblance whatsoever to the usual demonstration-style speeches, petitions and distribution of leaflets, everyone had a chance to participate regardless of their political views. Rather than Matsumoto, it was people like Yamashita and Ogasawara with their art and performances who made the event and the speeches a reality; and it was this group that created the carnivalesque atmosphere in which even people with no interest in politics played a role.

The demonstration as a site of changing values

As was the case with Ogasawara's participation in the 'Give back my bike' event, attendance at just one Amateur Revolt event made people realize that they had a right 'to voice those sorts of things' (Matsumoto and Futatsugi 2008: 140). In other words, being drawn into and participating in a festive and 'fun' gathering – even by accident – led to individuals on the streets encountering people making demands they would have previously thought unrealistic, such as 'Give back my bike' or 'Make rent free'. By being part of a group calling out slogans, these individuals came to understand the possibility of realizing the demands. It is thus possible that participation in a demonstration or 'uproar' can, in Matsumoto's words, be the moment that creates 'a post-revolutionary world in advance' (Matsumoto 2008a: 128; Karatani and Matsumoto 2012: 125–126). Through participation, people at demonstrations are able to experience a change in their values and thus be freed from the demands of various norms. Ultimately, apolitical people experienced the gatherings as a form of 'fun', even when others on the streets were chanting political slogans against the PSE Law, for example. In this way, Amateur Revolt was able to hold amorphous demonstrations that mobilized a diversity of participants with no prior connections.

It is clear that from one perspective the slogans chanted at Amateur Revolt demonstrations were entirely political. There must, for example, have been large numbers of participants who sympathized with the 'Give back my bike' demand – people who had been made to pay a fine in order to have an impounded bicycle returned. Slogans such as 'It's our right to have sex in a big room' and 'It's our right to stick drawing pins in the wall', which were devised by those who took part in the 'Make rent free' demonstration, make it clear that participants were in favor of the rally's key demand. Amateur Revolt's principle of daring to say what 'everyone wants to say, but no one says' (Matsumoto and Futatsugi 2008: 140) provided an opportunity for those who participated in street events to voice a variety of demands.

The messages of the anti-PSE Law demonstrations such as 'Can't the poor use air-conditioning?', 'Can't the poor listen to the radio?' and 'Can't the poor watch television?' were in fact extremely political. These demands were a contestation by 'people in poverty' over the fact that implementation of the PSE Law would have resulted in the city's poor residents being unable to purchase, and therefore unable to use, second-hand electrical goods. It is highly likely that even demonstration participants who were merely attracted by the 'fun' of the festive activities came in a broader sense to understand the political elements embedded in these messages. Thus, while the carnivalesque elements of Amateur Revolt demonstrations catered for both people who supported the political message and those attracted by the 'crazy uproar' and 'fun', there were undoubtedly cases where these elements overlapped to transform points of view.

Community born of protest

After taking part in a demonstration, some people eventually became involved in the operation of the Kōenji Amateur Revolt shop network. These included NORANERO and Mochizuki, referred to above. There was also a woman, AICON, who spoke to Matsumoto after the anti-PSE Law event. Meeting Matsumoto again at a different gathering, she accepted his offer to run a coffee shop during the daytime in Amateur

Revolt Shop No. Nine, which NORANERO operated as a bar at night. Leaving her part-time recycling shop job, she ran the coffee shop on the theme of 'revolution' that extolled 'anti-capitalism'. This involved, for example, serving Zapatista Fair Trade Coffee which she sourced from the IRA in Shinjuku (Matsumoto and Futatsugi 2008: 132–4). Another woman, yoyo, had felt that her 'heart was gradually being undermined' by working in a temp agency. Visiting Kōenji on occasion, she was moved by the fresh vegetables that were sold there by a farmer from Kanagawa Prefecture's Miura Peninsula in collaboration with one of the North-Center Shopping Street shop owners. This farmer had come to Koenji after reading a 1 January 2007 *Asahi Shimbun* article that introduced Amateur Revolt. In it, Matsumoto had been quoted as saying, 'If business wants to trample us underfoot, we must make another society for ourselves' (Manabe and Ōta 2007). Between 2007 and 2010, together with AICON and probably with Matsumoto's encouragement, yoyo ran a vegan café in Amateur Revolt Shop No. Nine using fresh vegetables from Miura Peninsula (Matsumoto and Futatsugi 2008: 162–3; *Kyoto Shimbun* 2009). yoyo said that she 'wanted to be able to bring together divided groups' such as city and country, rich and poor and adults and children through 'something that I like'. This 'something' was cooking (yoyo 2007). We might interpret this as yoyo's desire to use 'food' to bring about a change in people's values while putting into practice Matsumoto's idea of the need to 'make another society for ourselves'.

Various people overseas were also attracted to the Amateur Revolt interpretation of demonstrations and accordingly made connections with the group. Even before 2011, there was strong interest in Amateur Revolt among young activists throughout Asia and in places such as South Korea. This interest was the result of young Koreans being attracted by the 'easy-going features' that they discovered in Amateur Revolt. These young people felt alienated from the typical Korean demonstration that was characterized by large crowds, a high degree of 'intensity' and the expectation that participants be 'earnest' (Karatani and Matsumoto 2012: 123). In terms of dedication to the cause and the numbers of people mobilized, Japanese activists had reason to envy their Korean counterparts. However, and this may have also been the case in Hong Kong and Taiwan, there seemed to be little sense of intimacy among those taking part. Throughout Asia, Amateur Revolt's alternate spaces and methods and festive demonstrations with events that featured art and performance had a universal appeal that drew people to Kōenji. Key to this appeal was their take on demonstrations. Below, in addition to examining the fundamentals that mobilized people to take part in Amateur Revolt demonstrations and the elements that made the movement endure for fifteen years, I consider the common ideas and philosophies shared by those who appear at first glance to have nothing in common.

Networks created by rallies and Amateur Revolt's 'autonomy'

Everyday networks and 'chaos'

According to various people who operated the Tokyo metropolitan activist bases associated with Amateur Revolt, notice of the April 2011 anti-nuclear power demonstrations was disseminated via Twitter and various homepages to a diverse group of people with no common characteristics. It is possible that the use of the name 'Amateur Revolt' in these materials gave the impression that even 'amateurs' with no demonstration experience could participate (Yamamoto and Matsumoto 2012: 53). Even more important than this form of information dissemination, however, was the presence in inner Tokyo of the headquarters of multiple entities, such as the IRA, that had emerged post-2005 and were associated with Amateur Revolt. Through his everyday interactions with acquaintances who ran shops, had music and theatre backgrounds and worked in the arts, Matsumoto had built a network of relationships able to broadcast information instantly. He has pointed out that it was precisely the effectiveness of these personal networks that facilitated the spread of information through Twitter and the internet (Karatani and Matsumoto 2012: 128). In other words, people were mobilized by the strength of people-to-people relationships forged from everyday interaction through art, music and play. This was the result of Amateur Revolt members placing the highest value on the formation of bonds and the promotion of exchange between people in the context of everyday life.

In 2013, Yamashita relocated to Kyūshū. Although this led to the closure of a number of Amateur Revolt retail outlets, the group remains active and continues to hold demonstrations and similar events. This is because, as we have seen above, new members regularly join the group and members take turns at playing leadership roles within the movement. According to Matsumoto, without these changes in Amateur Revolt's membership, 'rules' and 'tacit constraints' would have emerged, with 'various things quickly tightening because of a status difference in those who joined first and those who joined later'. Matsumoto observed that this effect threatened even the anti-nuclear power movement. If that group 'became a single, unified block', he argued, 'it would lose its power to break down structures and should therefore disperse after every event to issue a renewed call for members before taking future action' (Matsumoto 2018c). Matsumoto and his colleagues were able to operate in this way because they viewed the 'chaos' generated by gathering such a diverse range of people together as 'fun'. To them, rather than being restrictive, the power generated by upheaval was enormously valuable to the movement. I will conclude by considering 'autonomy' (*jichi*) as a key idea informing Amateur Revolt's activities.

'Autonomy' and 'gathering'

Similarities between Amateur Revolt and the Occupy Movement have been noted above. Since members strongly advocate independence from rather than compliance with the system, the movement to take up residence in empty houses is sometimes called the Autonomous Movement. From his student days to the present, Matsumoto has strongly advocated a style of 'autonomy' similar to the European ideal. His declaration of the need to create 'a post-revolutionary world in advance' further expresses the idea of establishing something that stands independently from capitalism and the nation state. In reality, Matsumoto saw operating a recycling shop not merely as a means of making a living, but also as a way of distancing himself from the 'rip-off economy' of large-scale production and consumption and of developing an alternate economy and lifestyle. By broadening the lifestyle associated with recycling, he believed that it was possible to achieve 'economic autonomy through the control of things', that is, to live free from the meaningless consumption of goods and commodities (Matsumoto 2008a: 63–9).

Given that Yamashita began publishing NOPPIN News with a view to 'overturning Japan', his point of departure, too, was clearly some kind of antipathy towards conditions of control. It was perhaps this consciousness that saw Yamashita join forces with Matsumoto, who advocated strongly for autonomy and who was antagonistic towards all aspects of a system that sought to regulate and control the self. Nevertheless, Yamashita expressed his sense of 'autonomy' by 'living without having to work for someone else' through the ideal of a new lifestyle by means of which he removed himself from the forms of control that worked against him. Since 2011, Yamashita's clothing brand, 'Leaving-off half-way' (*Tochū de yameru*), has enjoyed good sales. Building on the opportunities this presented and in accord with 'the theory and practice of living enjoyably and supporting yourself doing things that you like', Yamashita began convening workshops entitled 'Learning to Leave-off Part-time Work' (*Baito yameru gakkō*) (Yamashita 2017), and published a book with the same title. With the successful sale of the clothing made by himself and his colleagues, Yamashita lowered prices, paid higher wages to employees and dropped his own profits to a bare minimum. He has made it known that through taking advantage of his own special skills, giving up part-time work in the employ of another and reducing his income to a bare minimum, he is 'practicing a form of anti-capitalism that focuses on the self'.

From a broad perspective, we can see that Amateur Revolt shares certain characteristics with the left. In addition, the group's desire to create ideal circumstances for the 'here and now', to declare the need to create 'a post-revolutionary world in advance' and to work in terms of equal and non-hierarchical relationships are principles shared with the 'New Anarchism' or 'Neo-Anarchism' (Tanaka 2015: 54–55; Obinger 2015: 95–97, 110). Nevertheless, even today Amateur

Revolt continues to resist being drawn into the confines of a defined ideology or movement in the classic sense. Instead, the group operates according to notions such as 'people who do what they like', 'amateurs', 'the poor' and 'fools', which they themselves value. Resistance to compliance with the norms and common practices of powerbrokers such as capital and the state saw Amateur Revolt create a movement that was beyond the comprehension of the social institutions that sought to constrain it. By refusing to do what they were told and by the various members doing as they pleased, Amateur Revolt projected an active image of undermining social order that was also comic and humorous. Matsumoto was particularly critical of the way in which organizations such as the Communist Party were attached to their title and a whole-of-movement ideology. He saw this as 'passing the buck', further declaring that 'it was a lie to claim that a good society was impossible if each member did as they pleased' (Karatani and Matsumoto 2012: 126–129). When we consider in tandem the opinions of the key Amateur Revolt members, Matsumoto and Yamashita, it becomes clear that each supports the autonomous practice of the individual who is not bound by a specific ideology.

A further activity valued by Amateur Revolt is connecting individuals. Matsumoto has stated that 'merely by coming together', particularly during events such as demonstrations, 'people who each do their own thing' are resisting authority. He further argues that because the authorities are able to do bad things by ensuring that individuals in a metropolis are isolated and divided, resistance can only occur when people gather as a group. Matsumoto has suggested that one attraction of the recycling shop is that it is a place that enables communication. From this perspective, Yamashita started sites both in shops and on the streets known as 'Zero Yen Shops' where free goods were offered. He did this because he enjoyed talking to the people who came to take the goods. He also set up a place known as 'Basshop' – a play on words involving the Japanese word for place, *basho*, and the word 'shop' – in front of Kōenji Station purely to enable people to gather together. In addition, there was a place in Kōenji called the 'Things-will-work-out-somehow Bar' (*Nantoka bā*).[3] This bar, which had a new manager each day, functioned to bring diverse people together. Although paying rent on the property, Matsumoto was unable to work in the bar every day. He therefore advertised for daily managers who paid the venue fee and bore the running costs for the bar on a particular day (Matsumoto 2016b: 78–87). At the time of writing, there have been a wide range of managers, including a Taiwanese activist and even Social Democratic Party lower house representative Fukushima Mizuho (Fukushima 2012; Matsumoto 2012a; Chokusō kafe 2012). Rather than running at a profit, the collaboratively operated bar functioned as a place where people could gather to form bonds. Central to this format were notions of 'autonomy' and 'gathering'. This emphasis on 'autonomy' and 'gathering' further contributed to a positive understanding of amorphousness as 'fun' rather than disorder.

Conclusion

In this chapter, I have examined how the amorphous movement known as 'Amateur Revolt' developed from values and attitudes opposed to integration into systems. The group instead valorized autonomy and groups of people gathering or assembling together. Demonstrations and events held by Amateur Revolt were free spaces open to a diverse range of people that became 'uproars' characterized by 'play' and 'fun'. The creation of 'uproar' and 'fun' was made possible when people of varying backgrounds – such as Matsumoto Hajime and Yamashita Hikaru – joined forces. From the outset, Matsumoto created a movement that was not a movement in the classic sense, while Yamashita performed and made art in sites not necessarily directly connected to the movement. In spite of their diverse perspectives, both were attracted to the idea of demonstrations as 'fun', and therefore networked to create an amorphous gathering that promoted a range of events that enabled people to gather together. Beginning in April 2011 with 15,000 people in attendance, Japan's anti-nuclear power demonstrations emerged from an amorphous movement similar to Amateur Revolt.

5 Twenty Years of Confrontation: Against the Ossification of US Military Bases in Okinawa

TORIYAMA Atsushi

Surge of the times: Perspectives on Okinawa's history

Across a twenty-year span from the mid-1990s, Okinawan society was rattled by plans for the construction of a new US military base within the prefecture. The progress of such construction plans, as outlined further in this paper, depended intrinsically upon decisions made by the prefectural governor and the prefectural and municipal assemblies, as well as the head of the municipality where the planned military base was to be located. In order to achieve their goals, social movements opposed to the base construction had to contend with the issue of majority formation within the system of indirect democracy. Consequently, accounts describing Okinawa's history of conflict over new base construction are rendered insufficient when perspectives are limited to approaches undertaken by existing anti-base movements, which tend to focus only on current conditions surrounding the (physical) site of planned base construction. It thus becomes crucial to locate descriptions in the correct historical context by elucidating corresponding changes in Okinawa's social consciousness.

On the consecutive demise of two political figures that exemplified Okinawa's post-war passage, Miyagi Etsujirō, a prominent researcher of the history and social consciousness of Okinawa, wrote in 2001:

> Post-war developments in Okinawa's politics have consistently evolved around problems surrounding US military bases (stationing of US military forces in Japan). To speak without fear of being disparaged for oversimplifying the situation, the solution lies in choosing either of the following options – to accept and resign oneself to the "reality" brought about by the presence of the US military and focus on materializing

possibilities permissible within those boundaries, or to criticize and prosecute that said "reality" in hope and pursuit of the possibilities that lie beyond. (Miyagi, E. 2001)

In the above quote, Miyagi was primarily referring to Senaga Kamejirō, former secretary-general of the Okinawa People's Party, who was largely regarded as the symbol of opposition during the period of US military administration, and Nishime Junji, who aided in the formation of the Liberal Democratic Party (LDP) of Okinawa over the same period, subsequently serving as the governor of post-reversion Okinawa for twelve years. In his observations, Miyagi avoids comparing the politicians through the use of typical polarizing axes, instead framing his explanation by highlighting the different ways in which both men have chosen to react to 'reality' and the ensuing question of whether to explore tolerable possibilities within set boundaries or to pursue prospects that may be available beyond. This particular outlook may be useful in relativizing arguments based primarily on the use of divergent axes (e.g. conservative/liberal, pro-American/anti-American, pro-base/anti-base), helping to free us from implicitly assuming a stable, static form of political force that is crystalized and unchangeable.

Furthermore, emphasis must also be placed upon the way Miyagi uses the term 'reality'. His intentional use of quotation marks implies the ongoing need to question how the term should be perceived, given the assumption that reality is the amalgamation of a singular, collective awareness. It is precisely because of the nebulous nature of this 'reality' that one is faced with the endless examination of how much may be wagered upon its possibilities.

Accounts of confrontations over new base construction that have taken place from the mid-1990s should be presented as a series of dynamic situations embodying inconsistent and variable conditions. Instead of reducing descriptions of Okinawa's journey of opposition to a struggle against static political forces, this paper aims to capture the amorphous turbulences of Okinawa's history as a chain of meandering outcomes formed through fission and contention.

Shift from oppositional stance to plans for a new military base

The 'Okinawa people's mass rally', a collective citizens' protest held on 21 October 1995, serves as a critical event in considering current circumstances surrounding the issue of US military bases in Okinawa. This mass demonstration was held in direct response to the gang rape of an Okinawan girl by three US military servicemen, which took place in September of the same year. Under the premise of voicing opposition to the repeated sexual offenses committed upon the local population across half a century, the mass demonstration called for a review of the US-Japan security alliance, as well as a reduction of the US military presence in Okinawa. Official data released by the event's organizers placed attendance rates at 85,000, making the rally the largest public citizens' gathering since the return of Okinawa to Japan in 1972. The event was also non-partisan: members of Okinawa's opposition parties joined hands with members of the main political party, prompting observers to draw comparisons to the 'All-island struggle' of the 1950s and christen the event 'the second wave' of Okinawa's protest movement.

Then Prefectural Governor Ōta Masahide, who took to the stage at the rally to address attendees, announced that he had refused to place his signature on documents to extend leases on private land rented to the US military, a system that enabled the mandatory expropriation of land by the US military in Okinawa. Not only was this an outright declaration of defiance against the repeated enforcement of a special measures law by Japan's central government to guarantee continued usage of land by the US military, Ōta's actions also signaled a clear objection to the continuation of more than five decades of the US military's protracted presence in Okinawa.

Most notably, however, was how the strong oppositional sentiment festering across Okinawan society at the time acted to propel Ōta to reject his role in obligatorily approving use of local land by the US military. This is clearly evident in Ōta's previous difficulty in officially declaring his stance, having been publicly quoted at the end of July 1995 saying '[the refusal to sign my approval] is a simple act, but one that cannot be done easily', and 'the matter [of eliminating US bases in Okinawa] must take into consideration its negative impact on Okinawa's economy' (Arasaki 2005: 150). Prior to this, in 1991, faced with the inevitable decision of the mandated authorization of US military land use, Ōta reluctantly conceded to the land expropriation after failing to make headway in repeated attempts at negotiations with the central government for the eventual return of leased land. Ōta's actions thus indicated an unwilling compromise in exchange for expectations of future progress on the issue of US military bases stationed in the prefecture (Okinawa Taimususha 1996: 56–57).

Ōta's open refusal was catalyzed by Okinawans' growing frustration with the presence of the US military triggered by the rape incident. Women were particularly vocal in their opposition to the military bases. Delegates arriving home from participating in the Beijing's Women Conference were accosted by news of the rape, sparking them to mobilize in direct opposition to prolonged years of exposure to acts of sexual violence perpetrated by the military, and prompting an examination of the larger question of why the perpetrators were even in Okinawa in the first place (Okinawa Taimususha 1996: 24).

On 28 September 1995, Ōta publicly announced his refusal to approve the lease renewal for the US military's continued use of private land, and was quoted as saying 'women who have participated in the mass rally were asking why they "weren't treated rightfully as human beings" [...] and why the people of Okinawa must be made to suffer intolerably' (Okinawa Taimususha 1996: 59). His comments were made in light of a potentially detrimental situation looming on the horizon for Okinawa: despite the end of the Cold War in the early 1990s, Japan and the US had announced plans to continue deploying some 100,000 servicemen in East Asia, casting a dark shadow over plans to reduce the size of the US military's presence in Okinawa.

During negotiations with Prime Minister Murayama one month after his official proclamation, Ōta commented on his decision, sharing his belief that he 'could not continue to authorize the ossification of military bases in Okinawa into the twenty-first century'. At a press conference two weeks later, he added, 'I hereby reject sacrificing the rights of

Okinawa, as well as the rights of our people to a humane way of life, as a means of ensuring peace for the [Japanese] mainland. We have sacrificed more than enough during the war [on Okinawa]' (Okinawa Taimususha 1996: 55–56). Ōta's comments were an open recognition of his deep, fundamental distrust of the central government's approach in pushing the negative outcomes of the US-Japan security alliance onto Okinawa, particularly in terms of the stationing of US forces in the prefecture.

In response, the Japanese government filed an execution of public duties lawsuit against Ōta in December 1995. After more than fifty years of repeated neglect and inaction, the government's move sparked awareness of the problems surrounding the stationing of US forces in Okinawa as a national political issue, garnering fresh attention to the ensuing responses from the US and Japanese governments. While managing to avoid a legal interregnum in the provision of leased land to the US military, the Japanese government was made to assume a conciliatory approach in the form of facilitating the realignment and reduction of US forces in Okinawa.

The Base Return Action Program (Beigun kichi henkan akushon puroguramu) initiated by prefectural authorities in January 1996 called for the materialization of the full reversion of all US military bases in Okinawa by the year 2015. Official responses by the Japanese and US governments were made clear in SACO's (Special Action Committee on Okinawa) midterm report released in April of the same year, which announced the full return of five out of a total of forty-one US-owned military bases in the prefecture and the partial return of an additional six facilities. Reversion, however, would only be carried out on the condition of replacement with alternative locations within Okinawa. Both the Japanese and US governments began pushing aggressively for the full return of Futenma Air Base, one of the targets of SACO's reversion plans, lobbying with an attitude of commitment to realigning and reducing the US military presence in Okinawa. Conversely, conditions that called for the provision of a suitable site for Futenma's relocation would trigger a series of serious, long-term consequences for Okinawan society.

Despite suggestions for Futenma to be merged with an existing base facility, both governments eventually settled on a plan to construct a floating maritime facility in the eastern waters off Okinawa's main island. In January 1997, the surrounding seas of Camp Schwab in Nago City were named as the proposed site of construction of the new replacement facility. Governor Ōta and the mayor of Nago City did not publicly voice objections to this move, moving instead to grant approval for the Naha Regional Defense Facilities Administration Bureau to conduct initial soil boring surveys of the planned site. The ambiguous stance of the Ōta administration towards this issue can be traced back to 8 September 1996, when a public referendum was held in Okinawa seeking a revision of the US-Japan security alliance, as well as the realignment and reduction of US military forces within the prefecture. Fifty-three % of the voting public participated in the poll, with an overwhelming 89% voting in favor of the move. Just two days later, however, in a dialogue with then Prime Minister Hashimoto, Ōta announced his compliance with the execution of his official duties in approving land lease renewal documents on 13 September. Arasaki Moriteru, in analyzing the historical significance of Ōta's decision, wrote:

> The prime minister's statements from Diet proceedings announced in the wake of the Hashimoto-Ōta dialogue promised nothing new with regards to the base issue apart from a verbal promise towards sincere endeavor. In concrete terms, this can be identified as the following – the government's commitment to budgetary measures worth five billion yen (50,000,000,000) under the Act on Special Measures for the Promotion and Development of Okinawa, and the establishment of the Okinawa Policy Council […]. Despite this, Ōta sounded his approval for the outcomes of his dialogue with PM Hashimoto, moving to resume executive duties in authorizing continued use of land by the US military. Just one year after publicly eschewing his role in the official sanctioning of US bases in Okinawa, the all-island opposition movement led by Ōta came to an abrupt end. The Okinawan people were thus left to resume the struggle on their own to fill the vacuum created by Ōta's departure. (2016: 97)

As a fait accompli stacked up against the unwillingness of Ōta and the mayor of Nago City to clarify their stance on plans for Futenma's relocation, a mounting sense of danger amongst residents of Nago City coalesced into the formation of a committee for the promotion of a citizens' referendum in June 1997. Efforts by the committee galvanized into a petition carrying the signatures of 46% of Nago's voting public calling for the enactment of legislation to hold a city-wide referendum. The sheer number of citizens petitioning for change prompted a shift in the policy of the city government, which had already begun moving towards conditional acceptance of plans for the construction of the replacement facility. In December 1997, citizens of Nago City went to the polls, but the referendum itself contained a critical alteration. The question originally carried only two response options – 'Agree' and 'Disagree' – but was later changed to include two additional categories: 'Agree, because environmental measures and improvements to the local economy may be expected' and 'Disagree, because environmental measures and improvements to the local economy may not be expected'. This resulted in a poll question with four response options. The leader of the movement behind the referendum, Miyagi Yasuhiro, recalled the event in an essay published ten years after the public poll:

> The distortion of the citizens' referendum into one that carried four choices triggered the desires of people who indicated that they would agree to the construction of the replacement facility if economic benefits could be expected. The mayor at the time, who appeared to oppose construction plans and displayed a neutral stance towards moves for the referendum, was actively involved in activities organized by the Citizens' Association for the Promotion of the Revitalization of Nago City [Nago-shi kasseika sokushin shimin no kai], a consolidated group comprising representatives from the construction industry, as well as commerce and industrial chambers. This group, which was in favor of conditional acceptance of the replacement facility, received flagrant patronage from the central authorities. In the small community that is Nago City, people who wielded power worked to gain favor for

their cause, creating a situation where fellow residents were pitted against each other, locked in mutual confrontation. (2008: 16–17)

Just days before the referendum, key members of the central government including the cabinet secretary descended upon Nago City in the name of conducting hearings on public opinion concerning the revitalization of Okinawa's northern region. In addition to copious efforts exerted by local groups that were fronted by members of the construction industry, staff members of the Naha Regional Defense Facilities Administration Bureau were sent in to conduct door-to-door canvassing of every household in Nago City. In response to massive mobilization by the pro-construction camp that included government bodies, residents opposed to the replacement facility formed a new committee (Committee Against Helicopter Base Construction / Kaijou heri kichi kensetsu hantai kyougikai), embarking on a campaign to drum up support at the grassroots level. Eventual outcomes of the referendum revealed that a combined percentage of 52.8% disagreed with the construction of the replacement facility, overshadowing the 45.3% who voted in favor of it (Asasaki 2016: 102–103). In recapitulating the Nago citizens' movement, Miyagi pays particular attention to the nature of citizen participation, which differed from conventional political campaigning, while reserving special mention for women and the significance of their role:

> Instead of voicing their personal opinions or engaging in debates on political ideology, women would often have conversations about "community development". The rape incident committed by US servicemen happened just two years before, and part of the reason could be attributed to a sense of dread that a facility, which would house the very same type of military personnel, was headed for the place they called home. Women who usually kept their distance from political elections and activities within political society felt an inherent responsibility to take action […]. I somehow feel that these women encapsulated the true meaning of the concept of having an "opinion", letting their voices be heard not through the use of faltering ideology, but rather through reality lived as members of the community. (Miyagi, Y. 2008: 113–115)

The structure of the anti-base protests exemplified by these women is clearly amorphous, albeit reinforced by a keen sense of crisis, mutually identifiable objectives and a common lived reality as residents faced with the prospect of a changing living environment brought about by the proposed construction of a replacement facility for Futenma.

Administrative permission and Henoko's obstruction

Days after the citizens' referendum, the mayor of Nago met with PM Hashimoto before indicating his acceptance of the replacement base, simultaneously announcing his decision to resign. Elections held to select the next mayor were conducted in February 1998, and the city opted to elect a candidate who promised to 'respect the judgment of the prefectural governor with regards to the replacement facility', edging out his competitor who openly campaigned against base construction.

Towards the end of the Nago mayoral election campaign, Ōta officially expressed that he was against construction plans for the replacement facility, triggering a knee-jerk response from the incumbent party that it was 'unequivocally against joining hands with the Ōta administration, which had broken its promise' to the central government. This caused widespread apprehension that budgetary plans driving promotion and development plans for Okinawa would be recalled if the prefecture continued to be led by Ōta (Miyagi, Y. 2008: 106). Such concerns were clearly manifested in gubernatorial elections held in Okinawa in November of the same year, where a political newcomer, Inamine Keiichi (chairman of the Okinawa Executive Association, 'Okinawa kei-ei-sha kyoukai'), with the full backing of Okinawa's local LDP chapter, embarked on a campaign emphasizing the use of slogans focused on highlighting the prefecture's economic stagnation and high unemployment rate of 9.2%. In addition to drawing attention to the shortcomings of the Ōta administration's confrontational stance against the central government with regards to the issue of military bases, Inamine's campaign promised that the planned base in Nago would only be leased to the US military for fifteen years; thereafter it would be converted into a shared facility for

Photo 5.1: Henoko seashore and fence before the beginning of construction in 2011. Source: taken by the author.

use as a joint military-civil airport (Arasaki 2005: 189–190). Inamine successfully won office, and with his appointment came change. The Okinawa Policy Council, whose workings had been suspended by the central government for more than a year, was resumed a day after election outcomes were announced, and arrangements were made to facilitate budgetary allocation for strategies to promote and develop Okinawa (Arasaki 2005: 192).

However, transformations in Okinawa concerned with budgetary policies for the prefecture's promotion and development cannot simply be attributed to this change in its political administration. With regards to the policy formation process, Arasaki wrote:

> During the 1990s, national policies aimed at promoting and developing Okinawa were the interwoven outcome spun from the central government's desire to continue containing US military facilities within Okinawa, in addition to the hopes of the Ōta administration, which envisioned a

base-free, economically thriving Okinawa through the assistance of the Japanese government, as well as the interests of key players in Okinawa's business circle, who were focused on reaping quick, short-term benefits. Originally a blueprint by the Ōta administration for the creation of a global city in Okinawa, plans lay momentarily frozen from Ōta's rebellion against the central government, only to be resurrected immediately upon the change in Okinawa's political stewardship. (Arasaki 2005: 192)

Plans for developing Okinawa into a global city were conceptualized by the Ōta administration in January 1996. Along with this economic blueprint, the Base Return Action Program was created in tandem to achieve the gradual and systematic removal of all US bases. Although the appellation of Ōta's visions for Okinawa ceased to exist with his electoral defeat, attempts by the central government to maintain channels for soothing tensions in Okinawa found continuation and fortification through new plans for promoting and developing the prefecture.

In November 1999, one year after Inamine's victory, his administration announced that the coastline along the ward of Henoko in Nago City would be most ideal for the construction of the replacement facility. Shortly after, the Japanese government declared that the Diet would set aside 100 billion yen across a ten-year period as budgetary allocation for the Program for the Promotion and Development of Northern Okinawa (Arasaki 2005: 193–194). Upon official acceptance of construction plans for Henoko by the mayor of Nago City one month later, the Diet moved to establish a number of executive committees that included the prefectural governor and respective municipal heads as constituent members. Through such central government moves that 'appeared to be made out of respect for the opinions of the local community, the responsibility for decision-making over matters that included the size of the Henoko facility, construction methods, policy-making and the use of returned land after the reversion of Futenma were all singularly pushed into the hands of local municipal officials' (Arasaki 2005: 195) in a circumspect bid to avoid an outright expression of the people's will, as seen during the Nago City referendum. Such circumstances were clear evidence that construction plans for Henoko were progressively used to win over the prefectural governor, as well as local heads and municipal assemblies. These moves placed great emphasis and reliance upon the crystalized state of organized political structures within the local community.

On the other hand, in his initial acceptance of base construction plans, the Nago City mayor pledged that his agreement depended on seven clauses that included utmost consideration for environmental preservation, a limited fifteen-year lease period and the conclusion of an official agreement governing terms of use for the planned facility, reiterating his intention to withdraw his acceptance if concrete steps were not taken to materialize these conditions (Arasaki 2016: 108). In actuality, not only was there no reliable indication that the US authorities would comply with the mayor's requests, there was also no attempt by the Japanese government to conduct bilateral negotiations to achieve this end. The issue of the fulfillment of such conditions was left in limbo; at the beginning of the 2000s, both the incumbent governor of Okinawa and mayor of Nago City won landslide victories in their re-election campaigns, signaling what was thought to be the 'lowest point of citizens' movements' within the prefecture (Arasaki 2005: 215). By then, formally organized anti-base protest movements usually fronted by members of opposition parties and labor unions had waned, considerably weakening their influence against the ossified structure of pro-base supporters who had begun winning over a large part of the local community.

Under such circumstances, a protest movement gained ground in Henoko, effectively halting construction work for the planned base. In April 2004, when the Naha Regional Defense Facilities Administration Bureau tried to conduct soil-boring surveys of the base site, concerned citizens arrived at the scene, initiating a long-term sit-in protest. In August of the same year, a US military helicopter crashed into the campus of a university located next to Futenma Air Base, exploding into flames. The incident reignited fears in the local community that the plans for the Henoko base would protractedly expose Okinawa to the dangers of hosting US military forces, triggering a new wave of dissent across the island. Despite such developments, the central government attempted to proceed with soil-boring tests in Henoko, installing scaffolds in shallow waters at the planned site. However, survey work continued to be drastically delayed by a series of non-violent acts of obstruction initiated by citizens, leading survey scaffolding to be removed by the Naha Regional Defense Facilities Administration Bureau in September of the following year. In his book, Arasaki speaks of the leaders of the obstruction movement:

> The struggle at Henoko represents an example of a "decidedly non-violent, efficacious fight solidified and buttressed by the consolidation of personal autonomy" [...]. Participants were mobilized not by organizations or groups of any kind, but came of their own personal accord, taking part on fixed days and times, while taking into consideration health conditions and daily living schedules. Some would stumble upon the protest by chance and stay to experience events that would forever alter their lives, while others came after getting to know of the experiences of other participants. At the heart of this movement were ties of solidarity amongst individuals that remained unseen and unaccounted for in statistical counts, and this network of support would go on to spread far beyond the shores of Okinawa. (Arasaki 2005: 221–222)

The protest movement that effectively put a halt to construction work on the planned Henoko base did not consist of crystallized forms of participation from specific organizations or local community groups. While the Inochio Mamoru Kai (Group for Life) organized by Henoko residents performed a central, functional role at the protest site, the movement was able to maintain its protest activities over an extended period of time, drawing strength from an amorphous and constant congregation of unconnected individuals, whose mobilization was neither systematic nor organized. Kinjō Yūji, the representative of Inochi no Kai, spoke of events at the time:

> I have always thought that this movement would not be limited to the community and be carried out not only by the local residents. Movements must involve the entire country, for if not, they would not be able to continue. Had this protest remained within Henoko, it would have been over in a matter of days. (Shin Okinawa Fōramu Kankou Kaigi 1996: 65)

Photo 5.2: The office of the Association for Protecting the Life of Henoko (Council to Stop Helicopter Base Construction) in 2011. The sign on the right reads, 'We will not allow the government to build a new base at Henoko. We will not allow the destruction of the quiet and rich environment. We will protect the rich sea where dugongs live. We will not allow the deployment of the MV Osprey in Okinawa. We will pass on our precious nature to our children and grandchildren'. Source: taken by the author.

Suspension of construction works for the new base in Henoko was achieved through protests undertaken not by organized, static congregations of local residents, but by an amorphous movement expanding far beyond the community, which exercised its efficacy even in a time when the local population of Henoko experienced deep divisions over the issue of the replacement facility.

Central government belligerence and a new wave of protests

In the wake of suspended construction works in the seas off Henoko, both the Japanese and US governments reached an agreement in October 2005, cancelling plans for the floating offshore military base and deciding instead on reclaiming land from Henoko's coastline to build a multi-functional facility. Not only would contents of this agreement potentially exacerbate the scale of damage to the lives of local residents in the vicinity and the environment, such details were decided upon without consultation with the prefectural governor or the mayor of Nago City. Both officials, who had officially agreed to conditional acceptance of a maritime facility in Henoko, were left with no room to negotiate. The agreement, which was concluded without consulting prefectural authorities, drew sharp criticism from Governor Inamine, who began calling for the removal of US Marine Corps from Okinawa (Arasaki 2016: 110).

In response, the central government enacted a law of special measures in April 2007 to facilitate the realignment of US forces stationed within the country, putting in place a system of subsidies in return for accepting realignment projects. Under this legislation, the minister of defense would select municipalities eligible for receiving subsidies, depending on their level of cooperation with realignment objectives. Miyagi Yasuhiro touches upon the historical significance of the change evident in the Japanese government's approach with the following observation:

> Towards the Ōta administration, which declared its opposition to plans for the Henoko replacement facility, the central government responded with clear, starvation-type tactics by suspending the convening of the Okinawa Policy Council. This invariably led Okinawa to change its approach, electing the conciliatory Governor Inamine, who conceded acceptance of Henoko on conditions of a limited, fifteen-year lease and joint civil use. Even as the Inamine administration maintained a state of politics that largely cooperated with the central government, it retained points of contention upon which it attempted to barter for

advantage. Eight years on, Okinawa would suffer from the gradual loss of conservative government heavyweights that included the inaugural Director-General of the Okinawa Development Agency, Yamanaka Sadanori, who were sympathetic to Okinawa's cause, giving way to a belligerent central government that was intent on forcing Okinawa to give up on its conditions for accepting realignment plans through the use of strong-arm tactics not unlike holdups at knifepoint. (2008: 79–80)

The government's fundamental shift in policy attitudes after 2005, as Miyagi puts it, points clearly at how central authorities nullified 'local consent' gleaned from years of prolonged negotiations to gain acceptance for the Henoko maritime facility, demolishing the foundations for compromise and cooperation. As the government transitioned from the Program for the Promotion and Development of Northern Okinawa to the system of subsidies within the Law of Special Measures for the Realignment of US Forces in Japan, Miyagi observes a series of *yo-gawari* (dynastic changes) as Okinawa underwent a change of government agencies from the development agency to the cabinet and lastly, the 'defense agency' (Arasaki 2016: 82). Here, the word '*yo-gawari*' bears larger in meaning and significance the experiences that have defined Okinawa and its history under the rule of different masters across time.

Policy changes after 2005 singularly dismissed the very 'local consent' that was to have formed the prerequisite for the replacement facility at Henoko. This consequently caused the crystalized pro-base stance which once successfully wooed the prefectural governor and municipal heads to transmute, paving the way for three large-scale non-partisan citizens' rallies to be held in Okinawa over a short time span.

The first of these mass mobilizations took place in September 2007, when public anger erupted at the ministry of education's move to impose changes and deletions of content concerning the Battle of Okinawa in its annual screening of textbooks designated for use in public schools. Earlier in the year in March, the ministry made recommendations for passages describing how soldiers of the Japanese Imperial Army had coerced civilians into committing mass suicide to be removed from history textbooks, prompting all local municipal assemblies in Okinawa to file a collective memorandum calling for the reversal of the decision. The prefectural assembly, which had earlier been informed of the ministry's decision to revise prescribed history textbooks, would proceed to approve the memorandum twice under the influence of Nakasato Toshinobu, who was the speaker of the prefectural assembly at that time. Nakasato, who survived the Battle of Okinawa as a child, would then go on to head the organizing committee for the citizens' rally of September 2007 (Arasaki 2016: 131–132).

A second citizens' rally followed shortly after in April 2010 to protest the construction of Futenma's replacement facility within Okinawa. The newly minted central administration, which was headed by the Democratic Party of Japan, stood by their campaign promise of moving Futenma's replacement to a location outside of Okinawa and Japan, paving the way four months later for a mayor with an anti-base stance to assume office in Nago City for the first time since 1997. Left in defeat, Okinawa's local chapters of the LDP-Kōmeitō coalition turned their backs on previous government plans for Futenma's replacement facility in Henoko, whose contents had been finalized in complete disregard of local opinion. Together, the disparate political parties of Okinawa came together to organize a non-partisan mass citizens' rally in protest of the Futenma replacement facility in Henoko.

The third such rally was a large-scale protest that occurred in September 2012 to object to the deployment of tilt-rotor US military aircraft, commonly known as Ospreys, to Futenma Air Base. The organizing committee for the 2012 rally traveled to Tokyo representing all local assemblies and municipal heads and personally handed a petition to the Abe administration, which had emerged victorious from general elections to regain control of the government. This move, which provided the initiative for prefectural politics to successfully overcome its discordant partisanship, set the momentum for the mobilization of citizen demonstrations that would once again be termed 'all-Okinawa' and 'island-wide'.

Despite these efforts, the central government proceeded with bilateral negotiations with the US, agreeing to press on with construction of the Futenma replacement facility and filing procedures for the approval of reclamation works in state-owned waters off Henoko to prefectural authorities in March 2013. Against such clear attempts to ram through with construction works, in December 2013 the Okinawa chapter of the LDP backtracked on advocating for the replacement facility to be located outside of Okinawa. This was followed shortly after by Governor Nakaima Hirokazu's dialogue with Prime Minister Abe at his official quarters, as well as his decision to approve land reclamation works at Henoko (Arasaki 2016: 148–151).

As the central government gradually revealed its aggressive stance in pushing ahead with construction at Henoko, Okinawa's pro-base movement began to see a departure of supporters that were once sympathetic to its cause. Nakasato, leader of the organizing committee for the citizens' rally protesting the issue of textbook revision in 2007, resigned from his position as the advisor of the LDP's Okinawa chapter in protest of its support for base construction, before declaring his departure from the political party in November 2013. He then threw his weight behind the incumbent mayor of Nago City, campaigning in support of his anti-base cause during elections held in January 2014. In a symposium held six months later, Nakasato reflected negatively upon ditched plans for the Futenma maritime facility, elaborating that 'the base would have become an Okinawa-owned asset after its limited fifteen-year lease. There were intentions to use this condition as an opportunity to subsequently drive all US Marines out of Okinawa, which was the reason why [I] supported the move [...]. But now, even this concession is no longer available' (Okinawa Kokusai Daigaku Okinawa Housei Kenkyūjyo 2015: 58). Nakasato's deep resentment can be traced back to the experience of having the hard-won concessions that were achieved by persistently prioritizing a cooperative attitude with the central government unilaterally withdrawn by the very same authorities. Nakasato's opposition varied in nature from the antipathy of those protesting against plans for Henoko from the outset, which accounts for why he became one of the most representative voices unifying 'all-Okinawa' in the 'island-wide' protest movements that subsequently took place. At the same symposium, Nakasato stated:

> I am convinced that the governments of Japan and the US have changed strategies for Okinawa and are poised to use Okinawa as the fortress that it was before the war, pushing it onto the frontlines if need be. If this is indeed the case, US bases should not be allowed to remain in Okinawa. In fact, I would also wish for Japan's Self-Defense Forces to leave the prefecture. (Okinawa Kokusai Daigaku Okinawa Housei Kenkyūjyo 2015: 48)
>
> Whatever the agreement between Japan and America, we must stand determinedly to say that we will neither accept it nor give in. For if not, this would most certainly be the end of Okinawa. And I will not stand for that to happen! (Okinawa Kokusai Daigaku Okinawa Housei Kenkyūjyo 2015: 80)

Nakasato continued by observing that in order to successfully subvert the central government's attempts to forcibly implement plans for the replacement facility at Henoko, the Okinawan people must consciously reject the use of 'colonialist strategies' where 'acrimony would be sowed amongst fellow residents and money used for the purpose of luring support for the government's cause' (Okinawa Kokusai Daigaku Okinawa Housei Kenkyūjyo 2015: 45).

Onaga Takeshi, the former top brass for the LDP's Okinawa chapter who provided key support for the Inamine and Nakaima administrations after 1998, echoed similar sentiments at a public discussion in April 2013:

> The people of Okinawa have been made to face the issue of hosting US bases, which have been placed here against their own accord, while engaging in divisive arguments about whether they should be prioritizing the local economy or the US forces. I can't help but feel angry that the rest of Japan remains condescending to our predicament [...]. It has always been my belief from some twenty years ago that our

current situation will persist as long as our people do not stand together in a unified movement against this, and I am convinced that the time has now come for us to do so. (Ryūkyū Shimpōsha 2018: 37–38)

Onaga was not merely generalizing in an attempt to spark unity amongst the voting populace. His comments were delivered at a point in time when the hard-won outcomes of Okinawa's compliance with the central government's wishes had been swiftly undermined, forcing upon its people the burden of having to stand up against the central government. This situation accounted for the urgency in Onaga's call for immediate action.

Onaga's words did not simply echo the sentiments of political parties or assemblymen seeking re-election. In retracing the events in Okinawa over a ten-year period following the citizens' referendum of Nago City, Miyagi's observations point clearly to the long-standing rifts and confrontations that local communities have had to endure:

> More than the number of local residents, the site of protests against base construction in Henoko has seen more continued participation from people living outside of Okinawa, who staunchly uphold their anti-base beliefs. I hold deep respect for their strong commitment and determination; as a resident of Nago City, I am faced with complex emotions each time I hear these protestors rightfully calling the Henoko base "a place built for murder". When a town as small as Nago is divided into opposing polarities, many ordinary folk try to carry on with their everyday lives while burying their honest thoughts and opinions deep within their hearts, naturally growing accustomed to avoiding mention of the issue even when conversing with their neighbors. These rightfully spoken words become vilification for the people themselves, which spread hurt and are hurt in return. (Miyagi, Y. 2008: 14)

The above observations not only ring true for the community of Nago, but also to varying degrees for the 'everyday lives' of people within the larger community of Okinawa, which is tainted with struggle and distress. Such daily realities are included in Onaga's reference to the 'divisive arguments' evident within Okinawan society, bringing new possibilities and potential to his call for a 'unified movement' of Okinawa's people. Onaga subsequently ran for office in November 2014, edging out the pro-base incumbent Governor Nakaima in a landslide victory with a margin of more than 100,000 votes.

Caught between the protests at Henoko which have persisted as a result of the amorphous mobilization of people from diverse backgrounds and the immovable pro-base organization which had won the community over was the mounting silence of local residents, whose steadily growing estrangement could no longer be ignored. Despite this, the antagonistic approach undertaken by the central government worked against it by weakening the once-crystalized pro-Henoko sentiment of the local political base, eventually culminating in Onaga's fateful departure from its influence.

Onaga's words, which not only pledged to permanently stem divisions surrounding the issue of US forces within Okinawan society, sought to reinterpret the estrangement between Henoko's protestors and ordinary residents, transforming it into momentum for the amalgamation of the Okinawan people to form a strong, unified front.

With Onaga's election as prefectural governor, the unstructured protests that continued at the proposed site for the replacement facility at Henoko found reinforcement within the framework of indirect democracy, coalescing with processes for majority formation. While the nature of the Henoko protests remained unchanged, the significance of their amorphousness was renewed in the tide of the opposition movement against the central government.

Prospects for the future

In January 2013, Onaga traveled to Tokyo in his capacity as the mayor of Naha City, displaying clear displeasure over the unilateral deployment of Ospreys in Okinawa. He declared, 'Okinawa was sacrificed in exchange for Japan's freedom, enduring administration under the US military government for twenty-seven years […]. During this time, Japan has behaved as if it had been maintaining domestic peace on its own, enjoying the fruits of rapid economic growth' (Ryūkyū Shimpōsha 2018: 30). Following these comments, Onaga further expressed distrust in the country of Japan and its people for continually making use of Okinawa, adding in a public debate three months later, 'In a way, I feel that the move to station US bases in Okinawa has been an "all-Japan" one, one chosen by the Japanese people to ensure peace and prosperity for the mainland' (Ryūkyū Shimpōsha 2018: 37–38).

Onaga's statements not only embody resistance against the continued stationing of most of Japan's US forces in Okinawa, but also highlight the peculiar difficulties faced by island regions in their isolation from the arc of economic progress enjoyed by the Japanese mainland. Given these conditions and the inherent fragility of local industries, the structure of crystalized support for the construction of the replacement facility at Henoko hints at how Okinawa's perennial vulnerability drives it to seek protection and assistance from the central government. Despite the many concessions made in exchange for financial aid, such danger continues to loom, evident from Miyagi's following observations concerning Nago City in the 2000s after the introduction of the Program for the Promotion and Development of Northern Okinawa:

> The major foundation of the revitalization project for Nago City was the implementation of a special economic zone for information technology and finance to woo investors to the region. Buildings that could be leased to private companies would be constructed using funding utilized from assistance schemes, whose inexpensive rental was incentive for technology firms (mostly call centers) to set up base in Nago […]. City officials would work to lure companies to invest with promises of cheap labor supply. Revitalization plans took off with the investment of tens of billions of yen, together with the city's provision of an affordable workforce in the form of waiting residents. (Miyagi, Y. 2008: 95)
>
> There are many young people who remain unemployed in Nago. One major factor for this is the decline of the city's key industry of agriculture, which triggers problems such as unemployment and poverty. Such excess labor would eventually be absorbed by the construction industry undertaking public works, which draws attention to the constant struggle

that people face in terms of unemployment and difficulties in finding new work, due to reasons such as company insolvency and bankruptcy. (Miyagi, Y. 2008: 95)

Against the backdrop of Japan's economic policy of market liberalization and the continued weakening of the domestic agricultural industry, the provision of public projects, which functioned as a stop-gap measure, began to wane from the 2000s. Given current conditions for revitalization and development, where the city of Nago has chosen to proceed with the installation of new business infrastructure that would become sources of employment for its affordable supply of labor in exchange for its acceptance of the Henoko replacement facility, forecasts for the future remain difficult. In the search for solutions to the nebulous nature of 'reality' as established at the start of this paper, one is also forced to come to terms with an accompanying set of interwoven and complex structural issues.

Counter to such developments is the rise of a booming international tourism market in Okinawa, as well as growing anticipation of new capital investment. Such buoyancy has been used contextually in the push for moves to reject base construction plans in Henoko. Taira Chōkei (chairman of Okinawa's Kariyushi group of hotels), key spokesperson for 'all-Okinawa' and 'island-wide' opposition movements, noted in a 2013 symposium that a 'market worth 1.9 billion yen exists within a four-hour radius from Okinawa, which is the reason why we have to leverage Okinawa's geographical superiority, transforming it from military to economic dominance. [...] Okinawa plays a crucial role as the gateway to Asia, and this role is poised to become more significant in future. Having military bases here will only serve to hinder our economic growth' (Okinawa Kokusai Daigaku Okinawa Housei Kenkyūjyo 2015: 68, 75). Taira's comments have been strongly echoed by Onaga, who shares similar sentiments:

> Okinawa no longer exists along the periphery of Japan. The possibilities for developing land reverted from military purposes has enormous potential for use as prime locations for domestic and international capital

investment, as well as the nurturing of industries such as tourism and IT [...]. The US bases of today are mere obstacles to the progress of Okinawa's economy. (Ryūkyū Shimpōsha 2018: 44)

Buoyant hopes that investors seeking to gain advantage from Okinawa's potential as an international tourist destination would invest in land returned by the US military have served as motivation behind the prefecture's attempts to break free from the illegitimacies it has sustained throughout its history. At the very foundations of this ideal stood Onaga, who shared his dream of an Okinawa that serves as 'the center of Asian dynamism', whose rich abundance would be derived from 'soft power in the form of pride for its natural environments, history and traditional culture' (Ryūkyū Shimpōsha 2018: 52).

Amorphous protests occurring in Henoko share one clear and common goal with the Onaga administration – the renouncement of plans for the construction of Futenma's replacement facility. However, when observational focus shifts from the opposition movement itself to the 'reality' envisioned beyond the objective of halting base construction, there exists no uniform collective vision for Okinawa's future, even within the 'all-Okinawa' and 'island-wide' protests led by Onaga himself. The amorphous nature of the movement's political intent thus contrasts starkly with the crystallized axis of its political coalescence.

Although this may very well be the manifestation of an Okinawa poised at the threshold of an unforeseeable future, it remains to be seen if the sudden expansion of international tourism will herald the beginnings of a society that continues to supply foreign investors with affordable labor, or one that opens itself up to a set of fresh possibilities. As the path to Okinawa's future becomes clearer, so will perceptions of its 'reality' that revolves around the stationing of US forces and military bases within the prefecture.

6 Opposing Hate Speech in Japan: Valuing Differences and Breaking New Ground for Human Rights

TANNO *Kiyoto*

Introduction

In Japan, *Honpō-gai shusshinsha ni taisuru futō na sabetsuteki gendō no kaishō ni muketa torikumi no suishin ni kansuru hōritsu* ('The Act on the Promotion of Efforts to Eliminate Unfair Discriminatory Speech and Behavior Against Persons Originating from Outside Japan'; hereafter, the 'Antihate Act') was simultaneously legislated and promulgated on 3 May 2016. The immediate enforcement was highly unusual, as most acts in modern times undergo a certain period of adjournment between their passage and commencement to allow for notification of the public. A notable exception was when many laws were put into effect on the day of promulgation early on in the Meiji Restoration.[1] This fast-tracking clearly points to the pressing need to regulate hate speech in Japan at the time. In fact, the act exerted an effect from the day prior to its commencement, on 2 May 2016, when the Yokohama District Court handed down a provisional disposition order to stop a hate speech rally on the basis of the Antihate Act.

The way in which the Antihate Act actually operates indicates that the National Diet as Japan's legislative branch, the court as the judicial branch and the ministry of justice as the executive branch have endorsed a completely new set of values concerning the rights of foreigners. Recognition has been given to the situation in which communities are formed in an amorphous manner where Japanese, foreigners and dual citizens blend together instead of the previously dichotomous understanding of the relationship between nationals (Japanese) and foreigners. This situation that entails completely new rights is being created by the social awareness that the rights of an entire community, including foreigners, must be defended if the rights of the Japanese members of the community are to be protected where the community is ethnically diverse and amorphously composed in terms of the legal status of its constituent members.

Historical process of fighting racial discrimination

In 1970, a young man disembarked from a train at Yokohama Station. He was Chonsok Pak (朴鐘碩) of Nishio City, Aichi Prefecture, to whom Hitachi had made an informal offer of employment as a high school graduate but withdrew it after discovering that he was an ethnic South/North Korean permanent resident of Japan ('Zainichi Korean'). He came to Kanagawa thinking that he might receive assistance in dealing with the job offer withdrawal because the prefecture had a large Japanese-born Korean population. The first people who approached him in Yokohama were students campaigning against the Vietnam War. The quick-thinking students contacted interested parties to form the 'Mr Pak Support Group' and began to provide him with assistance. This was the start of the Hitachi Employment Discrimination Trial, which became an important labor law precedent banning employment discrimination in Japan.[2]

Chonsok Pak is a second-generation Zainichi Korean who was born and raised in Japan and went to Japanese schools under his Japanese name, Shōji Arai. He grew up without even knowing how to pronounce his real name in Korean. He left his hometown to seek support from fellow Korean expatriates after his experience of employment discrimination, but it was Japanese people who reached out to him instead.[3] Jungdo Bei (裵重度) saw what was happening while he was living in Kawasaki and felt that Pak's problem was common to all Zainichi Koreans and that they were obliged to support him. Bei resolved that he would endeavor to eliminate prejudice and discrimination in everyday life as well as in employment. He met with Reverend Inha Li (李仁夏) of the Kawasaki Korean Christian Church, one of the proponents of the Mr Pak Support Group, to organize community study meetings on the issue.[4] Sengoku Yoshito (仙谷由人), one of Pak's lawyers in the Hitachi Trial, argued as follows:

> Racial prejudice is a matter of the human mind and is impossible to prove at trial. The court is where arguments are made to establish facts. How can an intellectual question be proven there?
> We cannot win the case if we fight over racial discrimination. We should simply argue that the making of an informal job offer constituted an employment contract under labor laws. (Bei 2011: 11)

In contrast, Bei and others insisted that the campaign would lose its meaning unless they claimed that it was employment discrimination on the basis of racial discrimination (Bei 2011: 11).[5] Based on this understanding, they started educational and communal support programs mainly for second-generation Zainichi Koreans and formed Seikyū-sha ('*seikyū*' is a concept traditionally used by Korean people to describe the Korean peninsula in an elegant way). It drew the participation of local youths, student volunteers and the staff and teachers of primary and secondary schools, culminating in the formation of the Minzoku sabetsu to tatakau Kanagawa Renraku Kyōgikai (Coordination Committee to Combat Racial Discrimination in Kanagawa). The committee's activity peaked at the time of the 1990 revision of the Immigration Law and led to a movement for the abolition of compulsory fingerprinting on 'alien registration cards' for foreigners even if they had not committed a crime.

In 1996, Kawasaki City became the first municipality to set up a *gaikokujin shimin daihyōsha kaigi* (foreign citizens' advisory council), the purpose of which was to provide an institutional channel for the local government to hear the voices of unenfranchised foreign residents. Many other local governments followed Kawasaki in establishing foreign citizens' advisory councils but most were defined as mayors' private advisory panels. This meant that while the views of foreign residents were heard, it was up to each individual mayor to decide whether to act on them or not. On the other hand, Kawasaki set up its advisory council under a city ordinance from the outset in order to guarantee that the mayor would not only hear the voices of foreign residents but also assume responsibility for responding to their proposals. Takao Yamada, the city official who played an important role in planning and developing Kawasaki's advisory council in its incipient stage, was one of the student activists Pak had first encountered in Yokohama.

Today's amorphous awareness and John Locke

The idea behind the approach that takes an unstable amorphous state as its starting point originated in thermal dynamics and spread to biology (evolutionary biology in particular), chemistry, game theory, evolutionary economics and many other areas, with general theoretical models supplied by complex systems theory and statistical mechanics. Thermal dynamics provided the concept of 'time', giving the diverse fields of subsequent research a new axis. This is the idea that the state of an object progresses irreversibly along the temporal axis[6] suggested by molecular biologist Jacques Monod in his discussion of 'chance and necessity' in life and DNA reproduction[7] and animal behaviorist Nikolaas Tinbergen in his examination of change in animal behavioral patterns within the stimulus-response mechanism.[8] While their analyses are conducted at different levels, they both address the presence of a common pattern in understanding biological change. In both cases, a certain change occurs, interacts with the environment and stabilizes as a common characteristic of a particular species.[9] In contemporary biology, what was discussed by Monod and Tinbergen is considered within larger biological chains. Tamiji Inoue and Makoto Katō consider that pollination mutualism observed between plants and insects and plants and animals is not only a particular plant's survival strategy but also forms part of the cycles of life in the tropical rainforest in which those plants exist (Inoue and Katō 1993).[10]

These views came to be recognized as useful in the field of social science from the 1980s. Humans certainly have language and communicate it via sound and writing. Moreover, people with agency vary their behavior at will from time to time. These attributes lead us to think that humans are completely different from insects and animals which repeat programmed behaviors. According to Robert Axelrod (1984), however, stable international order is achieved as a result of various treaties made by superpowers through Machiavellian negotiations and maneuvers in which they employ a tit-for-tat strategy where one party betrays the other only if the latter betrays the former. This is no different from the activity of bacteria and other primitive life forms or even the motions of inorganic matter. With this insight from the evolutionary biological perspective and the statistical dynamic implications, it is possible to explain social phenomena involving human intentions in the previously inexplicable social domain (Auyang 1998; Shiozawa 1997b).[11] In doing so, social scientists focus their attention on 'fluctuation', 'self-organization' and 'environment' (Shiozawa 1997a).

In my view, the primordial form of amorphous thinking in the social sciences can be found in John Locke's *Two Treatises of Government*. The publication is extremely famous as a fundamental work in examining the concept of the modern state and civil society and argues that people are equal on the grounds of natural rights. While claiming equality among individuals on the basis of natural rights in principle, Locke accepts the existence of differences between certain attributes of people in society such as kings, aristocrats, burgesses, masters, craftsmen, various professionals, husbands (men), wives (women), parents, children and so on.

In fact, in the first paragraph of the preface of *Two Treatises*, Locke declares the purpose for which he wrote this book as follows:

> These, which remain, I hope are sufficient to establish the Throne of our Great Restorer, Our present King William; to make good his title, in the Consent of People, which being the only one of all lawful Governments, he has more fully and clearly than any Prince in Christendom: And to justify to the World, the People of England, whose love of their Just and Natural Rights, with their Revolution to preserve them, save the Nation when it was on the very brink of Slavery and Ruine. (Locke [1689] 1960: 137)

His objective was to justify the ascension of William of Orange, who had assented to *The Bill of Rights* and ruled jointly with his wife Mary II, to the English throne.

The Bill of Rights of 1689 states as follows:

> And thereupon their Majestyes were pleased That the said Lords Spirituall and Temporall and Commons being the two Houses of Parlyament should continue to sitt and with their Majesties Royall Concurrence make effectuall Provision for the Setlement of the Religion Lawes and Liberties of this Kingdome soe that the same for the future might not be in danger againe of being subverted, To which the said Lords Spirituall and Temporall and Commons did agree and proceede to act accordingly. Now in pursuance of the Premisses the said Lords Spirituall and Temporall and Commons in Parlyament assembled for the ratifying confirming and establishing the said Declaration and the Articles Clauses Matters and Things therein contained by the Force of a Law made in due Forme by Authority of Parlyament doe pray that it may be declared and enacted That all and singular the Rights and Liberties asserted and claimed in the said Declaration are the true auntient and indubitable Rights and Liberties of the People of this Kingdome and soe shall be esteemed allowed adjudged deemed and taken to be and that all and every the particulars aforesaid shall be firmly and strictly holden and observed as they are expressed in the said Declaration And all Officers and Ministers whatsoever shall serve their Majestyes and their Successors according to the same in all times to come. (Parliament of England 1688)

The true liberties and rights of the people claimed by the religious and secular nobles and common people have been ancient and unquestionable and so regarded, admitted, determined, believed and understood. In Locke's words, they are the rights and liberties of the individuals with natural rights.

> God makes him in his own Image after his own Likeness, makes him an Intellectual Creature, and so capable of Dominion. For wherein so ever

else the Image of God consisted, the intellectual Nature was certainly a part of it, and enabled them to have Dominion over the inferior Creatures. (Locke [1689] 1960: 162)

To Locke, human beings were equal as God's creation and should be treated equally for the above reason.

However, the equality intended by Locke is neither a fact nor an aim. Locke's idea of human equality is a background condition for various standpoints and policy positions (Waldron 2002: 2). Accordingly, what is needed most is for humans to respect one another. Locke depicts connection between people on the basis of 'mutual respect'. This human connection is simultaneously one of relatedness and of distinctiveness and at the time manifested in the form of the division of labor.

In short, Locke understood that although people are individual beings with different attributes, when they build a society based on the principle of 'mutual respect' (that is, the idea that individuals have natural rights), their respect for differences will connect them organically and create an even larger and stronger society in a self-organizing fashion. His idea does not explain society by reducing it to individuals nor by seeing it as an aggregate of individuals. To rearrange Locke's idea by incorporating contemporary complex systems theory, as the relationships formed by individuals grow in complexity and depth of meaning, the individuals and the whole will blend together and create a fluctuating social condition which in turn will define the subsequent condition; a society can only be understood as the active expression of it.

How hate speech rallies were controlled in Kawasaki

The themes used by hate speech rally organizers in Kawasaki changed over time from the first rally held on 12 May 2013. Initially, the rallying cry was to 'Protect Kawasaki against anti-Japanese left-wingers and miscreant foreigners'.[12] It then gradually changed to 'Don't tolerate anti-Japanese behaviors' and to 'Purify Japan' by the time protesters tried to march into the large Korean community in Sakuramoto District.[13] It is not surprising that the hate speech rallies organized by Zaitokukai (an ultranationalist far-right association) were based on the 'Purify Japan' theme and there was nothing particularly new about the contents of the hate speeches at their demonstrations. What is more noteworthy is the fact that local residents organized an 'anti-war' rally on 5 September in opposition to the hate speech rally (see Photo 6.1).[14] When we examine the actual contents of the hate speeches, we can understand why the counteraction mounted by those on the receiving end had to be called 'anti-war'. The far-right extremists refered to Zainichi Koreans as 'enemies' and 'enemy aliens', justifying their call for their 'deaths' and 'killings'. They asserted that enemies would be killed in a state of war in any country.

Around the time of the September anti-war rally, 'education' in the art of protest rallying began in Sakuramoto District. Tomohito Miura, Director of Seikyū-sha (former director of Fureaikan, Kawasaki), felt the need to express the 'will of the community' but also recognized the need to conduct their counter-protest rallies lawfully by obtaining the requisite permission from the police. He carefully tried to avoid the situation in which people (especially youths) with no prior experience in activism were arrested simply because they did not know the relevant rules.[15] Moreover, this activism education assumed the eventual incursion of hate speech rallies into Sakuramoto.

The blocking of the far-right demonstrators' passage through Sakuramoto was put into practice on 31 January 2016. This was the result of a change to the planned rally route instituted by the police out of concern over the potential for a clash between the group and the counter-protestors mobilized on the day. The young and elderly counter-protestors staged a sit-in at an intersection to block the far-right demonstrators and local residents formed a human shield around the counter-protestors to protect them. The police traveling alongside the far-right demonstrators directed the organizers to turn back. In comparison, the 6 June 2016 action to prevent a hate rally had a completely different raison d'être. The far-right mobilization was

Opposing Hate Speech in Japan

Photo 6.1: *Sakuramoto anti-war demonstration. Source: Fureaikan Kawasaki City.*

originally largely motivated by revenge for the 31-January blockade of the intended march through Sakuramoto. For this reason, the group applied to the municipal government for the use of the same route. However, Kawasaki City Mayor Norihiko Fukuda rejected the application and refused the use of Fujimi Park by the far-right demonstrators as their departure point.

The characteristics of hate speech control in Japan

How can we interpret hate speech control in Japan? The Antihate Act does not define what constitutes hate speech nor provide any clause to prohibit it. The intent of the legislators of this law is stated in a book called *Heito supīchi kaishō hō – Seiritsu no keii to kihontekina kangaekata* (The Hate Speech Elimination Act: Enactment process and basic thinking) as follows:

This act takes the form of a philosophical law rather than a ban. Our greatest concern was, in essence, to maintain the constitutionally guaranteed right to freedom of expression, a principal value that we must protect. As the result of that consideration, we declare in the Preamble that unfair discriminatory speech and behavior towards non-Japanese residents will not be tolerated in order to strengthen our efforts to eliminate unfair discriminatory speech and behavior by spreading awareness among the general public and promoting their understanding and cooperation through further human rights education and awareness-raising activities. (Uozumi et al. 2016: 8)

Uozumi et al. also state the following about how to control hate speech and behavior:

We must not allow such speech and behavior, including at various levels of government. There are many existing laws and regulations [that can be used] for that purpose. We believe that this legislation will provide guidance in interpreting various laws such as the noise prevention ordinances and the defamation law. The governments can use their inhibitive power, including this *combination technique*. (2016: 39; emphasis added)

A careful examination of the hate-rally ban in Kawasaki with these points in mind demonstrates the characteristics of Japan's hate speech control methods. The national press linked the rally ban solely to the passage of the Antihate Act in the Diet. Let us think about this correlation. Although the hate rally's application to march through Sakuramoto on 5 June 2016 was rejected, permission for a new route from Nakahara Peace Park in Nakahara District, Kawasaki, was granted. Thus, the hate rally was still allowed to go ahead, just in a different place. The blocking of the hate rally in Sakuramoto cannot therefore be explained by the impact of the Antihate Act alone.

The hate rally was unable to pass through Sakuramoto because the Kawasaki branch of the Yokohama District Court issued a provisional disposition on 2 June to prohibit the hate rally from coming within 500 meters of Seikyū-sha headquarters, a local social welfare organization set up by Zainichi Koreans (Yokohama District Court Kawasaki Branch Decision on 2 June 2016, Heisei 28 (Yo) No. 42 Application for Provisional Disposition Injunction against Hate Rally). This application was made by Seikyū-sha under President Jungdo Bei. The planned rally route would have encroached on the injunction area. On the strength of the court decision, the mayor of Kawasaki City was able to make a ruling prohibiting the use of Fujimi Park.

Let us review the contents of the court decision. It argues for the validity of the injunction against the hate rally on the grounds of the International Convention on the Elimination of All Forms of Racial Discrimination (Heisei 7 (1995) Convention No. 26) as an international law as well as two domestic laws – the Antihate Act due to be enforced the following day and the Social Welfare Act (Shōwa 26 (1951) Law No. 45). It contains the findings of fact, including that Sakuramoto is widely known as a district with a high concentration of Zainichi Korean residents who live there peacefully; that Seikyū-sha provides a range of community support activities for local residents, from childcare and after-school care to aged care; and that there have been significant invasions of personal rights threatening the existence and dignity of the residents at a total of twelve hate rallies held in Kawasaki through the hurling of abusive slogans such as 'Die', 'Kill them', 'Go back to Korea', 'We'll kick all of you out', 'We'll choke you slowly' and 'Go home, Korean cockroaches'. On these facts, the court prohibited the staging of a hate rally within 500 meters of Seikyū-sha headquarters.

The birth and acceptance of amorphous social awareness

The injunction against the hate rally in Kawasaki was made possible by a new kind of social awareness. The judgment handed down by the Kawasaki branch of the Yokohama District Court declared that the personal rights of non-Japanese permanent residents of Japan should be protected under the Constitution by stating as follows:

Where infringement of personal rights is committed in the form of a gathering of infringers or demonstration by such groups, there is the need to consider a balance between it and the freedoms of assembly and expression provided by Article Twenty-One of the Constitution; therefore it is appropriate to assess the level of illegality in terms of correlation between the type and nature of the infringed right and the form and level of infringement if such an infringement is to be prohibited before it occurs. [...] The personal rights subjected to such an infringement are strong rights guaranteed and protected by the Constitution and other laws whereas the discriminatory speech and behavior as the infringing act [...] is clearly outside the scope of the constitutional guarantee of the freedoms of assembly and expression and amounts to abuses of rights under private law as well. Furthermore, considering that it is significantly difficult to restore the infringed personal rights after the fact, it is appropriate to deduce that the issuing of a preliminary injunction is permissible and the right to seek prevention of nuisance on the basis of personal rights is affirmed.

Historically, the principle of societal formation in modern Japan has been based on a structure consisting of layers of pseudo parent-child relationships with the emperor at the top. The relationship between the emperor and his subjects was likened to one between a gracious parent and his infants which was also the logic used in organizing the subjects under government control. The subjects were grouped together into registered households (*ie*), each of which was presided over by the head of the household (*koshu*: equivalent to the 'householder' under the current family registration system but of a completely different nature). Household members were subjected to the household head's authority to determine residence (that is, the household head decided where his family members should live) among other rights in total disregard of personal freedom. From 300 to 500 household heads were placed under the supervision of a village or town head and incorporated into each prefectural administration system. In this hierarchy, superiors acted as parents to their inferiors with the emperor as the parent of the whole nation. The vision of the Greater East Asia Co-Prosperity Sphere under the slogan '*hakkō ichiu*' (eight corners of the world under one roof) was planned as an overseas expansion of the Japanese pseudo parent-child paradigm under the emperor where the other nations and regions were unified under Japan rather than on an equal footing with it.

After World War II, the emperor's status was changed from sovereign to symbol of the nation and that of the Japanese people shifted from subjects to sovereigns under the Constitution. The old family system (*ie*) was rejected, and the household head's rights (*koshuken*) were abolished. The new family registers were compiled with the nuclear family – a married couple and their children – as the base unit and the householder had no special authority over other family members. Nevertheless, some vestiges of the old family system lingered even after the war, including Article 200 of the Penal Code that imposed harsher penalties on patricides, male-only inheritance of Japanese nationality, a remarriage prohibition period for women and different shares of inheritance for legitimate and illegitimate children (all these forms of discrimination have now been eliminated).

In my view, Japanese society both before and after World War II has always been designed as what I call a 'crystalline-structure society'. In modern Japan after the Meiji Restoration, the identity of the Japanese national was steadily developed. Individuals with that identity became atoms, and atoms are connected to each other in a way that mimics the parent-child relationship. The relationship between the emperor and his subjects was one of parent and child (*sekishi*), and the hierarchical relationship in the workplace was such that the superior was the pseudo parent (*oyakata*) and the inferior was the pseudo child (*kokata*). It was also the social custom that when a house was rented, the landlord became the parent and the tenant became the child. The landlord was also responsible to a certain extent for any mistakes the tenant made. However, each individual atom had the same 'Japanese' nature, and these atoms were regularly arranged around the emperor to create the pure crystalline structure of Japanese society that was the Empire of Japan. So, the pre-war crystalline structure applied the parent-child relationship to all hierarchical relationships. The practice of defining a person's rights in relation to the family register (*koseki*) did not change after the war. Even today, a Japanese person may draw up a will with a child as a beneficiary, but the notary public office will not accept it for registration without an official copy of the child's family register and certificate of residence. This logic is deeply involved in the determination of status of not only Japanese nationals but also foreigners, reflected in the preferential treatment of foreigners of Japanese ancestry over other foreigners (Tanno 2020: Ch. 4).

However, the reasoning used by the court in granting an injunction against the hate speech rally in Kawasaki went outside the limits of the family register logic, as follows:

> It is believed that the feeling, sentiment and belief held by non-Japanese residents living in Japan toward their own ethnicity and native country or region set the groundwork for the development of their personality and form the most fundamental part of their personal dignity and accordingly must not be violated by other residents in Japan and they must be treated with mutual respect. The announcing of an intent to cause harm to the life, body, freedom, reputation or property of the non-Japanese residents for the purpose of promoting or inciting discrimination against them specifically or agitating for the exclusion of non-Japanese residents on the grounds of their native country or region by defaming or severely insulting them are classified as discriminatory speech and behavior under Article Two of the Antihate Act. It is understood that such acts constitute unlawful acts as they are deemed as unlawful infringements on the personal right to lead a quiet and peaceful life at the aforementioned place of residence.

Protection of the individual's rights that warrant mutual respect is linked to protection of the rights of the family and local community to which the individual belongs. The personal rights of a foreign resident had been considered outside the reach of the Japanese Constitution.[16] The Kawasaki branch of the Yokohama District Court then determined that the right of foreign residents to live peacefully in their community was guaranteed by the Constitution, and to that effect, the ministry of justice's human rights bureau issued a human rights advisory to the offenders.[17] The lawsuit for an injunction against the hate speech rally stemmed from an earlier court action seeking redress for human rights violations suffered by three individuals (to be discussed in detail below).

The local community that deserves the state's protection is not formed by society based on parent-child relationships among citizens but by families formed through all kinds of relationships between Japanese and non-Japanese people and their identities. The relationships found in the local community are comprised of ties interwoven in a complex fashion between those with rights and those without rights. If we are to protect the rights of those who have them on this premise, we cannot keep ignoring those who supposedly have no rights. In fact, leaving the latter without rights can sometimes undermine the welfare of the former. Once we accept that a community is built on amorphous connections between diverse individuals, those who supposedly have no rights will have 'rights' in certain situations.

From foreigners' human rights to communities' rights

The judgment not to allow the hate speech rally to enter Sakuramoto handed down by the Kawasaki branch of the Yokohama District Court explained the non-Japanese permanent residents' right to live peacefully in their community on the grounds of personal rights guaranteed by Article Thirteen of the Constitution of Japan. Be it an administrative lawsuit or a civil complaint, legal actions involving foreigners are not usually mounted on the basis of Article Thirteen of the Constitution. This is because the article stipulates the individual's right to pursue happiness, and the court had seldom recognized the 'foreigner's right to pursue happiness' in the past. As discussed by Junji Annen in his '"Gaikokujin no jinken" saikō' (Rethinking 'foreigners' human rights'), although foreigners have human rights under the Constitution, theirs are not considered the same as those of Japanese nationals; accordingly, it has been considered acceptable to regulate the rights to freedom of choice in employment, place of residence and relocation on the basis of one's resident status under the Immigration Law and therefore foreigners' freedoms are curtailed within those limits even though these freedoms are normally considered basic human rights (Annen 1993).

A non-Japanese permanent resident in Ōita Prefecture filed a lawsuit seeking the right to life after the rejection of the claimant's application for social security to escape hardship caused by abuses committed by a brother-in-law (Heisei 24 (2012) Gyō (Hi) Case No. 45 Supreme Court Second Petit Bench Heisei 26 (2014) 18 July Judgment, in *Shōmu geppō* (Monthly litigations report), 61(2), pp. 356–391). However, the supreme court did not recognize the foreign resident's right to life at all on the grounds that even if some foreigners might have received social security benefits for administrative operational reasons in the past, Articles One and Two of the Public Assistance Act only cover Japanese citizens. Unless the provisions are revised, only Japanese citizens can claim their right to public assistance. The court held that the claimant as a non-citizen was not entitled to receive public assistance and hence had no right to apply for it. The claimant had Chinese nationality but was born, raised and married in Japan and had never been to her country of nationality. Japan does not even recognize the right to life of such persons. The passage of the Antihate Act has not changed this situation in which foreigners have no human rights and can make no demands on such basis.

Nevertheless, the Kawasaki court ruling upheld the 'personal rights of non-Japanese permanent residents'. Why was this decision possible? There is no doubt that the Antihate Act had a major impact in this regard. The issue of foreigners' human rights may be raised in relation to the Immigration Law, but foreigners' personal dignity has never been considered an issue. Their freedom in terms of employment choice and residence relocation is restricted, while the freedom to accompany their family members is predetermined by their visa category. These factors make it difficult to treat foreigners in general as 'individuals with dignity' in the first place.

The Antihate Act, however, supposes that foreigners' dignity naturally exists. The aforementioned legislators argue as follows:

> Hate speech includes speech and behavior aimed at the exclusion of a particular group of people from a local community and Japanese society on the grounds of their attributes such as ethnicity and nationality which they cannot change easily; it is absolutely unacceptable as it intends to severely harm personal dignity and divide local communities. (Uozumi et al. 2016: iii)[18]

> [It] inflicts serious damage on people's mind, body and life that deeply harms the dignity of the targeted minority people. It should be stopped, or it can spread hatred and prejudice throughout the society in which we live. (Uozumi et al. 2016: vii)[19]

Hate speech is not targeted at a specific individual. There is no evidence in court documents that far-right protesters named any individual when shouting abuses such as 'Kill' and 'Go home'. If defamatory speech or verbal assault is targeted at individuals, it is possible to penalize offenders or to provide redress or restoration to victims. If abuse is not directed at specific individuals, punishment or redress is impossible. A speech including phrases such as 'We won't get our hands dirty by taking the trouble to kill you; we calmly do things, legally, that will drive you to the brink of madness and back to what you call "Korean hell"' has been treated as a form of freedom of expression under Japanese law.

Sangyun Kim (金尚均) examines this structure in hate speech on the basis of interlocking 'vertical relationships' and 'lateral relationships'. In vertical relationships, where the 'individual' is attacked by the perpetrator and the former's status is diminished:

Category 1   the perpetrator is punished and their status is also diminished, or

Category 2   the victimized individual is afforded redress or restoration so that their status is restored to the previous level as much as possible. (Kim 2016)

However, where the victim is a 'group' of Zainichi Koreans rather than individuals, it includes men and women, young and old, the Korean-born first generation, the second and later generations with

Korean or North Korean nationality and those who were naturalized in Japan. This results in Category 3, where an attack is targeted at a group with diverse attributes, in the direction of lateral relationships. In this case, the group does not meet the necessary conditions for treatment as a victim under Japanese law (Kim 2016).

In the Kawasaki judgment, however, the vertical and lateral relationships were examined in the reverse direction. The three plaintiffs who sought redress for human rights violations included a first-generation Zainichi Korean woman (Plaintiff 1), a third-generation Zainichi Korean woman (Plaintiff 2) and the Japanese spouse of Plaintiff 2 (Plaintiff 3). Moreover, Plaintiffs 2 and 3 had children with dual nationality whose existence would have been taken into account in court deliberations even though they were not named as direct complainants in the bill of complaint about human rights violations.

A common thread in the plaintiffs' arguments was the issue of the identities of Zainichi Koreans. The individuals' identities became the issue of the identity of their families, which in some cases included members with Japanese (or dual) nationality. As new generations of Zainichi people continue to enter the world, families with no members with Japanese nationality are likely to become a minority. The personal rights of non-Japanese permanent residents under Article Thirteen of the Constitution were recognized in consideration of the 'lateral relationships'.

We must emphasize that recognition of the personal rights of non-Japanese permanent residents in the lateral relationships does not necessarily mean recognition of the 'personal rights of non-Japanese permanent residents' in general. As we have seen with the aforementioned Heisei 26 (2014) 18 July Supreme Court Second Petit Bench judgment on public assistance for a non-Japanese permanent resident, a foreign national as an individual is not entitled to claim any constitutional rights under law regardless of their personal circumstances. If the view expressed in the supreme court judgment continues to be upheld, the personal rights of non-Japanese permanent residents under Article Thirteen recognized by Yokohama District Court Kawasaki branch cannot be recognized for individuals. The

Kawasaki judgment pronounced that the personal rights of these people are protected under the Constitution where they exist as families that include Japanese nationals and form a certain community (that is, where they are understood to have 'lateral relationships').

Did foreigners' personal rights in the context of 'lateral relationships' emanate abruptly from the hate speech problem? I do not think so. Let us consider the fact that special permission for residency is granted in many cases where foreigners marry Japanese or permanent residents and have children with them. While the state sees no 'benefit' in cases where an issue can only be understood as an individual matter, its perspective shifts to the lateral relationship level in cases where an issue can be regarded as one experienced by the principal party and their family. If the issue is examined at this level, a path to grant 'benefit' can be opened. Although the 'benefit' of special residency permission cannot be discussed on the same level as 'dignity' under the Antihate Act, an analogy between them is significant. It points to the existence of the personal rights of an individual that are realized in communal living in the local community and the family.

Conclusion

We have seen above that the 'dignity' of others is the key that has enabled the previously unrecognized interests of certain people to be placed justly in society and individuals to be connected to the family and the local community. Incidentally, Locke's theory indicating a primordial form of amorphous thinking by treating society as an aggregation of people with diverse attributes has been subjected to strong criticism on the basis of misogyny because it is built on the foundation of the patriarchal social contract. Carole Pateman's *The Sexual Contract* (1988) is a major feminist critique of Locke. Further, *The Racial Contract* by Charles W. Mills (1997) argues that the theoretical framework of Pateman's feminist criticism is also applicable to the situation in which racial minorities find themselves. Pateman and Mills condemn the process in which a contract that is supposedly made on equal terms is not only unequal, but also disadvantages the subordinate party and formulates a general principle based on the relationships between the dominant parties, because this process is constantly converted to the domination of the weak by the strong (Pateman and Mills 2007).

On the other hand, Jeremy Waldron analyzes the meaning and limitations of Locke's theory from a different perspective in his argument on the necessity of controlling hate speech. Contemporary theorists treat Locke's idea about natural rights and government as if it were a universal theory, but *Two Treatises of Government* consists of his critique of Sir Robert Filmer who was a leading advocate for the divine right of kings at the time (*First Treatise*) and his discourse on the relationship between citizens and governments (*Second Treatise*). Social science has been primarily interested in the *Second Treatise*. In Japan, it was translated by Nobushige Ukai and published as *Shimin seifu ron* (Civil government theory) under the Iwanami Bunko (classic series) label in 1968, whereas the *First Treatise* was not included in the classic series until 2010. The situation is similar in the West, but Waldron argues that the *First Treatise* is more important than the *Second Treatise*, because the preconditions for the second part are explained in the first. For example, Locke scrutinizes God's definition of 'Man' itself in expounding on natural rights by refuting Filmer's thesis that God made Adam a king when He created him (which subsequently developed into the theory of the divine right of kings). Locke argues that Adam did not become a king until Eve was created, and even if he did become king prior to Eve, he would have held that position only over his children (and their descendants) with Eve. Although every person is said to have natural rights, Waldron stresses that 'every person' is limited to Christian rather than all human beings. Locke's view seems as if it were a universal principle, but his religious and cultural background is extremely important and presents as an almost tacit knowledge. The title of Waldron's book, *God, Locke, and Equality: Christian Foundations in Locke's Political Thought*, speaks for itself (Waldron 2002).

Waldron evaluates Locke's position on the status of women from a perspective that differs from that of Pateman and others. He stresses that although Locke treats patriarchal conjugal society as the basic social unit, he leaves room for a number of women's rights within the concept of 'contract' because wives and widows are allowed to own property independently of their husbands or families and wives share parental rights with their husbands. What is important here is how their rights are formulated. Waldron emphasizes that even though women's rights are placed within the family and determined according to their relationship with the patriarch, this is dictated by customs rather than logical necessity.[20]

In that case, we must ask where rights originate from and what it is for people to acquire them. In *Dignity, Rank, and Rights*, Waldron (2015) argues that elements of contemporary human rights have been formed through extension to lower-ranked people of what used to be attached to high-ranking public offices and the nobility that put people in these high offices. He claims that low-ranked people have been pulled up toward high ranks rather than that rights themselves have been broadened. What used to be enjoyed by only a small section of society has been afforded to wider segments of the population through the widening of the spectrum of 'respectable people'. Over the course of time, the membership which was accorded only to those of the same religious background has transcended that boundary and come to be determined according to the criterion of whether people are held in respect.

Consequently, the act of defaming or vilifying those who are held in respect constitutes not only harm to the respected people, but also an attack on society itself.

> There is a sort of public good of inclusiveness that our society sponsors and that it is committed to. We are diverse in our ethnicity, our race, our appearance, and our religions. And we are embarked on a grand experiment on living and working together despite these sorts of differences. Each group must accept that the society is not just for them; but it is for them too, along with all of the others. (Waldron 2012: 4)

For this reason, hate speech that attacks the dignity of others becomes an attack on a public good upon which society is built.

In 2019, Kawasaki City formulated Japan's first ordinance to ban hate speech with a penalty clause. Bill No. 157 on the enactment of an ordinance to rid Kawasaki of discrimination and create a community that respects human rights was passed unanimously by the municipal assembly on 12 December 2019.[21] Under the law, violators can face a penalty of up to ¥500,000 if they continue to engage in discriminatory speech after receiving three cautions. As mentioned earlier, the national Antihate Act has no penalty provision. Osaka Prefecture, which enacted an ordinance to ban hate speech ahead of Kawasaki, can force internet service providers to remove websites if they are found to have published hate speech, but it does not punish those who have articulated it. Punishment for violators of hate speech regulations is extremely uncommon in Japan.

The formulation of Kawasaki's antihate ordinance was supported by the mobilization of amorphous forces. The municipal government released the draft bill and asked for public comment from the broader community. Even though it was to be a municipal ordinance, the city sought submissions from all stakeholders, including non-locals who had connections with the city or its citizens as well as those interested in this issue. It gathered opinions from not only its citizens but also its potential visitors. When the bill was finalized, Kawasaki Mayor Norihiko Fukuda indicated at his regular press conference that he would aim for unanimous passage.[22] What we can learn from this approach is, to put it plainly, that a social movement that aims to respect differences is to act on the saying 'Two heads are better than one' and gathers the wisdom of a wide array of people transregionally or transnationally to present to the government.[23]

To enable such a movement to produce positive social outcomes, however, there have to be people or sections within the public bureaucracy to receive and accept the wisdom. In the past, in civic campaigns against pollution such as Minamata and the course of advancement of environmental control that followed, there were government workers who assumed the mission of translating civic demands into public policy in the public sector in addition to citizens' movements in the private sector. The success or failure of a social movement is greatly impacted by its ability to involve those who are tasked with incorporating private-sector input into public administration. When we focus on amorphousness as a criterion of analysis, we can not only examine the significance of giving consideration to diversity as a matter of social awareness, but also determine the probability of success on the basis of whether the movement has been able to involve the members of society who can turn it into policy. Nonetheless, the author must qualify this statement by adding that involving policy-makers does not always lead to the achievement of all of a social movement's objectives.

Acknowledgements
This work was supported by KAKENHI (16H05715), KAKENHI (17KT0063), and THE MITSUBISHI FOUNDATION.

Name order
The 'Japanese' convention of family name preceding given name is generally followed in this book. Departing from this style, this chapter uses the principle of given name followed by family name, with respect to both 'Japanese' and 'non-Japanese' names.

Unlike the previous chapters which focus on social movements launched by 'Japanese nationals', this chapter discusses and analyzes protests organized jointly by 'Japanese' and 'foreigners'. This complicates the name-order problem, because the historical background of the present situation must be given serious attention. The issues of Zainichi Koreans, for instance, cannot be discussed without due consideration for Japan's colonial past that forced Koreans to assume Japanese names. It is thus not acceptable to impose the 'Japanese' rules upon 'non-Japanese', a requirement that makes the name-order issue itself complex, problematic and amorphous.

Bearing this point in mind, this chapter universally applies the English-language convention of given name preceding family name, regardless of the individual's nationality, social status, occupational position or the historical period in which they lived.

Notes

Introduction

1 'Kyūjō kaeru na!' (2019); 2019.03.02 (2019).
2 'Panku rokkā rōdō kumiai' (2019).
3 Amamiya (2019).
4 March 11th of 2011 was the day of the Great East Japan Earthquake in Tōhoku that caused the accident at the Fukushima Dai-ichi Nuclear Power Plant. 'Post-3.11' is an oft-used expression for the era after the Fukushima disaster.
5 From here on, unless otherwise noted, the number of participants in rallies, demonstrations and the like is as announced by the organizers. It is normal for there to be a gap in numbers between those announced by the organizers and the police, and as the number of participants in the movement against the 2015 National Security Legislation drew enormous interest, there is need for further investigation in another setting on this question. In this regard, see Oguma (2016: 229, n. 2).
6 In 1960, the LDP government led by Prime Minister Kishi Nobusuke attempted to revise the Japan-US Security Treaty into a mutual one. When the LDP forced passage of the bill through the Diet, movements against the revision in Tokyo and around the country swelled. Although the bill passed the Diet, Kishi was forced to resign. Some intellectuals praised this mass participation as the naissance of civil society in Japan, and this event has often been mentioned as one of the most memorable moments in Japanese politics in the post-war era.
7 There were actually numerous participants who were accompanied by their children, to the extent that Hangenren set up a 'family area' near the Diet and adopted a system that made it easy for these people to take part.
8 The 'lost generation' is a term signifying people who graduated from school between 1993 and 2004 and had difficulties finding regular employment.

Chapter 1

1 Regarding the movement against the construction of a US military base in Henoko, Okinawa, see Chapter Five of this volume.
2 'Amorphous': https://www.merriam-webster.com/dictionary/amorphous. The definitions of 'amorphous' in the Oxford English Dictionary (1989, 2nd Ed., Vol. 1: 410) are more diverse, but basically they are the same as the definitions in merriam-webster.com, as follows: 'Having no determinate shape, shapeless', 'Belonging to no particular type or pattern; anomalous, unclassifiable', 'Not composed of crystals in physical structure; uncrystallized', 'Ill-assorted, ill-digested, unorganized'.
3 Tanno Kiyoto points out that a view of society as an amorphous entity can be dated back to John Locke. In Locke's view, according to Tanno, even when the individuals constituting society were motley and diverse, constructing society according to the principle of mutual respect can create a more robust society (see Chapter Six in this volume).
4 The Japanese anti-nuclear weapon movement diverged in 1965 when the Japan Congress Against Atomic and Hydrogen Bombs (Nihon gensuibaku kinshi kokumin kaigi, or Gensuikin) split from the Japan Council Against Atomic and Hydrogen Bombs (Gensuibaku kinshi nihon kyōgikai, or Gensuikyō) on the issue of how to evaluate the Soviet Union's nuclear test. Japan's anti-nuclear weapons movements have continued to work separately since then.
5 'Leftist political parties, leftist media and leftist intellectuals incit[ed] "elevated-consciousness-type" young people [young people's terminology making fun of their fellows who are serious or have social-mindedness] who consider it trendy to advocate peace' (Fukushima 2016: 27); 'SEALDs is clearly [something that] left-wing elderly people extolled as its "usual audience"' (Kitada, Kurihara and Gotō 2017: 138, statement by Kitada).

Chapter 2

1 For a discussion of the development of social movements from defeat in World War II until the period of high economic growth, see Kinoshita (2019).
2 The number of strikes in Japan peaked at 5,211 in 1975 and fell to 596 in 1985 (Kōsei Rōdōshō 2016).
3 Watanabe (1991) and Watanabe (ed.) (2004) discuss the growing conservatism of Japanese society in the 1980s from the viewpoint of the establishment of a company-centered society.
4 Work hours in Japan declined in the period of high economic growth – from 2,432 hours in 1960 to 2,065 in 1975. Following this, however, there was an upward shift, with figures again exceeding 2,100 hours in the 1980s and rising to 2,200 hours in the 1990s (Watanabe 1990).

5 Inoue (2013) also makes it clear that women were central to the operation of this movement.
6 An article in *Mainichi Shimbun* (2017) contains a graph showing the shifts in LDP membership numbers from 1989 to 2016.
7 JETRO (2019). In contrast with South Korea's 8,590 won (747 yen), Japan's average minimum wage for the 2019 financial year was 901 yen. Okinawa Prefecture had the lowest figure at 790 yen (Kōseirōdōshō 2020). (Japan's minimum wage system varies by region and occupation. Korea has a uniform system.)
8 Homepage of the Article Nine Association: http://www.9-jo.jp/en/index_en.html (last accessed 19 August 2020).
9 Iida (2018) has been consulted for data on the Article Nine Association.
10 Oguma and Kinoshita (2013) discuss notes written by around fifty former participants in the movement for the abandonment of nuclear power which reveal that women in particular were striving desperately to make their husbands and children aware of the dangers of radiation.
11 The number of participants in the movement for abandoning nuclear power generation is based on the Appendix in Kinoshita (2013c). This list records the regions, names and estimated numbers of participants in demonstrations that occurred throughout Japan from 11 March 2011 through to 2013. The figures for the numbers of participants in demonstrations are essentially based on those released by the organizers; in the case of smaller gatherings, the author has counted the numbers of participants in videos on YouTube and elsewhere.
12 Shinjuku ALTA building is a complex housing women's clothing shops, cafes and studios for events and TV shows. The square in front of the ALTA building (ALTA Square) is a place where the younger generation meet twenty-four hours per day, 365 days per year.
13 In Kinoshita (2013b), I discussed in detail the nature of the post-3.11 anti-nuclear movement.
14 A documentary film about the spread of these anti-nuclear power demonstrations contains a collection of interviews with those who took part, including myself (Oguma 2015).
15 Based on Higuchi (2018).
16 The increasingly amorphous nature of these social movements is consistent with the elements of the 'new anarchism' proposed by cultural anthropologist David Graeber (2004: 7), as follows: 1) that one's means must be consonant with one's end; 2) that one cannot create freedom through authoritarian means, and; 3) as much as possible, one must oneself, in one's relation with one's friends and allies, embody the society one wishes to create.
17 In the 2015 movement against the revision of the National Security Legislation, the social movement run by the new generation – SEALDs

(Students Emergency Action for Liberal Democracy) – gained the most attention, but the older generation, who were mobilized in groups such as the Article Nine Association, sustained the mobilization efforts of the social movement. In a way, this movement became large-scale as a result of the left-wing and liberal forces – who had previously been in conflict with each other – effecting a general mobilization based on post-war democratic ideas. Consequently, this movement can be thought of as the 'last opportunity' in which the ageing and declining post-war style of social movement coexisted with the new style of social movement suited to modern society.

Chapter 3

1 Tamura and Tamura (2016: 172) noted that the main points of the SEALDs statement closely resemble those of the 1955 declaration delivered at the time of the founding of the LDP.
2 The Article Ninety-Six Association is a movement started by supporters of the Constitution who oppose the proposal made in 2013 by Abe Shinzō to reduce the Diet majority necessary for the proposal of constitutional revision from two-thirds of members, as required in Article Ninety-Six, to one half. The Save Constitutional Democracy Association is a movement established in 2014 with researchers and scholars as core members, in order to resist the Abe administration's political denial of the Constitution. Conversely, this organization aspires to revive politics grounded in constitutional recognition. *Sekai* (The World) is a critical analysis magazine established in 1946 which is representative of the liberal faction in Japanese critical circles.
3 This point was also made in the Shutoken hangenpatsu rengō (Tokyo Metropolis Anti-Nuclear Power Alliance) demonstration, ' "Saikidō hantai! Shushō kantei mae kōgi" [We oppose reactor restarts! Protest outside the prime minister's official residence] 8 nenme e' (Towards the eighth year) (http://coalitionagainstnukes.jp/?p=12518).

Chapter 4

1 The expression '*Shirōto no ran*' is translated here as 'Amateur Revolt' in accordance with the English term given on the collective's original website: http://keita.trio4.nobody.jp/index_com.html. While this translation is also used by Brown (2018), both Nakamura (2008) and Cassegård (2013) translate the term as 'Amateur Riot'. Obinger (2015) uses the German, 'Aufstand der Amateure', which means 'amateur uprising' or 'revolt'.

2 See Note 12 of Chapter Two by Kinoshita.
3 For the current locations and opening schedule of *Nantoka bā*, see the following website of 'Nantoka BAR': https://www.shirouto.org/nantokabar/

Chapter 6

1 Another period when an exceptionally high number of acts were promulgated and enforced on the same day was between Japan's defeat in World War II and the enforcement of the San Francisco Peace Treaty on 28 April 1952. Many of them related to foreign visitors, including the Alien Registration Ordinance, which was the last imperial ordinance, and the Immigration Control Act for border control.
2 The lower court ruling on this case was handed down by the Yokohama District Court on 19 June 1974 (Yokohama Chisai Shōwa 45 (1970) (Wa) Case No. 2118). The issue was also raised in the National Diet because Hitachi's internal document revealed its practice of not employing 'Communist Party or Minseitō sympathizers', 'avid Sōka Gakkai members' and 'the mentally or physically handicapped', in addition to 'not actively employing foreigners'. This elicited sharp objections in the House of Representatives Judicial Affairs Committee (The 72nd Diet Session House of Representatives Judicial Committee Meeting Minutes No. 28). Hitachi decided not to appeal in light of the opinions expressed at the Diet session and the district court judgment became final.
3 See Pak (1974) for his life history prior to the employment discrimination trial.
4 Circumstances during this period are detailed in Che et al. (1974).
5 See 'Dai 2-kai Fureaikan no ayumi' (History of Fureaikan, episode 2) for this exchange (http://www.city.kawasaki.jp/kawasaki/cmsfiles/contents/0000026/26446/23kouza02.pdf, last accessed 17 August 2019).
6 Irreversible progression or change along the temporal axis is not limited to thermodynamic phenomena. Examples of the irreversible processes that progress over certain periods of time include a biological phenomenon in which eggs develop into embryonic cells that become differentiated into separate organs, and a chemical reaction where two or more chemical substances transform into another while releasing heat (a typical example is organic chemical synthesis). These processes appear to be completely different depending on which level we look at (that is, behavior at the genetic or atomic level, enzymic or crystalline level or cell or rock level). Another feature is described as follows:

> One of the most interesting aspects of dissipative structures is their coherence. The system behaves as a whole, as if it were the site of long-range forces. In spite of the fact that interactions among molecules do not exceed a range of some 10^{-8}cm, the system is

structured as though each molecule were "informed" about the overall state of the system. (Prigogine and Stengers 2017: 171)
7 According to Monod, DNA structure is replicated almost perfectly, but the occurrence of crossing over at a certain rate, that is, an accidental change, is inevitable. This accident leads to species divergence, and the new species becomes established as the changed DNA structure continues to be replicated almost perfectly thereafter (conversion from chance to necessity) (Monod 1972).
8 Tinbergen (1969) considers that a behavior that is repeated in the stimulus-response mechanism becomes a fixed pattern and leads to the establishment of a behavioral pattern peculiar to a species.
9 Kunihiko Kaneko points out that the level of analysis and the meaning of interaction vary greatly from one academic discipline to another by stating, 'When cell biologists say that "Cells interact with one another", they think of, for instance, an interaction between molecules via receptors to influence one another. On the other hand, ecologists would think of a predator-prey relationship between individuals as an interaction. Physicists and chemists would picture the exertion of forces such as intermolecular attraction and electromagnetic force as an interaction' (Kaneko 2014: 16).
10 Similarly, William Agosta (2002) sheds light on insect behaviors for the purpose of securing food, finding a mating partner or evading a predator by analyzing their pheromones from an organic chemistry viewpoint. He explains the release of various chemical substances by insects in terms of interaction between the environment and genetic mutation and argues that the range of such interaction stretches to the general environment.
11 Kaneko talks about the problem of employing statistical mechanics as it negates the possibility of theorizing about irreversibility on the following grounds:
Statistical mechanics is a branch of physics that came about after the establishment of thermodynamics to study consistency between the microscopic and macroscopic levels and cannot exist independently of thermodynamics. Behavior at the micro level does not automatically conduce an understanding of behavior at the macro level. While thermodynamics allows the argument for and the quantification of the irreversibility of a change from one state to another, statistical mechanics has yet to offer a theory of irreversibility itself. (Kaneko 2014: 35)
12 The fourth rally, held on 2 February 2012, and fifth on 22 February 2012 used slightly different slogans – 'Denounce Anti-Japan in Kawasaki' in the former and 'Nationwide Great People's Rally to Regain Takeshima (Liancourt Rocks)! (Kanagawa)' in the latter.
13 The title of the eleventh rally, held on 8 November 2015, was 'From Kawasaki! Purify Japan Rally (Don't Tolerate Anti-Japan)', while that of the twelfth

rally on 31 January 2016 was 'From Kawasaki Japan Purification Rally "Part 2" (Don't Tolerate Anti-Japan)'.
14 A video of this anti-war rally can be viewed on YouTube (https://www.youtube.com/watch?v=0PGTNR_TJTI, last accessed 19 August 2020).
15 He was particularly concerned that youngsters might be provoked by aggressive hate speech.
16 See Tanno (2019) for details on this point.
17 See *Asahi Shimbun* (https://www.asahi.com/articles/ASJ8251J8J82UTIL027.html, last accessed 19 August 2020) and other press reports for details of this human rights advisory. Although the issuing of the advisory was widely reported, its wording is not known as it was sent to specific individuals only.
18 These words can be found in 'Kantōgen' (prefatory note) by Yūichirō Uozumi who chaired the 190th Diet Session House of Councillors Judicial Committee.
19 These words can be found in 'Hajimeni' (Introduction) by Katsuo Yakura, member of the 190th Diet Session House of Councillors Judicial Committee. Similar expressions can be found in 'Jobun' (Preface) by Yoshifu Arita, member of the 190th Diet Session House of Councillors Judicial Committee. Arita declares that the principle of human dignity is applicable to permanent residents as well by stating as follows: 'Hate speech denies human dignity and equality. We pledge to use this legislation as a springboard and advance our actions to turn the International Convention on the Elimination of All Forms of Racial Discrimination into reality on Japanese soil hand in hand with the people who put their bodies on the line to stop discrimination, the victims and the hard-working experts' (Uozumi et al. 2016: xi).
20 The customs also dictate the position of each family in the social hierarchy and the ranks of individuals and their occupations. On the other hand, Pateman argues that the 'every person' in the premise of 'Every person has natural rights' is limited to males and that women are subsumed in 'every person' as members of a family governed by a man; all social relationships are defined on the basis of men's dominance of women founded on conjugal society as sexual contract.
21 Kawasaki Antihate Bill No. 157 aimed at the creation of a discrimination-free community in conjunction with Bill No. 155 on the enactment of an ordinance to amend part of the ordinance for the installation of Kawasaki City's sub-organs (in part related to the civic culture office). While Bill No. 157 was passed unanimously, the additional resolution to the bill was passed by majority vote and was not unanimous.
22 The mayor's comment was reported in *Kanagawa Shimbun* on 16 November 2019 (https://www.kanaloco.jp/article/entry-209022.html, last accessed 19 August 2020).
23 See the city's website (http://www.city.kawasaki.jp/templates/pubcom/250/0000108585.html, last accessed 19 August 2020) for the outcome of the public comment about Kawasaki's Antihate Bill.

Bibliography

'2019.03.02 Abe seiken fuzaken na! Abe seiken hantai! Kyūjō kaeru na!' [2 March 2019. Abe regime, don't fool around! Don't change Article 9! NO to the Abe regime! 2 March Suginami demonstration] (2019). Accessed at https://www.youtube.com/watch?v=hV-QnpD8AUA.

Agosta, W. C. (2000). *Thieves, deceivers, and killers: Tales of chemistry in nature*. Princeton: Princeton University Press.

Amamiya, K. (2018). 'Manuke o mamore', Kōenji saikaihatsu hantai parēdo no maki [Volume on 'Protect the Fools!', the Kōenji anti-redevelopment parade]. *Magajin kyūjō: Amamiya Karin ga yuku! dai 460 kai* [Article Nine Magazine: Amamiya Karin goes forth! No. 460], 26 September. Accessed at https://maga9.jp/180926/.

Amamiya, K. (2019). Kaosu! Kōenji saikaihatsu 'Chotto matta!' ibento no maki [Volume on chaos! 'Wait a moment!' event on Kōenji redevelopment]. *Magajin kyūjō: Amamiya Karin ga yuku! dai 495 kai* [Article Nine Magazine. Amamiya Karin goes forth! No. 495], 11 September. Accessed at https://maga9.jp/190911-2/.

Andō, T. (2013). *Nyū refuto undō to shimin shakai: 'Rokujū nendai' no shisō no yukue* [The new left movement and civil society: The whereabouts of '60s' thought]. Kyoto: Sekai Shisōsha.

Andō, T. (2019). *Datsugenpatsu no undōshi: Cherunobuiri, Fukushima, soshite korekara* [A history of anti-nuclear power generation movements: Chernobyl, Fukushima, and hereafter]. Tokyo: Iwanami Shoten.

Annen, J. (1993). 'Gaikokujin no jinken' saikō [Rethinking 'foreigners' human rights']. In Y. Higuchi and K. Takahashi (eds), *Gendai rikken shugi no tenkai (jō): Ashibe Nobuyoshi sensei koki shukuga* [Development of contemporary constitutionalism (Vol. 1): In commemoration of the seventieth birthday of Professor Nobuyoshi Ashibe], pp. 163–182. Tokyo: Yūhikaku.

Anpo kanren-hō ni hantai suru mama no kai @ Ōsaka [Mothers Against National Security Legislation @ Osaka] (2016). Zadankai: Mukanshin datta mama tachi ga tachiagatta [Roundtable discussion: Once-uninterested mothers have arisen]. *Harappa: Hoiku o kangaeru nakama no zasshi* [Harappa: Journal of Companions Who Care About Childcare], 374, pp. 2–5.

Arasaki, M. (2005). *Okinawa gendaishi (shimban)* [Modern history of Okinawa, new edition]. Tokyo: Iwanami Shoten.

Arasaki, M. (2016). *Nihon ni totte Okinawa to wa nani ka* [What Okinawa means to Japan]. Tokyo: Iwanami Shoten.

Arikawa, T. (2016). *Songen to mibun: Kenpōteki shii to 'Nihon' to iu mondai* [Dignity and status: Constitutional thinking and the 'Japan' problem]. Tokyo: Iwanami Shoten.

Asahi Shimbun (2006a). 'Furukutemo tsukaeru': PSE-hō hantai demo ['It's okay to use old things': The anti-PSE Law demonstration], 19 March.

Asahi Shimbun (2006b). PSE māku nakutemo, chūko denki hanbai ōkei, Keisanshō tenkan: 'Chūkohanbaiten ga seihin o uketotta' ato de 'hanbaiten ga kensa' zentei [It's okay to sell second-hand electrical appliances even without a PSE mark, policy change by the METI assuming 'second-hand store safety-checks of appliances' after 'acquiring goods'], 25 March.

Asahi Shimbun (2008). 'Toshikoshi haken mura', Hibiya kōen ni 31 nichi kaison: Shoku to jūkyo teikyō ['New Year's Eve Temporary Employee Village', village opening on the 31st in Hibiya Park: Food and housing provided], 30 December. Accessed at http://www.asahi.com/special/08016/TKY200812290186.html.

Asahi Shimbun (2009). Seizōgyō haken/ukeoi, 40 mannin shitsugyō mitōshi: Gyōkai dantai shisan [Manufacturing industry temporary and contract workers, forecast 400,000 unemployed: Business industry estimate], 27 January. Accessed at http://www.asahi.com/special/08016/TKY200901270287.html.

Asahi Shimbun (2011a). Kairo de 100 mannin demo. Yodōshi tsuzuku mikomi [One-million-strong demonstration in Cairo. Anticipated to continue throughout the night], 2 February. Accessed at http://www.asahi.com/special/meastdemo/TKY201102010627.html.

Asahi Shimbun (2011b). Shinsaigo no seiji ni hachiwari fuman [80% of people are dissatisfied with politics after the earthquake], 26 December. Accessed at http://www.asahi.com/special/08003/TKY201112250192.html.

Asahi Shimbun (2013). Nyūsu Q3: 'Minasan wa 12 banme no senshu': Kokoro toraeta DJ porisu [News Q3 'You are the twelfth player': DJ Police won the hearts and minds of the people], 7 June.

Asahi Shimbun (2015). Uocchi Anpo Kokkai: Demo no kin'yōbi: Datsugenpatsu kara hajimatta [Watch the Diet session on the National Security Legislation: Demonstrations on Friday, the beginning was anti-nuclear power plants], 12 September.

Asahi Shimbun (2016). Seiken itten, kaizen e iyoku kyōchō: Burogu 'Hoikuen ochita' kyōkan hirogaru [Government changed its position, emphasizing its eagerness for advancement: Spreading empathy for the blog 'We flunked the nursery school entrance exam'], 9 March.

Asahi Shimbun (2017). Genkō kempō 'nihon ni totte yokatta' 89% [89% of people said the Constitution of Japan is good for Japan], 2 May. Accessed at https://www.asahi.com/articles/photo/AS20170501004416.html.

Asahi Shimbun (2018). Rōso soshiki ritsu 17%, kako saitei o saishin [Labor union

organization rate 17%, new record low], 19 December. Accessed at https://www.asahi.com/articles/ASLDM3SLDLDMULFA00S.html.
Auyang, S. Y. (1998). *Foundations of complex-system theories in economics, evolutionary biology, and statistical physics.* Cambridge: Cambridge University Press.
Axelrod, R. (1984). *The evolution of cooperation.* New York: Basic Books.
Bauman, Z. (2000). *Liquid modernity.* Cambridge: Polity Press.
Beck, U. (1992). *Risk society: Towards a new modernity.* London: Sage Publications.
BeFlat: 10 dai no jinken jōhō nettowāku [BeFlat: Human Rights Information Network for Teens] (2009). Bimbō de yutaka na jinsei o ikiru: Shirōto no ran, Matsumoto Hajime san [Living a plentiful life while poor: Amateur Revolt, Matsumoto Hajime], April. Accessed at https://www.jinken.ne.jp/be/meet/matsumoto/index.html.
Bei, J. (2011). Dai 2-kai Fureaikan no ayumi [History of Fureaikan, episode 2]. Accessed 17 August 2019 at http://www.city.kawasaki.jp/kawasaki/cmsfiles/contents/0000026/26446/23kouza02.pdf.
BLOGOS Henshūbu (ed.) (2015). 'Kotoshi no natsu de shinunjanaika to omotteta': SEALDs menbā ga furikaeru 'Anpo hantai undō' ['In the summer of this year I thought I might die': The 'Anti-National Security Legislation Movement' as recalled by SEALDs members]. Accessed at https://blogos.com/article/141783/.
Brown, A. (2018). *Anti-nuclear protest in post-Fukushima Tokyo: Power struggle.* London: Routledge.
Cassegård, C. (2013). *Youth movements, trauma and alternative space in contemporary Japan.* Leiden: Brill.
Che, S., Pak, C., Satō, K., Li, I., Takanami, T., and Wada, J. (1974). Zadankai Hitachi kyūdan eno ayumi [Panel discussion on the path to the condemnation of Hitachi]. In Paku-kun o kakomu kai (ed.), *Minzoku sabetsu – Hitachi shūshoku sabetsu kyūdan* [Racial discrimination: Condemnation of employment discrimination by Hitachi]. Tokyo: Aki Shobō, pp. 3–58.
Chiavacci, D., and Obinger, J. (2018). Towards a new protest cycle in contemporary Japan?: The resurgence of social movements and confrontational political activism in historical perspective. In D. Chiavacci and J. Obinger (eds), *Social movements and political activism in contemporary Japan: Re-emerging from invisibility.* London: Routledge, pp. 1–23.
Chokusō kafe (2012). Chokusō kafe@nantoka bar 2012.11.11 [Chokusō café at Nantoka bar 2012.11.11], 11 November. Accessed at https://www.youtube.com/watch?v=M7NVyx8fY-c.
Dalton, R. J. (2014). *Citizen politics: Public opinion and political parties in advanced industrial democracies* (6th ed.). Thousand Oaks: Sage.
Della Porta, D. (2015). *Social movements in times of austerity: Bringing capitalism back into protest analysis.* Cambridge: Polity.
Fraser, N. (2009). Feminism, capitalism and the cunning of history. *New Left Review*, 56 (Mar/Apr), pp. 97–117.

Fukushima, K. (2016). *SEALDs to Higashi Ajia wakamono demo tte nanda!* [What are SEALDs and youth demonstrations in East Asia?]. Tokyo: Īsuto Puresu [East Press].
Fukushima, M. (2012). Nantoka bar de ichinichi tenchō [One-day-manager at the Nantoka Bar], 22 August. Accessed at https://ch.nicovideo.jp/mizuho-fukushima/blomaga/ar2817.
Furuya, T., and Okuda, A. (dialoguists) (2015). *Aikoku tte nanda?: Minzoku, kyōdo, sensō* [What is patriotism?: Ethnicity, native place and war). Tokyo: PHP Kenkyūjo.
Graeber, D. (2004). *Fragments of an anarchist anthropology*. Chicago: Prickly Paradigm Press.
Hasegawa, K. (2018). Continuities and discontinuities of Japan's political activism after the Fukushima disaster. In D. Chiavacci and J. Obinger (eds), *Social movements and political activism in contemporary Japan: Re-emerging from invisibility*. London: Routledge, pp. 115–136.
Hashiguchi, S. (2011). *Wakamono no rōdō undō: 'Hatarakasero' to 'hatarakanaizo' no shakaigaku* [The young people's labor movement: The sociology of 'Let us work' and '[We] shan't work']. Tokyo: Seikatsu Shoin.
Hashimoto, T. (2012). Anna demo kurai de yononaka o ugokasu koto ga dekiru nara, boku no ima made no rōryoku wa nan dattan da? Yononaka sonna amaku nai [If that sort of demonstration can change society, what's all my effort until now been worth? Society's not that easy-going]. Accessed at http://blogos.com/article/132262/.
Hattori, N. (2016). Hi o mamori, ba o atatameru [Stoking the fire, keeping the place warm]. *Gendai Shisō* [Contemporary Thought], 44(7), pp. 56–65.
Henmi, Y. (2016). Intabyū: Jiryū ni Aragau [Interview: Against the trend of the world]. *Asahi Shimbun*, 21 January.
Higashi, K. (2004). 'Teikō naki sanka' to 'sanka naki teikō' wa, tsunagareru ka [Can 'non-resistant participation' and 'non-participatory resistance' be linked?]. *PEOPLE'S PLAN*, 28, pp. 22–29.
Higuchi, N. (2016). *Japan's ultra-right*. Melbourne: Trans Pacific Press.
Higuchi, N. (2018). 3/11 igo no shakai undō: Dare ga sanka shita no ka [Post-3.11 social movements: Who participated?]. *2018 nendo Nihon Seiji Gakkai Hōkoku* [Report of the 2018 Japanese Politics Conference].
Hirabayashi, Y. (2013). Nani ga 'demo no aru shakai' o tsukuru no ka?: Posuto 3/11 no akutivizumu to media [What makes a 'society with demonstrations'?: Post-3.11 activism and the media]. In S. Tanaka, H. Funabashi and T. Masamura (eds), *Higashi Nihon daishinsai to shakaigaku: Daisaigai o umidashita shakai* [The Great East Japan Earthquake and tsunami and sociology: A society that gave rise to a great disaster]. Kyoto: Minerva Shobō, pp. 163–195.
Honda, H. (2014). Seiji no kōzō [The structure of politics]. In H. Honda and T. Horie (eds), *Datsu genpatsu no hikaku seijigaku* [The comparative

politics of abandoning nuclear power generation]. Tokyo: Hōsei Daigaku Shuppankyoku, pp. 71–89.

Hōsō o kataru kai monitā gurūpu (2012). Terebi wa dō tsutaetaka 'Sayonara genpatsu 10 mannin shūkai' [How TV broadcasted 'Farewell to Nuclear Power Plants 100 Thousand Assembly']. *Sogo Journalism Kenkyū*, 222, pp. 36–37.

Ide, M., Suzuki, K., Takeuchi, M., Hattori, S., and Redwolf, M. (E. Oguma moderator) (2013). Kantei-mae kara no shōgen [Testimony from outside the prime minister's official residence]. In E. Oguma and C. Kinoshita (eds), *Genpatsu o tomeru hitobito: 3/11 kara kantei-mae made* [People who stop nuclear power generation: From 3.11 to outside the prime minister's official residence]. Tokyo: Bungei Shunjū, pp. 11–20.

Iida, Y. (2018). *Kyūjō no kai – Atarashii nettowāku no keisei to soseisuru shakai undō* [Article Nine Association: Establishing new networks and social movements undergoing revival]. Tokyo: Kadensha.

Inoue, H. (2013). A reconsideration of 'new social movements' in 1980s Japanese society: The 'Ikego Forest Conservation Movement' I. *Nagoya Bunri Daigaku Kiyō dai 13 go* [Nagoya Bunri University Bulletin, vol. 13]. Accessed at https://www.jstage.jst.go.jp/article/nbukiyou/13/0/13_KJ00008386379/_pdf.

Inoue, K. (2006). PSE-hō 'Akumademo minaoshi o' gyōsha ra, sara ni shomei katsudō [Those who say, 'We need to reexamine everything about this law', in addition to petition-raising activism]. *Asahi Shimbun*, 25 March.

Inoue, T., and Katō, M. (eds) (1993). *Hana ni hikiyoserareru dōbutsu tachi: Hana to sōfunsha tachi no kyōshinka* [Animals attracted by flowers: Coevolution of flowers and pollinators]. Tokyo: Heibonsha.

Ishida, T. (1961). *Gendai soshiki ron* [Contemporary organizational theory]. Tokyo: Iwanami Shoten.

Itō, M. (2012). *Demo no media ron: shakai undō shakai no yukue* [Discourse of demonstration as media: The whereabouts of social movement society]. Tokyo: Chikuma Shobō.

JETRO (2019). The minimum wage (hourly wage) in 2020 has risen 2.87 percent to 8,590 won, 8 August. Accessed at https://www.jetro.go.jp/biznews/2019/08/d031629e14d52d41.html.

Kan, N., and Oguma, E. (interviewer) (2013). Kantei no naka kara no shōgen [Testimony from inside the prime minister's official residence]. In E. Oguma and C. Kinoshita (eds), *Genpatsu o tomeru hitobito: 3/11 kara kantei-mae made* [People who stop nuclear power generation: From 3.11 to outside the prime minister's official residence]. Tokyo: Bungei Shunjū, pp. 161–192.

Kanagawa Shimbun (2019). Zenkai icchi de seiritsu o: Sabetsu kinshi jōrei teishutsu muke Kawasaki shichō [Kawasaki mayor to submit anti-discrimination ordinance for unanimous approval], 19 November. Accessed 19 August 2020 at https://www.kanaloco.jp/article/entry-209022.html.

Kaneko, K. (2014). *Seimei towa nani ka – Fukuzatsu-kei seimei kagaku e dainihan* [What is life: Toward complex-systems biology, second edition]. Tokyo: Tokyo Daigaku Shuppan Kai.

Karatani, K., and Matsumoto, H. (2012). Taiwa: Seikatsu to ittaika shita demo wa tegowai [Dialogue: The strength of demonstrations that merge with the everyday life]. In J. Setouchi, S. Kamata and K. Karatani, et al., *Datsugenpatsu to demo-Soshite, minshushugi* [Abandoning nuclear power generation and demonstrations: And, democracy]. Tokyo: Chikuma Shobō, pp. 116–129.

Kasai, K., and Noma, Y. (2016). *San-ichiichi go no hanran: Hangenren, shibakitai, SEALDs* [Post-3.11 rebellion: The Metropolitan Coalition Against Nukes, Corps of Racist- Bashers and SEALDs]. Tokyo: Shūeisha.

Kawamoto, Y. (2013). Shinkoku ni uketomerareta 'Tadachi ni eikyō wa nai' [The 'there is no immediate impact' that was seriously accepted]. *WEB RONZA*, 8 March.

Kawasaki, K., and Asano, T. (eds) (2016). *'Wakamono' no yōkai* [The dissolution of 'young people']. Tokyo: Keisō Shobō.

Kim, S. (2016). Abstract of a presentation at Kawasaki City Labor Union Hall in August 2016. Unpublished.

Kinoshita, C. (2013a). Mumei no musū no hitobito to tsunagatte ikitai [I want to join up with a countless number of nameless people from here onward]. In E. Oguma and C. Kinoshita (eds), *Genpatsu o tomeru hitobito: 3/11 kara kantei-mae made* [People who stop nuclear power generation: From 3.11 to outside the prime minister's official residence]. Tokyo: Bungei Shunjū, pp. 47–49.

Kinoshita, C. (2013b). Hangenpatsu demo wa donoyouni tenkai shitaka [How did the anti-nuclear power generation demonstration develop?]. In E. Oguma and C. Kinoshita (eds), *Genpatsu o tomeru hitobito: 3/11 kara kantei-mae made* [People who stop nuclear power generation: From 3.11 to outside the prime minister's official residence]. Tokyo: Bungei Shunjū, pp. 305–313.

Kinoshita, C. (2013c). Kanmatsu furoku: 2011-nen ikō no hangenpatsu demo, risuto [Appendix: A list of anti-nuclear power generation demonstrations after 2011]. In E. Oguma and C. Kinoshita (eds), *Genpatsu o tomeru hitobito: 3/11 kara kantei-mae made* [People who stop nuclear power generation: From 3.11 to outside the prime minister's official residence]. Tokyo: Bungei Shunjū, pp. 1–38.

Kinoshita, C. (2017). *Popyurizumu to 'min'i' no seijigaku: San-ichiichi go no minshushugi* [The politics of populism and the 'will of the people': Post-3.11 democracy]. Tokyo: Ōtsuki Shoten.

Kinoshita, C. (2019). *'Shakai o kaeyō' to iwaretara* [When someone says 'Let's change society']. Tokyo: Ōtsuki Shoten.

Kitada, A., Kurihara, Y., and Gotō, K. (2017). *Gendai Nippon rondan jijō: Shakai hihyō no 30 nen shi* [Opinion forum in contemporary Japan

for adademic and journalistic debate: Thirty years of social critique]. Tokyo: Īsuto Puresu [East Press].
Klein, N. (2007). *The shock doctrine: The rise of disaster capitalism.* New York: Picador.
Klein, N. (2015). *This changes everything: Capitalism vs. climate.* New York: Simon & Schuster.
Kobayashi, I. (2003). Gēmu kankaku de henka o okose [Make a change like playing games]. *Asahi Shimbun,* 2 March.
Kobayashi, T. (2016). *Shinia sayoku to wa nani ka: Han-anpo hōsei, han-genpatsu undō de shutsugen* [What does 'senior left-wingers' mean? Participating in the anti-National Security Legislation and anti-nuclear power generation movements]. Tokyo: Asahi Shimbun Shuppan.
Komori, Y., Kurosawa, I., Motoyama, J., and Saigō, M. (2016). *Akirameru koto o akirameta: Sengo nanajūichi-nenme no demokurashii* [I gave up giving up: Democracy in the 71st year after the war]. Kyoto: Kamogawa Shuppan.
Konomachi Ākaibuzu [City archives] (2017). Chūō sen ensen de hanahiraita sabukaruchā [The subculture that blooms along the Chūō Line], 30 May. Accessed at https://smtrc.jp/town-archives/city/koenji/p07.html.
Korpi, W. (1978). *The working class in welfare capitalism: Work, unions and politics in Sweden.* London: Routledge & Kegan Paul.
Kōseirōdōshō [Ministry of Health, Labor and Welfare] (2016). *Rōdō sōgi tōkei chōsa* [Statistical survey of labor disputes]. Accessed at https://www.mhlw.go.jp/toukei/list/14-22.html.
Kōseirōdōshō [Ministry of Health, Labor and Welfare] (2017). Zuhyō-2-1-18: Setaikōzōbetsu sōtaiteki hinkonritsu no suii [Changes in the relative poverty rate by household structure]. *Heisei 29 nendo ban Kōseirodō hakusho* [2017 Health and Labor White Paper]. Accessed at https://www.mhlw.go.jp/wp/hakusyo/kousei/17/backdata/01-02-01-18.html.
Kōseirōdōshō [Ministry of Health, Labor and Welfare] (2018). Rōdō Kumiai Kiso Chōsa [Basic survey of labor unions].
Kōseirōdōshō [Ministry of Health, Labor and Welfare] (2020). Chiiki betsu saitei chingin no zenkoku ichiran [List of the minimum wage in all of the prefectures]. Accessed at https://www.mhlw.go.jp/stf/seisakunitsuite/bunya/koyou_roudou/roudoukijun/minimumichiran/.
Krauss, E. S., and Simcock, B. L. (1980). Citizens' movements: The growth and impact of environmental protest in Japan. In K. Steiner, E. S. Krauss and S. C. Flanagan (eds), *Political opposition and local politics in Japan.* Princeton: Princeton University Press, pp. 187–227.
Kyoto Shimbun (2009). Daitenkan – ikikata ga kawaru – Dai 2 bu: hito to machi ga tsunagaru tanoshisa – 'Shirōto no ran' kyōkan hirogaru [Great conversion – lifestyle change – part 2: The pleasure of connecting people and town – growing sympathy towards 'Amateur Revolt'], 16 February.
'Kyūjō kaeru na! Abe seiken NO! 2019/3/2 Suginami demo' [Don't change Article Nine! NO to the Abe regime! 2 March 2019 Suginami demonstration]

(2019). Accessed at http://www.mkimpo.com/diary/2019/abe_no_suginami_19-03-02.html.
Lash, S., and Urry, J. (1987). *The end of organized capitalism*. Maddison: University of Wisconsin Press.
Locke, J. ([1689] 1960). *Two Treatises of Government*. Reprinted in P. Laslett (ed.), Locke: *Two Treaties of Government*. Cambridge: Cambridge University Press (Japanese edition of Second treaties of two treaties of government: N. Ukai (trans.) (1968). *Shimin seifuron*. Tokyo: Iwanami Shoten.
Locke, J. ([1689] 1968) *Shimin seifu ron*, Nobushige Ukai (trans.). Tokyo: Iwanami Shoten. (Japanese translation of J. Locke ([1689] 1960). *Second treaties of two treaties of government*.)
Locke, J. ([1689] 1975). *An essay concerning human understanding*. Reprinted in P. H. Nidditch (ed.), *John Locke: An essay concerning human understanding*. Oxford: Clarendon Press.
Machimura, T., and Satō, K. (2016). Chōsa no gaiyō: Datsu genpatsu o mezasu shimin katsudō eno apurōchi [A research outline: The approach to the citizens' activities towards the abandonment of nuclear power generation]. In T. Machimura and K. Satō (eds), *Datsu genpatsu o mezasu shimin katsudō: 3.11 shakai undō no shakaigaku* [Citizens' activities towards abandoning nuclear power generation: Sociology of 3.11 social movements]. Tokyo: Shin'yōsha, pp. 15–32.
Mainichi Shimbun (2017). Jimintō; tōin 1,000 nin kakutoku noruma [LDP: Quota to acquire 1,000 party members], 27 June. Accessed at https://mainichi.jp/articles/20170628/k00/00m/010/114000c.
Mainichi Shimbun (2018). Sugita giin jishoku jimintou-mae ni 5000 nin ga atsumaru [5,000 people call for representative Sugita Mio to resign], 28 July. Accessed at https://mainichi.jp/articles/20180728/k00/00m/040/076000c.
Mainichi Shimbun (2020). Higashinihon-daishinsai, anotoki no 'kyou' 3 gatsu 27 nichi [The Great East Japan Earthquake, 'today' of that time, 27 March], 27 March. Accessed at https://mainichi.jp/graphs/20200316/hpj/00m/040/011000g/5.
Manabe, H., and Ōta, M. (2007). Rosuto jenerēshon 1: Samayou 2000 mannin [Lost generation 1: The footloose 20 million]. *Asahi Shimbun*, 1 January.
Matsumoto, H. (2008a). *Binbōnin no gyakushū: Tada de ikiru hōhō* [The poor strike back: How to live for free]. Tokyo: Chikuma Shobō.
Matsumoto, H. (2008b). *Binbōnin dai-hanran: Ikinikui yononaka to tanoshiku tatakau hōhō* [The great rebellion of the poor: How to enjoy pushing back against a hostile world]. Tokyo: Aspect Inc.
Matsumoto, H. (2012a). 2 gatsu 27 nichi, Taiwan hōkokukai & chokusō kafe kyūshutsu sakusen [Report on visit to Taiwan and relief operation for Chokusō Café], 27 February. https://ameblo.jp/tsukiji14/entry-11175111901.html?newwindow=true.
Matsumoto, H. (2012b). Zenbu no genpatsu o tomeru made [Until we stop all

the nuclear power plants]. In J. Setouchi, S. Kamata and K. Karatani, et al., *Datsugenpatsu to demo- Soshite, minshushugi* [Abandoning nuclear power generation and demonstrations: And, democracy]. Tokyo: Chikuma Shobō, pp. 12–13.

Matsumoto, H. (2016a). 'Sekai ōbaka shūketsu kinen! Sakoku hantai parēdo' kaisai! Tsuini mugen kōryū no saikuru ga mawarihajimeta! ['Celebrating a gathering of the fools of the world! Holding a parade against the national isolation policy!' The cycle of never-ending exchange begins at last!]. *Magajin kyūjō: Matsumoto Hajime no nobinobi daisakusen, dai 95 kai* [Article Nine Magazine: Matsumoto Hajime's peaceful great strategy, No. 95], 5 October. Accessed at http://www.magazine9.jp/article/matsumoto/30442/.

Matsumoto, H. (2016b). *Sekai manuke hanran no tebikisho: Fuzaketa basho no tsukurikata* [Rebellion handbook for the fools of the world: How to create a place to joke about]. Tokyo: Chikuma Shobō.

Matsumoto, H. (2017). Ajia ken no ugō no shū ga Souru ni shūketsu [Rabble-rousers from across Asia gather in Seoul!]. *Magajin kyūjō: Matsumoto Hajime no nobinobi daisakusen, dai 105 kai* [Article Nine Magazine: Matsumoto Hajime's peaceful great strategy, No. 105], 27 September. Accessed at https://maga9.jp/nobinobi170927/.

Matsumoto, H. (2018a). Kōenji ikki 2018! [Kōenji riot 2018!]. *Magajin kyūjō: Matsumoto Hajime no nobinobi daisakusen, dai 109 kai* [Article Nine Magazine: Matsumoto Hajime's peaceful great strategy, No. 109], 24 January. Accessed at https://maga9.jp/180124-2/.

Matsumoto, H. (2018b). Kōenji saikaihatsu hantai parēdo: Buji subete shūryō [The Kōenji anti-redevelopment parade – all ended well]. *Shirōto no ran 5gō-ten, tenshu nikki* [Amateur Riot: Diary of the owner of Shop No. 5], 26 September. Accessed at https://ameblo.jp/tsukiji14/.

Matsumoto, H. (2018c). Manuke bunkaken tsui ni sekidō o koeru! NO LIMIT Jakaruta ga yatte kuru [Fools' culture finally crosses the Equator! Here comes NO LIMIT Jakarta]. *Magajin kyūjō: Matsumoto Hajime no nobinobi daisakusen, dai 118 kai* [Article Nine Magazine: Matsumoto Hajime's peaceful great strategy, No. 118], 21 November. Accessed at https://maga9.jp/181121-6/.

Matsumoto, H. (2019). Mata Suginami! Abe seiken hantai no daikibo demo ga hassei! [Suginami again! Large-scale demonstration against the Abe regime occurs!]. *Magajin kyūjō: Matsumoto Hajime no nobinobi daisakusen, dai 120 kai* [Article Nine Magazine: Matsumoto Hajime's peaceful great strategy, No. 120], February 13. Accessed at https://maga9.jp/190213-6/.

Matsumoto, H., and Futatsugi, S. (eds) (2008). *Shirōto no ran* [Amateur Revolt]. Tokyo: Kawade Shobō Shinsha.

Matsumoto, H., Higuchi, T., Kinoshita, C., and Ikegami, Y. (2012). Nisen jūninen nigatsu nijūhachinichi Kōenji 'Shirōto no ran' to Uōrugai o musubu'

kiroku [Record of the linking of the Kōenji 'Amateur Revolt' and Wall Street, February 28, 2012]. *Shibungi: Chiiki bunka ichi no tameno sōgō zasshi* [Quadrante: Areas, cultures and positions], 14, pp. 9–33.
Melucci, A. (1989). *Nomads of the present: Social movements and individual needs in contemporary society*. Philadelphia: Temple University Press.
Meyer, D. S., and Tarrow, S. (1998). A movement society: Contentious politics for a new century. In S. M. David and S. Tarrow (eds), *The social movement society: Contentious politics for a new century*. Lanham: Rowman and Littlefield Publishers Inc., pp. 1–28
Mills, C. W. (1997). *The racial contract*. Ithaca: Cornel University Press.
Miyagi, E. (2001). Sengo seiji taigen shita futari – Senaga Kamejirō to Nishime Junji (Ge) [Two people who have experienced post-war politics: K. Senaga and J. Nishime (vol. 2)]. *Ryūkyū Shimpō*, 29 December.
Miyagi, Y. (2008). *Okinawa rapusodi* [Okinawa rhapsody]. Tokyo: Ochanomizu Shobō.
Miyazaki, S. (2019). 'Kodomo' no seiji hatsugen [Political talk of 'children']. *Asahi Shimbun*, 1 November.
Monod, J. (1971). *Chance and necessity: An essay on the natural philosophy of modern biology*. New York: Alfred A. Knopf.
Mōri, Y. (2009). *Sutorīto no shisō: Tenkanki toshite no 1990 nendai* [Street thought: The 1990s as a turning-point]. Tokyo: NHK Shuppan.
Mori, H., and Kubo, Y. (2016). Atsuryoku dantai seiji no zendankai: Yūkensha chōsa to rieki dantai chōsa no bunseki [The precursor to pressure-group politics: Analysis of voter surveys and interest-group surveys]. In Y. Tsujinaka (ed.), *Seiji hendōki no atsuryoku dantai* [Pressure groups in a political transition period]. Tokyo: Yūhikaku, pp. 13–37.
Muramatsu, M. (1994). *Nihon no gyōsei: Katsudō-gata kanryōsei no henbō* [Japan's administration: The transformation of active bureaucracy]. Tokyo: Chūō Kōronsha.
Nakamura, M. (2013). 'Demo wari' de chiiki kangen shiyō [Let's restore regional areas with 'demonstration discount']. In E. Oguma and C. Kinoshita (eds), *Genpatsu o tomeru hitobito: 3/11 kara kantei-mae made* [People who stop nuclear power generation: From 3.11 to outside the prime minister's official residence]. Tokyo: Bungei Shunjū, pp. 77–79.
Nakamura, Y. (director) (2008). *Shirōto no ran* [Amateur Revolt], 80 mins., documentary film. Accessed at https://www.youtube.com/watch?v=2ovV47QWrDM.
Narumi, K. (2019a). 'Kōenji' de saikaihatsu ga nakanaka susumanai haikei-karuchā no machi wa dono yō ni shite umareta ka [How did it emerge: Kōenji, the culture town where redevelopment makes little progress?]. *Tōyō Keizai onrain* [Toyo Keizai Online], 7 February. Accessed at https://toyokeizai.net/articles/-/264096?page=3.
Narumi, K. (2019b). Dīpu na machi: Kōenji ga'furugi' 'awaodori' de yūmei ni natta wake [Deep town: 'Second-hand clothes' and '*awa odori*' dancing

made Kōenji famous]. *Āban raifu metro* [Urban Life Metro], 25 May. Accessed at https://urbanlife.tokyo/post/11231/3/.
Nihon Keizai Shimbun (2011). Hamaoka-genpatsu teishi o motomete Tokyo de demo [2,500 people participated in a demonstration in Tokyo against the Hamaoka nuclear plant], 10 April. Accessed at https://www.nikkei.com/article/DGXNASDG1001U_Q1A410C1CR8000/.
'No Limit Tokyo Autonomous Zone' (2016). Event n.d. Accessed at http://nolimit.tokyonantoka.xyz/events/.
'No Limit Tokyo jichiku' [No Limit Tokyo Autonomous Zone] (2016). Accessed at http://nolimit.tokyonantoka.xyz/.
Noma, Y. (2012). *Kin'yō kanteimae kōgi: Demo no koe ga seiji o kaeru* [Friday protest in front of the prime minister's official residence: Voices of demonstration will change politics]. Tokyo: Kawade Shobō Shinsha.
Noma, Y. (2018). *Jitsuroku: Reishisuto o shibaki tai* [True record: The Corps of Racist-Bashers]. Tokyo: Kawade Shobō Shinsha.
Oberschall, A. (1978). Theories of social conflict. *Annual Review of Sociology*, 4, pp. 291–315.
Obinger, J. (2015). *Alternative Lebensstile und Aktivismus in Japan: Der Aufstand der Amateure in Tokyo* [Alternative lifestyle and activism in Japan: Amateur Revolt in Tokyo]. Wiesbaden: Springer.
Oda, M. (2006). We are the three (only)!. Accessed at https://www.youtube.com/watch?v=kROFCjoWcYw.
Offe, C. (1985). *Disorganized capitalism*. Cambridge: The MIT Press.
Oguma, E. (2002). *'Minshu' to 'aikoku': Sengo Nihon no nashonarizumu to kōkyōsei* ['Democracy' and 'patriotism': Post-war Japan's nationalism and the public]. Tokyo: Shin'yōsha.
Oguma, E. (2012a). Rekishi no henka no genba [Sites of historical change]. In J. Setouchi, S. Kamata and K. Karatani, et al., *Datsugenpatsu to demo: soshite, minshushugi* [Abandoning nuclear power generation and demonstrations: And, democracy]. Tokyo: Chikuma Shobō, pp. 140–143.
Oguma, E. (2012b). *Shakai o kaeru ni wa* [To change society]. Tokyo: Kōdansha.
Oguma, E. (2013). Mōten o saguriateta shikō: 3.11 igo no sho-undō no tsūshi to Bunseki [Trials that found the blind spot by groping: A complete history and analysis of the movements after 3.11]. In E. Oguma and C. Kinoshita (eds), *Genpatsu o tomeru hitobito: 3.11 kara Kanteimae made* [People who stop nuclear power generation: From 3.11 to outside the prime minister's official residence]. Tokyo: Bungei Shunjū, pp. 193–304.
Oguma, E. (2015). *Shushō kantei no mae de* [Tell the prime minister]. Directed and produced by E. Oguma. Accessed at https://www.uplink.co.jp/kanteimae/index_en.php.
Oguma, E. (2016). Nami ga yosereba, iwa ga shizumu: Fukushima genpatsu jiko go ni okieru shakai undō no shakaigakuteki bunseki [When the wave comes, the rock submerges: Sociological analysis of social movements

after the accident at the Fukushima nuclear power plant]. *Gendai Shisō* [Contemporary Thought], 44(7), pp. 206–233.
Oguma, E., and Kinoshita, C. (eds) (2013). *Genpatsu o tomeru hitobito: 3.11 kara Kantei-mae made* [People who stop nuclear power generation: From 3.11 to outside the prime minister's official residence]. Tokyo: Bungeishunjū.
Oguma, E., and Ueno, Y. (2003). *'Iyashi' no nashonarizumu: Kusa no ne hoshu undō no jisshō kenkyū* [The nationalism of 'healing': Empirical research on grassroots conservative movements]. Tokyo: Keiō Gijuku Daigaku Shuppankai.
Okinawa Kokusai Daigaku Okinawa Housei Kenkyūjyo [Okinawa Institute of Law and Politics, Okinawa International University] (ed.) (2015). *Towareru Okinawa aidentiti towa nanika* [What is the Okinawan identity in question?]. Naha: Okinawa Taimususha.
Okinawa Taimususha (ed.) (1996). *50nenme no gekidō* [The 50th year of strife]. Naha: Okinawa Taimususha.
Okuda, A. (2015). Demo suru tabi ni pakuraretetara ore, kokkai ni ittenai su yo [If we'd been arrested each time we held a demonstration, I wouldn't have gone to the Diet building]. *NONUKES voice*, 6, pp. 73–87.
Okuda, A., and Inose, K. (interviewer) (2015). Yūki, aruiwa kake toshite [As courage, or as risk-taking]. *Gendai shisō* [Contemporary Thought], Rinji zōkan-gō [special edition], October, pp. 45–51.
Okuda, A., Kuramochi, R., and Fukuyama, T. (2015). *2015-nen Anpo: Kokkai no uchi to soto de—Minshushugi o yarinaosu* [The 2015 National Security Legislation: Remaking democracy – inside and outside the Diet building]. Tokyo: Iwanami Shoten.
Okuda, A., Oguma, E., and Redwolf, M. (2016). 'Kanteimae' kara 'Kokkaimae' e [From 'in front of the prime minister's official residence' to 'in front of the Diet']. *Gendai Shisō* [Contemporary Thought], 44(7), pp. 30–55.
Ōsawa, M. (2015). SEALDs no shūhen kara: Hoshusei no naka no kakushinsei [From the SEALDs environs: Reformism within conservatism]. *Gendai Shisō* [Contemporary Thought], Rinji zōkan-gō [special edition], October, pp. 52–54.
Our Planet TV (2011). Sinjuku arutamae hiroba ni nimannin [20,000 people in ALTA Square], 14 June. Accessed at http://www.ourplanet-tv.org/?q=node/1110.
Pak, C. (1974). Minzoku jikaku eno michi – Shūshoku sabetsu saiban jōshinsho [My road to racial self-awareness: Submission to employment discrimination trial]. In Paku-kun o kakomu kai (ed.), *Minzoku sabetsu – Hitachi shūshoku sabetsu kyūdan* [Racial discrimination: Condemnation of employment discrimination by Hitachi]. Tokyo: Aki Shobō, pp. 237–260.
Panku rokkā rōdō kumiai [Punk Rocker Labor Union] (2019). Accessed at https://www.tunecore.co.jp/artist/P-R-L-U?id=316654&lang=ja or https://www.tunecore.co.jp/artist/P-R-L-U.

Parliament of England (1688). *Bill of rights*, Chapter 2 1 Will and Mar Sess 2. Accessed at http://www.legislation.gov.uk/aep/WillandMarSess2/1/2/introduction.
Pateman, C. (1988). *The sexual contract*. Cambridge: Polity Press.
Pateman, C., and Mills, C. W. (2007). *Contract and domination*. Cambridge: Polity Press.
Pekkanen, R. (2006). *Japan's dual civil society: Members without advocates*. Stanford: Stanford University Press.
Prigogine, I., and Stengers, I. (2017). *Order out of chaos: Man's new dialogue with nature*. London: Verso.
Redwolf, M. (2013). *Chokusetsu kōdō no chikara: 'Shushō kantei-mae kōgi'* [The power of direct action: 'Protesting outside the prime minister's official residence']. Tokyo: Crayon House.
Redwolf, M. (2015). Futatabi datsugenpatsu no kōru no bakuhatsu o!: Kongo no chō-tōha shimin undō no yukue [A second explosion of abolish nuclear power chants: The direction of a citizens' movement that transcends party politics]. *NONUKES voice*, 6, pp. 58–67.
Ryūkyū Shimpōsha (ed.) (2018). *Tamashiino seijika Onaga Takeshi hatsugenroku* [Chronicles of the words of politician Onaga Takeshi]. Tokyo: Kōbunken.
Saigō, M. (2015). 'Dare no kodomo mo, korosasenai' watashitachi no demosu kuratia [Our 'Never let anyone's child be killed' people's power]. *Sekai* [The World], December, pp. 140–143.
Saigō, M. (2018). 'Anpo hōsei ni hantai suru mama no kai': Tachiagatte kara to, kore kara [The 'Group of mothers opposed to the National Security Legislation': After it arose, and from here forward]. *Heiwa undō: riron to jissen* [Peace movements: Theory and practice], 566, pp. 2–16.
Samalavičius, A. (2008). An amorphous society: Lithuania in the era of high post-communism. A. Simanaviciute (trans.). First published in *Kulturos barai* (February 2007). Accessed at https://www.eurozine.com/an-amorphous-society/.
Satō, K., Harada, S., Nagayoshi, K., Matsutani, M., Higuchi, N., and Ōhata, H. (2018). San-ichiichi go no undō sanka: Han-/datsu-genpatsu undō to han-anpo hōsei undō e no sanka o chūshin ni [Post-3.11 movement participation: Focusing on participation in the anti-/abandoning nuclear power generation and anti-National Security Legislation movements]. *Tokushima daigaku shakai kagaku kenkyū* [Social Sciences Research, Tokushima University], 32, pp. 1–77.
'Sayonara genpatsu issenman-nin akushon' [Goodbye nuclear power generation ten-million-person action] (2019). Accessed at http://sayonara-nukes.org/.
SEALDs (Students Emergency Action for Liberal Democracy) (2015). *Minshushugi tte kore da!* [This is what democracy looks like!]. Tokyo: Ōtsuki Shoten.
SEALDs (2016). *Minshushugi wa tomaranai* [Democracy will not stop]. Tokyo: Kawade Shobō Shinsha.

Shimbun Akahata (2012). Genpastu nakuse jyū-nana mannnin [170,000 people participated in the no nuke rally], 17 July. Accessed at https://www.jcp. or.jp/akahata/aik12/2012-07-17/2012071701_01_1.html.

Shimomura, Y. (2011). Tōkyō, Kōenji ni okeru furugi ko'uriten no shūseki: Daitoshi shōgyō chi'iki no kōshin ni okeru' jakunen jieigyōsha [The agglomeration of second-hand clothing stores in Kōenji, Tokyo: Young independent retailers in the regeneration of urban commercial areas]. *Nihon toshi shakai gakkai nenpō* [The Annals of the Japan Association for Urban Sociology], 29, pp. 77–92. Accessed at https://www.jstage.jst. go.jp/article/jpasurban/2011/29/2011_77/_pdf/-char/en.

Shin Okinawa Fōramu Kankō Kaigi (ed.) (1996). *Kēshi-Kaji* [The returning wind], vol. 51.

Shiozawa, Y. (1997a). *Fukuzatsu-kei keizaigaku nyūmon* [Economics of complex systems]. Tokyo: Seisansei Shuppan.

Shiozawa, Y. (1997b). *Fukuzatsusa no kiketsu – Fukuzatsu-kei keizaigaku shiron* [Economic essays on complexity and complex systems]. Tokyo: NTT Shuppan.

Shiraishi, H. (2011). *Media o tsukuru: 'Chiisa-na koe' o tsutaeru tame ni* [Creating media: To convey the 'little voices']. Tokyo: Iwanami Shoten.

Shutoken hangenpatsu rengō [Metropolitan Coalition Against Nukes] (n.d.). Saikidō hantai! Shushō kantei mae kōgi [We oppose reactor restarts! Protest outside the prime minister's official residence], 8 nenme e' [Towards the eighth year]. Accessed at http://coalitionagainstnukes.jp/?p=12518.

Solnit, R. (2010). *A paradise built in hell: The extraordinary communities that arise in Disaster.* New York: Penguin Books.

Sōmushō [Ministry of Internal Affairs and Communications] (2012). Topikku: Arabu kakumei to sōsharu media [Topic: Arab revolutions and social media]. *Heisei 24 nendo ban jōhōtsūshin hakusho* [Telecommunications white paper for the 2012 fiscal year]. Accessed at https://www.soumu. go.jp/johotsusintokei/whitepaper/ja/h24/html/nc1212c0.html.

Sono, R. (2011). *Boku ga Tōden mae ni tatta wake* [Why I stood in front of TEPCO]. Tokyo: San-Ichi Shobō.

Steinhoff, P. (2018). The uneven path of social movements in Japan. In D. Chiavacci and J. Obinger (eds), *Social movements and political activism in contemporary Japan: Re-emerging from invisibility.* London: Routledge, pp. 27–50.

'Stop Hamaoka nuclear plant' blog (2011). Nanohana kakumei-shimin ga Nagoya de demo [450 citizens demonstrate in Nagoya]. Accessed at http:// stophamaokanuclearpp.com/blog/?p=5.

Suga, H. (2012). *Hangenpatsu no shisō-shi: Reisen kara FUKUSHIMA e* [The history of the thinking behind opposition to nuclear power: From the Cold War to FUKUSHIMA]. Tokyo: Chikuma Shobō.

Sugimoto, Y., and Mouer, R. (1995). *Nihonjinron no hōteishiki* [The Japanology equations]. Tokyo: Chikuma Shobō.

Tahara, M. (2019). Honkon demo ni higashi Ajia no wakamono: Kokkyō koeta chika suimyaku [The youth of East Asia at Hong Kong demonstrations: Subterranean border-crossing]. *Tōkyō Shimbun*, 18 July.
Takabatake, M. (1979). Taishū undō no tayōka to henshitsu [The diversification and transformation of mass movements]. In Nihon Seijigakkai [Japanese Political Science Association] (ed.), *Nenpō seijigaku 1977: gojūgonen taisei no keisei to hōkai: zoku gendai Nihon no seiji katei* [The annuals of the Japanese Political Science Association 1977. The formation and disintegration of the 1955 system: The political process in contemporary Japan, continued]. Tokyo: Iwanami Shoten, pp. 323–359.
Takagi, Y., Suenobu, S., and Miyazawa, T. (eds) (1957). *Jinken sengen shū* [Collection of human rights declarations]. Tokyo: Iwanami Shoten.
Takahashi, G., and SEALDs (2015). *Minshushugi tte nanda?* [Tell me what democracy looks like?]. Tokyo: Kawadeshobō Shinsha.
Takahashi, M., and Matsumoto, H. (2012). Fukushima no koto o wasurete kureru na [Do not forget about Fukushima]. In J. Setouchi, S. Kamata and K. Karatani, et al., *Datsugenpatsu to demo: soshite, minshushugi* [Abandoning nuclear power generation and demonstrations: And, democracy]. Tokyo: Chikuma Shobō, pp. 44–51.
Takakusagi, K. (ed.) (2016). *Beheiren to shimin undō no genzai: Yoshikawa Yūichi ga nokoshita mono* [The Citizen's League for Peace in Vietnam and the present situation of citizens' movements: Yūichi Yoshikawa's legacy]. Tokyo: Kadensha.
Takatsuka, M. (2015). Tokubetsu intabyū: 'Sensō shitakunakute furueru demo' shusaisha, Takatsuka Mao-san [Special interview: Demonstration of 'I hate war so much it makes me shiver' organizer, Ms. Mao Takatsuka]. *Onnatachi no nijūisseiki* [The Women's 21st Century], 83, pp. 46–48.
Tamura, T., and Tamura, D. (2016). *Rojō no shintai, netto no jōdō. Sanichiichi go no atarashii shakai undō: han-genpatsu, han-sabetsu, soshite SEALDs* [Bodies on the road, effect on the net. New post-3.11 social movements: Anti-nuclear power generation, anti-discrimination and SEALDs]. Tokyo: Seitōsha.
Tanaka, H. (2015). Atarashii anākizumu wa naze 'atarashii' no ka: Shisō to undō no henyō ni kansuru shiteki kōsatsu [What is 'new' about 'new anarchism'?: A historical consideration of transformation in thought and activism]. *Rekishi kenkyū* (Journal of Historical Studies), 39–76.
Tanno, K. (2018). *'Gaikokujin no jinken' no shakaigaku – Gaikokujin eno manazashi to gisō sashō, shōnen hikō, LGBT, soshite heito* [Sociology of foreigners' human rights in Japan: Perception of foreigners, forged visas, juvenile delinquency, LGBT and hate]. Tokyo: Yoshida Shoten.
Tanno, K. (2019). Gaikokujin no 'shitizunshippu' – Gyōsei un'yō to shakai undō no aidani umareru shimin ken [Foreigners' 'citizenship': Civil rights arising between administrative application and social activism]. *Fukushi shakaigaku kenkyū* [Journal of Welfare Sociology], 16, pp. 13–28.

Tanno, K. (2020). *'Kokuseki no kyōkai' o kangaeru – Nihonjin, Nikkeijin, Zainichi o hedateru hō to shakai no kabe, zōho kaitei ban* [Considering the 'borders of nationality': Legal and social barriers separating Japanese, Japanese descendants and Korean residents, enlarged and revised edition]. Tokyo: Yoshida Shoten.

Tinbergen, N. (1969). *The study of instinct.* Oxford: Oxford University Press.

TNN (2011). *Demo iko! Koe o agereba sekai ga kawaru; Machi o arukeba shakai ga mieru* [Let's go to a rally! If we raise our voices, the world will change; if we walk through the town, we will be able to see society]. Tokyo: Kawadeshobō Shinsha.

Tominaga, K. (2017). *Shakai undō to wakamono: Nichijō to dekigoto o ōkan suru seiji* [Social movements and young people: Politics that swings between the everyday life and incidents]. Kyoto: Nakanishiya Shuppan.

Tomisawa, A. (2011). Tochō-mae no hanami de sanbyakunin ga han-genpastu songu o utatta yoru [300 people sing an anti-nuclear song at the cherry blossom viewing in front of the Tokyo metropolitan government], 5 April. Accessed at https://www.excite.co.jp/news/article/E1301939720954/.

Toyama, K. (2010a). Shirōto no ran: zenshi, Yamashita Hikaru intabyū 03 [The prior history of Amateur Revolt: Yamashita Hikaru interview 03], 11 January. Accessed at https://ameblo.jp/toyamakoichi/entry-10431684864.html?frm=theme.

Toyama, K. (2010b). Shirōto no ran: zenshi, Yamashita Hikaru intabyū 04 [The prior history of Amateur Revolt: Yamashita Hikaru interview 04], 12 January. Accessed at https://ameblo.jp/toyamakoichi/entry-10432532071.html?frm=theme.

Toyama, K. (2010c). Shirōto no ran: zenshi, Yamashita Hikaru intabyū 05 [The prior history of Amateur Revolt: Yamashita Hikaru interview 05], 13 January. Accessed at https://ameblo.jp/toyamakoichi/entry-10433357497.html?frm=theme.

Toyama, K. (2010d). Shirōto no ran: zenshi, Yamashita Hikaru intabyū 12 [The prior history of Amateur Revolt: Yamashita Hikaru interview 12], 20 January. Accessed at https://ameblo.jp/toyamakoichi/entry-10438556320.

Toyama, K. (2010e). Shirōto no ran: zenshi, Yamashita Hikaru intabyū 13 [The prior history of Amateur Revolt: Yamashita Hikaru interview 13], 21 January. Accessed at https://ameblo.jp/toyamakoichi/entry-10439239729.html.

Toyama, K. (2010f). Shirōto no ran: zenshi, Yamashita Hikaru intabyū 18 [The prior history of Amateur Revolt: Yamashita Hikaru interview 18], 26 January. Accessed at https://ameblo.jp/toyamakoichi/entry-10441186863.html?frm=theme.

Toyama, K. (2010g). Shirōto no ran: zenshi, Yamashita Hikaru intabyū 19 [The prior history of Amateur Revolt: Yamashita Hikaru interview 19], 27 January. Accessed at https://ameblo.jp/toyamakoichi/entry-10443992789.html?frm=theme.

Toyama, K. (2010h). Shirōto no ran: zenshi, Yamashita Hikaru intabyū 20 – saishūkai [The prior history of Amateur Revolt: Yamashita Hikaru interview 20 – final installment], 28 January. Accessed at https://ameblo. jp/toyamakoichi/entry-10444799302.html?frm=theme.
Tsukio, Y. (1991). *Posuto jōhō shakai no tōrai: Jūnen go o kaeru nanatsu no gijutsu kakushin to wa?* [The advent of the post-information society: What are the seven technological innovations that will change the next decade?]. Tokyo: PHP Kenkyūsho.
Ueno, C. (2015). Shitte ita no ni nani mo shinakatta watashi mo kyōhansha datta [Although I knew but did nothing, I was an accomplice, too]. *NONUKES voice*, 6, pp. 40–48.
Ueno, C., and Kitada A. (2015). '1968' to '2015' no aida: Anpo hōan hantai undō no atarashisa to keishō shita mono [Between '1968' and '2015': Innovation and continuity in the anti-National Security Legislation movement]. at *PURASU* (at Plus), 26, pp. 4–37.
Uozumi, Y., Nishida, S., Yakura, K., Miyake, S., Arita, Y., Nihi, S., and Tani, R. (2016). *Heito supīchi kaishō hō – Seiritsu no keii to kihontekina kangaekata* [Hate Speech Elimination Act: Enactment process and basic thinking]. Tokyo: Daiichi Hōki.
van der Steen, B., Katzeff, A., and van Hoogenhuijze, L. (2014). Introduction: Squatting and autonomous action in Europe, 1980–2012. In B. van der Steen, A. Katzeff and L. van Hoogenhuijze (eds), *The city is ours: Squatting and autonomous movements in Europe from the 1970s to the present*. Oakland: PM Press, pp. 1–19.
Waldron, J. (2002). *God, Locke, and equality: Christian foundations in Locke's political thought*. New York: Cambridge University Press.
Waldron, J. (2012). *The harm in hate speech*. Cambridge: Harvard University Press.
Waldron, J. (2015). *Dignity, rank, and rights*. New York: Oxford University Press.
Watanabe, F. (2012). *Ai to Yūmoa no shakai undō ron: Makki shihonshugi o ikiru tameni* [Social movements for love and humor: In order to live in late capitalism]. Kyoto: Kitaōji Shobō.
Watanabe, O. (1990). *Yutakana shakai Nihon no kōzō* [The structure of Japan, the wealthy society]. Tokyo: Rōdō Junpōsha.
Watanabe, O. (1991). *Kigyō shihai to kokka* [Company dominance and the state]. Tokyo: Aoki Shoten.
Watanabe, O. (1996). Kaikyū no ronri to shimin no ronri [The logic of social class and the logic of citizenship]. In Rekishigaku Kenkyūkai (ed.), *Kōza sekaishi 12: Watakushi-tachi no jidai* [World history course 12: Our times]. Tokyo: Tokyo Daigaku Shuppankai.
Watanabe, O. (ed.) (2004). *Nihon no jidaishi 27: Kōdo seichō to kigyō shakai* [Japanese historical periods 27: High growth and corporate society]. Tokyo: Yoshikawa Kōbunkan.

Yamada, M. (2016). *Seiji sanka to minshu seiji* [Political participation and democratic politics]. Tokyo: Tokyo Daigaku Shuppankai.
Yamamoto, H., Katano, Y., Kanaya, M., Tamaki, E., and Nomiya, D. (2004). 'Shimin' no kōbō: Iraku sensō kōgi undō ni miru gendai Nihon shakai ['"Citizens" offence and defense: Contemporary Japanese society seen in the Iraq War protest movement]. *Sofia*, 52-53, pp. 65–90.
Yamamoto, T., and Matsumoto, H. (2012). Taiwa: Mirai o kaeru tame no akushon [Dialogue: Action for changing the future]. In J. Setouchi, S. Kamata and K. Karatani, et al., *Datsugenpatsu to demo: Soshite, minshushugi* [Abandoning nuclear power generation and demonstrations: And, democracy]. Tokyo: Chikuma Shobō, pp. 52–63.
Yamashita, H. (2017). *Baito yameru gakkō* [Learning to leave-off part-time work]. Tokyo: Taba Books.
Yokota, H. (2016). *SEALDs senkyō: 'Yatō wa kyōtō !'* [A SEALDs election: 'Opposition parties fighting together!']. Tokyo: Ryokufū shuppan.
Yoshida, R. (2016). Ano hi no ato: Rojō nite [After that day: On the streets]. *Gendai Shisō* [Contemporary Thought], 44(7), pp. 96–104.
yoyo (2007). Konnichi wa! [Hello!]. *VEGE shokudō nikki* [VEGE refectory diary], 2 November. Accessed at http://vegecanteen.seesaa.net/index-11.html.
Yui, D. (2019). *Heiwa o warera ni: Ekkyō suru Betonamu hansen no koe* [Give peace a chance: Border-crossing voices against the Vietnam War]. Tokyo: Iwanami Shoten.

Index

Abe administration, 12, 91, 93, 100, 106, 159, 193
Abe regime
  Anti-Conspiracy Law, 106
  anti-intellectualism, 88
  petitioned re Osprey aircraft, 159
  policies, 6, 89
  protests against, 1–4, 6, 100
  support for, 93
Abe seiken NO!, 1
Abe seiken NO: jikkō Iinkai, 100
Abe, Shinzō
  'Abe's power surge', 97
  constitutional reform, 11
  dialogue with Nakaima, 160
  impersonations, 2
  opposition to, 21, 89–91
ACT March 11th Japan, 43
Act on Special Measures for the Promotion and Development of Okinawa, 148
Act on the Promotion of Efforts to Eliminate Unfair Discriminatory Speech and Behavior Against Persons Originating from Outside Japan *see* Antihate Act
Act on the Protection of Specially Designated Secrets, 47, 50, 84
  see also Special Secrecy Law; State Secrecy Law
AEQUITAS, 93
Afghan War, 60
AICON, 136
All-Campus Joint Struggle movement *see* Zenkyōtō movement
All-Out Action Implementation Committee, 99
Amateur Revolt
  as amorphous social movement, 114–42
  anti-nuclear power demonstrations, 5–7, 9, 33–4, 130, 132, 138, 142
  anti-PSE Law demonstration, 126–8, 133–6
  beginning, 6
  effect of Iraq War, 67
  'Give back my bike' demonstration, 124–5, 132–136
  hidden network, 116
  Hirano, 49
  history, 114–15, 124–6
  imitated by overseas movements, 34
  influence of Arab Spring, 33
  international connections, 137–8
  international speakers, 130

Irregular Rhythm Asylum (IRA), 131–2, 137–8
   'Make rent free' demonstration, 128–9, 136
   Matsumoto, 3–5, 41, 43, 115–20, 123–42
   membership, 115–16
   new ideas, 20
   'No Limit Tokyo Autonomous Zone,' 130–31
   Ogasawara, 120–3, 125, 127, 131–5
   playful demonstrations, 124–36, 142
   recycling, 3, 5–6, 114, 119–20, 123, 126–7, 131, 139–41
   Shop No. One, 131, 133
   Shop No. Five, 2–4
   Shop No. Nine, 131, 137
   Shop No. Eleven, 133
   similarity to European movements, 5–6
   sound demonstrations, 2–4, 34
   style, 3–4, 6–7
   'submerged network,' 4
   'Three people' demonstrations, 126
   Yamashita, 116, 120–5, 127–8, 130–5, 139–42
amorphization of identity, 29–33
amorphization of society, 24, 26–9, 33, 37, 64
amorphous, definitions, 24, 26, 37–8
amorphous social awareness, 177–81, 189
amorphous social movements, 45–58, 61, 79, 109–13
amorphousness, 37–9

androcentrism, 35
'Angry durmmers,' 21, 50
Annen, Junji, 181
Anpo protests, 1960, 45, 84, 89, 102
Anpo Treaty, 90
anti-bomb movements, 15, 55, 99
anti-capitalism, 137, 140
Antifa, 2
anti-fascist protestors, 2
anti-globalization movement, 67
Antihate Act, 167, 175–7, 180, 182, 185, 188
anti-intellectualism, 88
Anti-National Security Legislation Mothers Against War *see* Mama no Kai
anti-nuclear power movement *see also* Hangenren
   2011 demonstrations, 5–6, 72, 138, 142
   2012 demonstrations, 109, 111
   Angry drummers, 50
   effect of Chernobyl, 63
   festive atmosphere, 21
   global, 36
   Hydrangea Revolution, 33
   impact of Fukushima accident, 40–5, 69–75
   Matsumoto, 7, 41, 43, 115, 130
   'New Wave,' 102
   'ordinary people,' 22
   representative post-Fukushima movement, 8–10
   use of social media, 29
   varied activities, 102

Index

anti-poverty movement, 19, 67–8, 93
anti-PSE Law demonstration, 126–8, 133–6
anti-racism *see also* Antihate Act
  Angry drummers, 50
  Corps of Racist-Bashers, 13
  demonstrations, 173
  dignity, 177, 180, 182–3, 185, 187
  against hate speech, 8, 25, 50, 167–89
  history, 75–7
  post Fukushima accident, 59
  regulations, 33, 57, 103, 167, 175, 177–8, 180–3, 188
  rights court cases, 167, 176–7, 180–2, 185
  slogans, 174, 177, 183
  structure, 183–4
anti-redevelopment movement, 7, 130
anti-war movements, 1, 4, 21, 67, 102, 174–5
Arab Spring, Egypt, 33
Arai, Shōji, 168
Arasaki, Moriteru, 148, 152, 155
Arita, Yoshifu, 35
Article Nine, 1–2, 11–12, 67, 87
Article Nine Association, 1, 12, 66–7
Article Ninety-Six, 11
Article Ninety-Six Association, 88
Asahi Shimbun, 75, 101, 107, 127, 137
Association for Protecting the Life of Henoko, 156
Association of Scholars Opposed to National Security Legislation, 12, 87, 97

Association of the Pathetic, 20
atsumari, 5, 116
Autonomous Movement, 139
'autonomy,' 5, 7, 116, 118, 139–40, 142
Axelrod, Robert, 171

baby-boomers, 22
Base Return Action Program, 147, 153
Basshop, 141
Battle of Okinawa, 158–9
Bauman, Zygmunt, 38
Beck, Ulrich, 38
Beheiren
  call for participants, 45–6
  Citizen's League for Peace in Vietnam, 16, 45
  Citizen's League of *Cultural Groups* for Peace in Vietnam, 45
  crowd sizes, 102
  international reach, 35–6
  non-hierarchical, 18
  'ordinary citizens,' 30
  Takahashi, 46
Bei, Jungdo, 168–9, 177
Betonamu ni heiwa o! Shimin rengō, 45
Bill No. 157, 188
Bill of Rights (England), 172
Binbōnin daihanran shūdan, 119
Binbōnin Shimbun, 118
birthrate, decline in, 65
'brotherhood politics,' 68
Brown, Alexander, 115

Camp Schwab, 148
capitalism, 27, 35, 60–1, 91
Cassegård, C., 115
Change.org, 110
chanting slogans, 1–3, 10, 21, 82, 85, 89–91, 96, 100, 135–6, 173, 177
'chaos as connecting people,' 131, 138–9
Chernobyl nuclear power plant, 8–9, 36, 40, 61, 63, 102
'Cherry Blossom viewing Rally,' 70
chōrōshū, 6
'citizens,' 29–32
Citizens' Association for the Promotion of Revitalization of Nago City, 149
'Citizens' Group that Will Not Forgive Special Privileges for Koreans in Japan', 13, 31 *see also* Zaitokukai
Citizen's League for Peace in Vietnam *see* Beheiren
Citizen's League of *Cultural Groups* for Peace in Vietnam *see* Beheiren
Citizens' Nuclear Information Center, 43
Civil Alliance Calling for Peace and Constitutionalism, 55, 98
Civil Alliance for Peace and Constitutionalism, 97
CNIC (Citizens' Nuclear Information Center), 43
cognitive precariat, 24, 81
Cold War, 33, 75, 78

collective self-defense, 11, 90
Committee Against Helicopter Base Construction, 150
communism, 35
Communist Party, 1, 45, 64, 68, 97–9, 103, 135, 141
'community,' 5
'company,' the, 28, 52–3, 63
conservatism, 18, 90–3
Constitution
  Article Nine, 1–2, 11–12, 67, 87
  Article Thirteen, 181, 184
  Article Twenty-One, 178
  Article Ninety-Six, 11
  LDP promoted reforms, 12
  post-war peace, 15
  public opinion, 64
  rallies to protect, 7, 11–13, 94, 100
  SEALDs on, 90
Constitutional Democratic Party, 1
constitutionalism, 100–1
consumer culture, 62–3
Coordination Committee to Combat Racial Discrimination in Kanagawa, 169
'Cross out the national flag' campaign, 90
crowd-funding, 36
'crystalline,' 37–8
crystalline-structure of Japanese society, 32–3, 52–3, 179
'curry struggle,' 118

Dame-ren, 20
dankai no sedai, 22

*Datsu genpatsu nau. Datsu,'
    denpatsu-kei ibento karendā,* 42
Datsu-genpatsu Suginami, 111
democracy, 29, 88–90
'democracy or dictatorship,' 89
Democratic Party, 53, 66, 68, 96–7, 159
democratization movements, 69
demonstrations
  1995, October 21st, 145
  2004, April, 154
  2007, September, 158–9
  2010, April, 159
  2011, April, 5–6, 9, 20, 41, 70–2, 115, 138, 142
  2011, March 27th, 70
  2011, June 11th, 9, 40, 72
  2011, June 15th, 73
  2011, September, 40
  2011, September 11th, 9
  2011, September 19th, 72
  2012, February, 73
  2012, March, 10
  2012, July, 10, 74
  2012, September, 159
  2013, May 12th, 173
  2013, September 5th, 174
  2013, September 8th, 76
  2014, February, 54
  2015, August 30th, 51, 86
  2016, January 31st, 174–5
  2016, June 5th, 176
  2016, June 6th, 174
  2018, July 27th, 76
  2019, March 2nd, 1–5, 7

active groups, 104
anti-nuclear power, 5–10, 33–4, 36, 109, 111, 130, 132, 138, 142
anti-racist, 8
broadening of issues, 112
crowd sizes, 13, 102–3, 109, 111, 145
Friday protests, 9–10, 23, 33–4, 36, 48
parades, 20
participants, 21–4, 40–1, 50–60, 71, 74, 77, 82
participation rate, 18, 109
police response, 104–5
public opinion, 105
visibility, 100–5
denationalization, 33–6
Denuclearization Suginami, 46, 111
'De-nuke now. De-nuke-related event calendar,' 42
deregulation of the labor market, 64
Dignity, Rank, and Rights (Waldron), 187
'disaster capitalism,' 60–1
diversity, 32, 53–4, 83, 116, 135, 189

Echigo, Kaori, 43
'economic conscription,' 94
economic stagnation, 81, 151
Edano, Yukio, 44
Egypt, 33, 69, 72
'elders,' 5–7
elections
  1998 gubernatorial, 151
  2009, December, general, 68
  2011, local, 69

2012, December, general, 11
2012, lower house, 9, 97
2013, upper house, 97–8
2014, lower house, 97, 99
2016, upper house, 98
voter turn-out, 96
erotomaniac daimyō, The, 129
'Executive Committee for NO to the Abe Administration,' 100

Facebook, 46, 48, 69, 106, 112
family registers, 179–80
feminism, 17, 35
Filmer, Sir Robert, 186
fingerprinting of foreigners, 169
first person expression, 85
'flower demonstrations,' 108
Fordism, 27
foreign citizens' advisory councils, 169–70
Fraser, Nancy, 35
Freeter movement, 19, 52, 115, 117
'Friday protest in front of the prime minister's official residence,' 9, 29, 33, 36, 47, 74–5
'Fridays for Future' movement, 34, 54, 57
Fugitive Offenders and Mutual Legal Assistance in Criminal Matters Legislation (Hong Kong), 36
Fukuda, Norihiko, 175, 188
Fukuoka Youth Movement (FYM), 48
Fukushima Dai-ichi nuclear power plant accident *see also* anti-nuclear power movement
effects on anti-nuclear power movement, 69–75, 84
evacuations, 40
government misinformation, 44
impact, 40–5
psychological effects, 44
reminder of nuclear dangers, 36
Fukushima, Mizuho, 142
Fukuyama, Tetsurō, 96
Futenma Air Base, 147–9, 151, 153–4, 159–60, 166
FYM (Fukuoka Youth Movement), 48

gaikokujin shimin daihyōsha kaigi, 169
Gakusha no Kai, 12, 55
'gatherings,' 3–7, 116, 141–2
General Council of Trade Unions of Japan, 45, 102
Genpatsu yamero!!!!!, 9, 83
genshiryoku mura, 41
Gensuikin, 55, 99
Gensuikyō, 55, 99
General Freeter Union (Frītā zenpan rōdō kumiai), 129
'Give back my bike' demonstration, 124–6, 132–5
globalization, 35, 66, 75
God, Locke, and Equality: Christian Foundations in Locke's Political Thought (Waldron), 186
'Goodbye nuclear power' rally, 72
Goodbye Nuclear Power Ten Million People's Action, 99

Index

Great East Japan Earthquake, 40, 69, 84 *see also* Fukushima Dai-ichi nuclear power plant accident
Great Hanshin-Awaji Earthquake Disaster, 19, 65
Greater East Asia Co-Prosperity Sphere, 178
Greens (the), 1
Gunma, 72

hakkō ichiu, 179
Hamaoka Nuclear Power Plant, 70
Hangenpatsu Suginami, 46
Hangenren
  ACT March 11th Japan, 43
  bridge for Gensuikin and Gensuikyō, 55
  claims made by, 82–3, 90
  composition, 46–7
  crowd sizes, 103
  on demonstrations, 105
  Denuclearization Suginami, 111
  Friday rallies, 9–10, 23, 33, 36, 48, 74, 102, 108
  influence on SEALDs, 48, 108
  membership, 23, 57
  no nationwide structure, 51
  'NO NUKES DAY,' 99
  Noma, 49
  Norimichi, 20
  not 'citizens,' 32
  opposition to Abe, 100
  on police, 104
  purpose, 112
  'quiet demonstrations,' 102

Redwolf, 13, 23, 83
  single issue principle, 83
  TNN and, 47
  Yasumichi, 13
'hard to survive,' 94
Hashimoto, Ryūtarō, 148, 151
Hashimoto, Tōru, 103
hate speech *see* racism
Hate Speech Elimination Act: Enactment process and basic thinking, 175
Hatoyama government, 68–9
Hattori, Norimichi, 20
Heito supīchi kaishō hō, 175
Henmi, Yō, 91
Henoko military base, 1–2, 69, 152–65
Higuchi, Naoto, 77
Hinomaru flag, 90
Hirano, Taichi, 47, 49
Hitachi Employment Discrimination Trial, 168–9
Hong Kong protests, 6, 33, 36, 80
Honma, Nobukazu, 93, 100
Horie, Takashi, 8, 24
Hōsei University, 117–19
'hot-pot struggle,' 118–19, 124
housewives, 9, 15, 22, 63
human rights, 176, 180–2, 187–8
Hurricane Katrina, 60–1
Hydrangea Revolution, 33

'I hate war so much it makes me shiver,' 46
Ikegami, Yoshihiko, 36

ikizurai, 94
ikizurasa, 93
Inamine, Keiichi, 151–3, 157, 161
individualization, 38–9, 62
Inochio Mamoru Kai, 155
Inoue, Tamiji, 170
Instagram, 46
International Convention on the Elimination of All Forms of Racial Discrimination, 177
internationalism, 35
internet
  'De-nuke now. De-nuke-related event calendar,' 42
  facilitation of activism, 33, 51, 56, 69, 74, 82, 102, 109–10, 138
  facilitation of international activism, 33
  hate speech, 188
  as source of Fukushima information, 43–4
Iraq War
  opposition to, 20–1, 40, 60, 67, 122
  participation in, 66
Irregular Rhythm Asylum (IRA), 130–1, 136, 138
Ishiba, Shigeru, 103
Ishida, Takeshi, 15
Ishihara, Shintarō, 70, 103
Itō, 133–4
Itō, Masaaki, 22

Japan Congress Against Atomic and Hydrogen Bombs, 99

Japan Council Against Atomic and Hydrogen Bombs, 99
Japan National Railways, 62
Japan Socialist Party, 1, 4 *see also* Social Democratic Party
Japanese Trade Union Confederation, 68
Jasmine Revolution, Tunisia, 33, 69
jichi, 5, 116, 139
jiritsu, 5

Kajiwara, Robert, 34
Kan government, 69
kantei mae, 107
Katō, Makoto, 170
Katō, Yūji, 104
Kawasaki, 168–70, 173–7, 180–1, 184–5, 188
Kawasaki Korean Christian Church, 168
Kim, Sangyun, 183
kindaika=heiwa ishiki, 14
Kinjō, Yūji, 155
Kinoshita, Chigaya, 8, 24, 29
Kiryūsha (Quiriusha) bookshop, 132
Kishi government, 60
Kishi, Nobusuke, 190
Klein, Naomi, 37, 60
Kōchi, 48
Kōenji NEET Union, 124, 129
'Kōenji Riot', 130
Kōenji, Tokyo
  Amateur Revolt, 6, 114, 130
  demonstrations, 1, 9, 33, 71–3
  'live houses,' 121

Matsumoto, 3, 5
  opposition to redevelopment, 6
  second-hand shops, 121
  Things-will-work-out-somehow Bar, 141
  Yamashita, 120–2
Koike, Akira, 98
Koizumi government, 66, 68
kokkai mae, 107
kokumin, 30
Kokumin namen na, 32
Kōmeitō, 97, 159
Komori, Yōichi, 85
Korea normalization treaty, 17
Koreans, Japan resident, 8, 31, 75–6, 168–9, 174, 177, 183–4
'*kotatsu* struggle', 118
K-POP fans, 51–2, 76
Kumamoto, 48
Kyūjō kaeru na!, 1
Kyūjō no Kai, 1, 12

labor movements, 29–31, 35, 52, 62, 64
labor unions
  anti-Abe demonstrations, 1
  broadening of aims, 15, 27
  call for reactor restarts, 53
  collaboration in restructuring, 63
  company-specific, 28, 52
  decline in, 28, 64
  Freeter, 52
  participation rate, 28
  post-war, 30
  rally attendance payments, 110
  rally sizes, 102
  seen as discriminatory, 31
  Sōhyō, 45
  welfare measures, 68
Law of Special Measures for the Realignment of US Forces in Japan, 158
'Learning to Leave-off Part-time Work,' 140
'leave-it-up-to-them democracy,' 42, 45, 51
'Leaving off half-way,' 140
'Lehman Shock,' 57, 66–7
Let's go to a rally! If we raise our voices, the world will change; if we walk through the town, we will be able to see society (TNN), 47
LGBT protestors, 2, 59, 76
Li, Inha (Rev.), 168
Liberal Democratic Party
  2014 election, 99
  Constitutional reform, 12
  defeated 2009, 68
  economocentrism, 16
  end of one-party rule, 64
  Ishiba, 103
  leaders, 66
  membership, 64
  nuclear power, 53
  returned to power 2012, 11, 97
Liberal Democratic Party of Okinawa, 144, 151, 159–61
'liquid modernity,' 38–9
Locke, John, 171–3, 185–7
London Blitz, 61

Machida, Kō, 127
Machida, Machizō, 127
'Make rent free' demonstration, 128–9, 135–6
Mama no Kai, 12, 40, 48–9, 52, 55–6, 85, 97, 111–12
manga, 127, 133
Matsumoto, Hajime
  Amateur Revolt, 3–5, 41, 43, 115–20, 122–42
  anti-redevelopment movement, 7
  connection with elders, 5–7
  'post-revolutionary world in advance,' 135, 139–40
  on reason for activism, 43
  workers as 'model slaves,' 116
  Yamashita and, 120, 122–4, 128, 139
media
  failure to report protests, 21, 34–5
  international, 34–6
  reporting of Fukushima accident, 43
  reporting of protests, 10–11, 13, 18, 22, 35, 74–5
Meiji era, 15, 167, 179
Melucci, A., 4
MeToo movement, 34, 59
Metropolitan Coalition Against Nukes *see* Hangenren
Mexico City Earthquake, 61
Mills, Charles W., 185
Minzoku sabetsu to tatakau Kanagawa Renraku Kyōgikai, 169
misogyny, 185
Miura Peninsula, 137

Miura, Tomohito, 174
Miyagi, Etsujirō, 143–4
Miyagi, Yasuhiro, 149–50, 157–8, 162, 164–5
Miyazaki, Sayaka, 54
Mochizuki, 132, 136
'model slaves,' 116
'modernization = peace consciousness complex,' 14
Monbukagakushō, 108
Monod, Jacques, 170
Mōri, Yoshitaka, 20, 134
Motoyama, Jinshirō, 47, 85, 92, 96
'Movement against the Construction of US Military Housing in the Ikego Forest,' 63
Mr Pak Support Group, 168
Mubarak, Hosni, 69
Murayama, Tomiichi, 146
music as political tactic, 2–3, 6, 10, 20–1, 82, 100, 125–7, 130, 135

Nagano, 72
Nagatsuma, Akira, 97
Naha Regional Defense Facilities Administration Bureau, 148, 150, 154–5
Nakaima, Hirokazu, 160–1, 163
Nakasato, Toshinobu, 158–61
National Confederation of Trade Unions, 68
National Diet building, 9–11, 13, 29, 33, 36, 45, 47–50, 56–7, 76, 86, 95–6, 98, 102–3, 105–8, 112

Index

National Liaison Council for the Elimination of Nuclear Power, 99
National Security Legislation (US-Japan Security Treaty) 2015, 48–9, 51, 55, 59, 76–7, 82, 89, 109, 111
  Association of Scholars Opposed to National Security Legislation, 12, 87, 97
  Mama no Kai, 12, 40, 48–9, 52, 55–6, 85, 97, 111–12
  opposition to, 11–14, 16, 21, 24–5, 30, 32, 46–51, 55–7, 59–60, 76–7, 81–91, 94–5, 98–9
  passing of, 97
  size of protests, 103
National Trade Union Council, 68
'nationals,' 29–30, 32–3, 36
nativism, 65
natural rights, 171–2, 186
Negri, Antonio, 23
neighborhood associations, 16
Neo-Anarchism, 140
neoliberalism, 60, 66–8, 78
New Anarchism, 140
New Clean Government Party, 97
New Socialist Party, 1
'New Year's Eve Temporary Employee Village,' 68
New York Times, The, 35
'News for the Poor,' 118, 120
Nishime, Junji, 144
Nishinari Riot, Osaka, 128–9
'No Limit Tokyo Autonomous Zone,' 130, 132

'No Limit Seoul Autonomous Zone,' 130
'NO NUKES DAY,' 99
No Nukes More Hearts, 47
No Nukes Plaza Tokyo, 47
Noda, Yoshihiko, 10, 88
Noma, Yasumichi, 13, 46, 49, 51
Nonaka, Hiromu, 66
NOPPIN News, 121, 140
NOPPIN Shimbun, 121
NORANERO, 131, 136–7
North Korean kidnapping issue, 65
NPO Law, 19
nuclear power *see also* anti-nuclear power movement
  calls for restart of reactors, 53
  cessation of nuclear power generation, 10
  failure to stop reactor restarts, 82, 88
  fuel reprocessing, 70
  opposition to restarts, 88–9, 91
  power stations, 8, 10
  suspension of non-operational reactors, 10
'nuclear village,' 41, 53, 78
nursery school blog, 106, 110

Obinger, J., 115
Occupy movement, 72
Occupy movement (US), 33, 72–3
Occupy Tokyo, 57
Occupy Wall Street, 57, 68
Ogasawara, Keita, 120–3, 125, 127, 131–5

Oguma, Eiji, 22–3, 42, 44, 83, 100, 102
Ōi nuclear power plant, 10, 88–9
Ōita Prefecture, 182
Okinawa
  Act on Special Measures for the Promotion and Development of Okinawa, 148
  'All-island struggle,' 145
  'all-Okinawa' movement, 159, 161, 165–6
  Association for Protecting the Life of Henoko, 156
  Base Return Action Program, 147, 153
  Camp Schwab, 148
  Citizens' Association for the Promotion of Revitalization of Nago City, 149
  Committee Against Helicopter Base Construction, 150
  demonstrations, 145, 154, 158–9
  floating maritime facility, 148, 157, 160
  Futenma Air Base, 147–9, 151, 153–4, 159–60, 166
  Henoko military base, 1–2, 69, 152–65
  'island wide' movement, 159, 161, 165–6
  Law of Special Measures for the Realignment of US Forces in Japan, 158
  Nago City, 148–51, 153–4, 157, 159–60, 162, 164–5
  Naha Regional Defense Facilities Administration Bureau, 148, 150, 154–5
  opposition to US bases, 1–2, 25, 34, 69, 143–66
  prefectural referendum, 2019, 47
  Program for the Promotion and Development of Northern Okinawa, 153, 158, 164
  referendum 1996, 148
  referendum 1997, 149–50
  return of some bases, 147
  returned to Japan, 145
  SACO (Special Action Committee on Okinawa), 147
  yo-gawari, 158
Okinawa Development Agency, 158
Okinawa Executive Association, 151
Okinawa People's Party, 144
Okinawa Policy Council, 148, 152, 157
Okuda, Aki, 46–7, 50–1, 87–9, 91–3, 104
Onaga, Takeshi, 161–6
'one-day joint struggles,' 102
Ōno, Itaru, 92
Osaka, 48, 188
Ōsawa, Mami, 92, 94
Ōta, Masahide, 145–9, 151, 153, 157
'Outdoor Sleeping Appreciation Society, The,' 117

Pak, Chonsok, 168, 170
Pateman, Carole, 185–6
peace movement, 1, 3, 7, 12, 14, 29, 102

Index

Penal Code, Article 200, 179
People's Council to Stop the Revised Security Treaty, 45
PM's official residence, 9, 29, 33, 36, 47, 74–6, 105–8, 112
political parties, 110
'Poor People's Great Rebellion Collective,' 119, 122, 124
post-war democracy, 14–17, 29–30, 33, 60–1, 64–7, 87–8
post-war social movements, 62–6
'Potsdam student councils,' 17, 29
Potsudamu jichikai, 17
Prime Ministerial and Expert Advisor Open Colloquium, 109
'professional citizens,' 31
Program for the Promotion and Development of Northern Okinawa, 153, 158, 164
progressive national movement, 14, 30
'Protect Japan from Abe Shinzō!,' 91
Public Assistance Act, 182
Punk Rocker Labor Union, 4
punk subculture, 4, 6, 120–1, 127, 133, 135
puro shimin, 31

Rabanderia (Lavanderia) café, 132
Racial Contract, The (Mills), 185
racial discrimination, 169, 177, 188
racism *see also* anti-racism
 demonstrations, 174, 176
 against foreigners, 167–89
 growth of, 65
 hate speech against Japan-resident Koreans, 8, 13, 31, 65, 75–7, 173–5, 183
Redwolf, Misao, 13, 23, 83, 89, 104–5, 108
renewable energy, 91
Rengō, 53
resource mobilization theory, 39
RLL (Radical Laughter Left), 128

SACO (Special Action Committee on Okinawa), 147
SADL (Small Axe for Democracy and Life), 48
Saigō, Minako, 40, 48–9, 56, 112
Sakamoto, Ryūichi, 126
Sakurai, Makoto, 51
San Francisco Earthquake, 61
SASPL (Students Against the Secret Protection Law), 11, 46–7, 49, 54, 56, 83–4
Save Constitutional Democracy Japan, 88
SEALDs (Students Emergency Action for Liberal Democracy)
 anti-anti-intellectualism, 88
 anti-nuclear beginnings, 11–12, 46–7
 call on parties to join hands, 97–8
 chanting, 21
 claims made by, 83–4, 86–7, 90–1
 connection with international activism, 33
 democracy, 89–90
 on demonstrations, 104–5

'Don't underestimate nationals', 32
Fukushima accident as impetus, 40
Honma, 100
inspired by Hangenren, 108
intergenerational cooperation, 87
membership, 49
as motivator to new activists, 55
Motoyama, 47, 96
no nationwide structure, 51
not 'citizens,' 32
not university based, 28, 53–4
opposition to National Security
   Legislation, 12, 51, 55
ordinary people, 36
origins, 83–4
and political parties, 99
purpose, 112
regional versions, 48
SEALDs KANSAI, 48, 54
SEALDs RYŪKYŪ, 47–8
SEALDs TŌHOKU, 48, 54
SEALDs TŌKAI, 48, 54
Shibata, 50
slogan, 96–7
student loan debts, 93
Ushida, 56
Yamada, 44
Seikyū-sha, 169, 174, 177
Sekai, 88
Self-Defense Forces, 11–12, 90, 161
Senaga, Kamejirō, 144
Sengoku, Yoshito, 169
Sensō shitakunakute furueru, 46
September 11 terrorist attacks, 60
Sexual Contract, The (Pateman), 185

Shibakitai, 13, 35, 46, 48–9, 51, 56
Shibata, Mana, 50
Shi'i, Kazuo, 97
Shimin rengō, 55, 97
Shimin seifu ron (Ukai), 186
Shinchō Yonjūgo, 76
Shinjuku ALTA building, 72, 122,
   126, 135
Shinjuku Ward, Tokyo, 70, 75, 127,
   131–2, 137
Shin-Ōkubo, Tokyo 75–6, 119–20,
   124
Shirōto no ran see Amateur Revolt
shizuka na demo, 102
shushō kantei, 105
Small Axe for Democracy and Life,
   48
Social Democratic Party, 1, 64, 141
Social Welfare Act, 177
Socialist Party, 1, 45, 64, 99, 102
societal formation, history of, 178–9
'Society to Preserve the Run-down
   Feel of Hōsei University,' 117–18
socioeconomic class, 31
Sōgakari kōdō, 12, 99
Sōhyō, 45
solidarity, 36
Solnit, Rebecca, 60–1
'sound demonstrations,' 2–4, 20, 34,
   40, 133
sound trucks, 2–4
South Korea, 6
Soviet Union, 61
Special Action Committee on
   Okinawa, 147

Special Secrecy Law, 89, 91, 93
squatter movement, 114–15
stagnation, political, 14, 17, 19, 29, 59
State Secrecy Law, 84
state-managerialism, 35
'Stop nuclear power!!!!!,' 9, 83
'struggle to live, the,' 93–4
student based issues, 17, 117–19
student loan debts, 93–4
student movement late 1960s, 4–5, 14, 16–18, 62
Students Against the Secret Protection Law *see* SASPL (Students Against the Secret Protection Law)
Students Emergency Action for Liberal Democracy *see* SEALDs (Students Emergency Action for Liberal Democracy)
Sugawara, Hikari, 54
Suginami housewives, 15
Suginami Ward, Tokyo, 1, 4, 73, 111, 114, 129
Sugita, Mio, 76
Sumatra Earthquake, 60
Sunflower Movement (Taiwan), 33
Suwahara, Takeshi, 84
Suzuki, Norifumi, 129

Taira, Chōkei, 165
Taiwan, 6, 33–4, 36
Takabatake, Michitoshi, 14
Takahashi, Gen'ichirō, 84–5
Takahashi, Taketomo, 46
Takatsuka, Mao, 46

Takeuchi, Yoshimi, 89
Tanaka, Hikaru, 25, 67
Tanno, Kiyoto, 8, 25, 33
Tanpoposha, 47
Teens Stand Up To Oppose War Law *see* T-ns SOWL (Teens Stand Up To Oppose War Law)
'Tell me what democracy looks like?,' 97
TEPCO *see* Tokyo Electric Power Company (TEPCO)
textbooks, censorship of, 158–60
'Three people' demonstrations, 125–6
Thunberg, Greta, 34, 54
Tinbergen, Nikolaas, 170
TNN, 47–9
T-ns SOWL (Teens Stand Up To Oppose War Law), 12, 48, 51
Tochigi, 72
Tokyo Electric Power Company (TEPCO), 34, 41, 43
Tokyo Station, 108
Toriyama, Atsushi, 25
Tottori, 48
Treaty on the Prohibition of Nuclear Weapons, 91
Tunisia, 33, 69
TwitNoNukes (TNN) *see* TNN
Twitter, 29, 46, 49, 69, 111, 138
Two Treatises of Government (Locke), 171, 186

Uchida, Tatsuru, 91
Ueno, Chizuko, 85, 87
Ukai, Nobushige, 186

Umbrella Movement (Hong Kong), 33
unemployment, 67–8, 151, 164–5
universities
  1960s activism, 16
  SEALDs not unviersity-based, 28–9, 50, 53–4
  student based issues, 17, 117–19
  student solidarity, 50, 53
  University of Tokyo, occupation of, 102
Uozumi, Y., 176
US military *see also* Okinawa
  bases, opposition to, 1–2, 25, 34, 143–66
  Osprey aircraft, 159, 163
  sexual offenses, 145–6, 150
Ushida, Yoshimasa, 56, 92, 104
US-Japan Security Treaty *see* National Security Legislation
US-Japan Security Treaty Joint Struggle Council, 74
Ustream broadcasts, 43, 109

Vietnam War, 16–17, 67
volunteer movements, 65

Waldron, Jeremy, 186–7
Washington Post, 35
WDW (We Disagree with War), 48
We Disagree with War (WDW), 48
Westphalianism, 35
women protestors, 1–2, 15, 22, 146, 150–1

women's movements, 59
women's rights, 187
'workers,' 29–32, 46
World Conference for Abolishing Nuclear Power 2012 YOKOHAMA, 109

Yamada, Nodoka, 44
Yamada, Takao, 170
Yamanaka, Sadanori, 158
Yamashita, Hikaru
  Amateur Revolt, 116, 120–5, 127–8, 130–5, 139–42
  Basshop, 141
  Kōenji, Tokyo, 120–2
  'Learning to Leave-off Part-time Work,' 140
  'Leaving off half-way,' 140' 139
  Matsumoto and, 120, 122–4, 128, 139
  Things-will-work-out-somehow Bar, 141
Yokohama District Court, 176–7, 180–1, 184
youth movements, 4–5, 8, 16, 18, 20, 22–3, 55
YouTube, 95, 109, 126, 128, 192
yoyo, 137

Zainichi, 75, 168–9, 174, 177, 183–4
Zaitokukai, 13, 51, 174
Zapatista Fair Trade Coffee, 136
Zenkyōtō movement, 17, 28–9, 51, 87
Zero Yen Shops, 141